SCOTLAND'S OPEN ROAD

SCOTLAND'S
OPEN ROAD

AGNES W. S. INNES

PHOTOGRAPHS BY
DAVID INNES

With a map

ROBERT HALE · LONDON

PRINTED IN GREAT BRITAIN BY
LOWE AND BRYDONE (PRINTERS) LTD., LONDON

To
All Our Caravan Friends
Past, Present and Future

Contents

Illustrations

Illustrations

When the Wanderlust Calls:
The Caravan and our life in it

Caravanning, boating, fishing, exploring, photography and writing make up our life—my husband David's and mine—and give us one of roving from April until October each year. And it is of those happy months, and some of the places we visit and love that I am going to tell you about.

Long ago we realized that only a caravan could give us the freedom we wished, yet it had to be one so well fitted out as to be a miniature home, completely self-contained yet mobile; and that we achieved when we designed 'Golden Eagle'.

But this was a problem. First came a list of wants, then a general interior plan, next an acceptable shape and to take a 12-foot boat on the roof. Following that came the big question: the probable weight of the caravan plus the movable contents.

After weeks of work everything was decided. Our mobile home would have to be 18 feet long and 7 feet wide. Unloaded it would weigh about 23 hundredweights. The movable contents and boat with loading cradle would be about 7 hundredweights.

For stability and strength we chose the horse-box type of close-coupled, four-wheel undergear, and to carry 50 per cent more than load. (Legally it comes under the same regulations as the more conventional two-wheel type.)

For good towing, and to counter heavy kitchen-end weight, the wheel grouping was set back from the centre. The ball-hitch and towbar are of standard type, but for extra comfort in long-distance running D.B. hydraulic twin stabilizers are fitted between the caravan and car; these make the outfit travel as one solid unit.

We have two cars each fitted to pull the caravan; one, now ageing, but a well-tried favourite, is an Austin Westminster Countryman, 2·65 litre. The other is a Vanden Plas, 4 litre

R. Princess, which is fully automatic, has all the newest aids and gadgets, and the 4-litre Rolls-Royce engine makes pulling a heavy caravan anywhere easy. Although this is a high-powered car and always well-loaded, we find it quite economical.

To load the boat the caravan is tipped by the front jacks, or legs, on its end. The loading cradle is now fixed to roof rails, then the boat is fitted to the cradle, the end of which is lifted, and the whole is run along the roof rails and locked in position.

Inside 'Golden Eagle' we have three separate rooms, each opening off a tiny entrance hall: the lounge, which becomes a bedroom by night; the kitchen, and the toilet-room. The lounge has a settee-bed with sponge-rubber seat and foam-plastic mattress. This is very comfortable and is 'made' in the morning like an ordinary house bed before being closed up. Another useful part of our dual-purpose furniture is my writing desk, the flap of which lifts to reveal a large mirror and dressing table. Opposite this is an alcove with a radiator, and above it a serving hatch to the kitchen, all topped by an 8-inch electric clock. Our walnut-topped table and the chairs fold and can be carried out of doors for meals in the sunshine.

Our work and hobbies mean carrying a fairly comprehensive amount of equipment and make good storage important. Compactness was obtained by using drawers, of which there are twenty-eight. Twelve are in the sideboard-writing desk unit, and those extend right in to the nose of the caravan, making them much larger than they appear. Two are shallow, lined with green baize and fitted for cutlery; another is fitted to take sewing materials, like a fitted workbox, and also has sections for stockings, gloves, handkerchiefs, etc., so those items never become jumbled together. Inside the large roomy wardrobe, which is insulated against dampness from condensation, there is a large, square hat drawer.

In the kitchen at floor level there are two very efficient cold drawers, which are sectioned and fitted, one to take meat, fish, cheese, butter and fats, bacon, and milk, all in separate compartments, the other to take fruit and vegetables. A current of air passes from below the floor into those drawers and out into the kitchen; this can be regulated or excluded as required.

There is an egg drawer with trays, a fitted kitchen-cutlery

drawer, and a laundry drawer which holds everything for iron-
ing; clothes line, pegs, and soaps all in their own sections. Beneath
the sink is a deep drawer and a cupboard for cleaning materials.
Beneath the cooker is the pot cupboard and a 12-volt accumu-
lator for general lighting (5 lights). Above one tier of drawers
are the store cupboards, and above them a handy shoe rack,
while other wood-fronted shelves between the windows hold
bottled fruits and jams. In the corners are handy, deep bins for
pails, etc.

In our toilet-room, besides the chemical-toilet, there is a pull-
out wash-hand basin, and behind the basin a roomy toilet acces-
sory cabinet and a fire extinguisher. Drinking water is carried in
two-gallon containers. Washing water is on tap from an eight-
gallon tank which also collects all rain water from the roof.

We had christened our mobile home 'Golden Eagle' after the
'Royal Bird of Good Omen' of our ancient Scottish kings,
and because in it we would be able to live near the fastnesses
beloved by that regal bird.

We had no idea at first what the caravan would do for us and
mean to us as time went on. One of the most important things it
has given us are friends up and down the country. It is wonderful
to be welcomed back even after several years' absence from a
place. Like the Saturday we arrived on our usual pitch beside
Loch Ken in Kirkcudbrightshire, and within half-an-hour an
elder of Kells Kirk jumped off his bicycle beside us. He had seen
us pass through New Galloway, and had come to tell us that
next day was their communion service and to invite us to attend.
As our Scottish Presbyterian churches only hold communion
twice—or at most four times—a year it is always an important
day in the church, which is usually packed, leaving no room for
the late-comer.

Another instance which warms my heart is when we stop as
usual for a few days at the foot of Glen Coe when travelling north
or south by that western route. We not only receive a grand
welcome from our slate-quarry manager friend and his wife but
also from the post mistress, who beamingly tells us that she knew
we were coming when letters began to arrive for us. It was here
that one day our friend asked why we called the caravan 'Golden
Eagle', and quick as lightning her husband replied, "Because the
golden eagle is the king of birds and this is the queen of caravans."

But we were always even more heart-warmed as we brought 'Golden Eagle' to rest at Ardmair in Ross-shire, and there were our old friends the Macdonalds hurrying along from their croft with outstretched hands to welcome us back, and their collie dog outstripping them with wagging tail to show his pleasure in a happy reunion. Then our two feathered friends came to add their shrieking welcome; that pair of gulls which wait so patiently for our return every time we go fishing.

Besides our local friends, we have made and are still making countless caravanning friends from every part of Britain, and many from abroad. Because of my writing in many magazines, with the articles well illustrated by David's photographs, many showing 'Golden Eagle', people often consider themselves our friends, although they have never met us.

One day recently a man knocked on our door and said, "This *is* the 'Golden Eagle'! I am from London. My caravan is in the next field." Then he drew a sheaf of papers from an inside pocket. "These are your articles in that magazine over eleven years. Because of them we took up caravanning and have followed your routes and found them wonderful; and now we have found you and 'Golden Eagle'."

Another caravanner came round the last bend, and, seeing us parked far below, shouted in glee to his wife.

"The caravan, for a pound!" They too had chased around for years hoping to catch up on us somewhere.

Another caravanner who found us at Ardmair and interested us very much was an art master from a college in Ohio. After saving for some time, he, with his wife and four small children, had come over for a holiday. Meantime he had amassed a great deal of information from my articles about the most beautiful parts of Scotland to visit. He also thanked me for making it plain to him what type of caravan to have and what features would be necessary in the car to pull it. He had hired a caravan on arrival, and chose a Land-Rover for his power-unit. They had little time beside us because every day was so planned that they had to run to schedule to fit it all in.

Taking only one other instance of overseas visitors who have, surprisingly, become fast friends, there was the German couple with their fifteen-year-old son who brought their caravan to rest beside us last summer. They stayed three weeks and, being kindred spirits, friendship was inevitable. They also had a boat, but because they brought the whole outfit from Germany via Hull weight was a consideration and their boat was small, so the German lady sometimes accompanied us in our boat. She and I had good walks together, and how interesting it was to learn the German names of wild flowers and give her our English or, sometimes, Scottish names.

She said her husband did not eat fish but she did, yet her husband was an ardent fisherman. One day she offered to smoke our mackerel for us, and we were intrigued because David has long wished he could smoke fish. Her 'smoker' was small and ingenious, an oblong pan, 13 inches by 7 inches, in which was spread oak sawdust; a small tin with asbestos wick and methylated spirits heated it from underneath. Above was placed the grid with the filleted fish, over which fixed a lid. It took only eight minutes to smoke and that gives time to set the table before we feast on that succulent, steaming-hot fish straight from the smoker.

Mrs. R. was to send me a smoker from Germany on their return home and tell me the cost, but her husband told David that he thought the Ullapool fishing-tackle shop sold them. We were off post-haste and David returned with his smoker. He has since improved it by adding another rack to take a second layer of fish, and it has been most successful and has added quite a new dimension to our way of cooking fish.

We derive great interest in what other caravanners like to do on holiday. The caravanners who come to the haunts that we frequent are usually lovers of simple things; of birds and wild flowers, of trees and wild animals, of beautiful sunsets and rainbows after rain. Many have been artists who find their caravan— right on the spot—the perfect answer for the peace and relaxation necessary for good work. There was the caravanner who had mostly rain during her fortnight's stay, yet her paintings were superb. They were water-colours, yet of such richness of purples, greens, golden-brown and deep reds that the mountains with their fissure-riven faces looked alive and vital, more so than they appear when drenched in sunshine.

Another caravanner's interest was in gathering tiny pieces of seaweeds. Until she showed me I had no idea that there were seaweeds in such glorious colours; cherry-red, soft pink, saffron-yellow, browns, greens, some dark and rich, some vivid and startling and rich gold. She dried those minute pieces and pressed them, and said she used them to make trees, flowers, etc., in her pictures, building around them.

Others gather shells, the flat, fan-shaped, scallop-like shells being great favourites. One friend brought home over a hundred and sold them for 6d. each at her Girl Guide sale.

"People use them for ashtrays and soap dishes," she told me, "and they are in demand for snacks at cocktail parties and buffet suppers."

Much of my own treasure trove consists of beautiful chunks of stone, often pink and white marble or pink and green and silver granite, or bits of quartz, sometimes sparkling with gold or silver. I use them as paper weights or as ornaments, but most of the large pieces have gone to make my rockeries, especially the rockery around the water garden at home. David has also used the flat, colourful stones from Ardmair beaches embedded on top of a long cement border edging the rose bed by the summerhouse walk. They are beautiful after a shower, as water brings up their vivid colourings.

Tiny, iridescent stones I often use on top of flower pots of geraniums and bulbs and ferns in the sun-lounge and these I find invaluable round the stems of newly planted cuttings, so that when watering I do not dampen the little stems before they are rooted, as this sets up rot.

When in the caravan I often get cuttings of plants, especially geraniums and pelargoniums, from crofters and cottagers, so that now I have a wonderful and varied collection. All that comes through caravanning. Sometimes people who are not caravanners ask if caravanning is not just a change of sink. I do not find it so. There is practically no housework, the little there is can be done in ten minutes.

On tour we stop for meals when and where we like, and that is usually where our windows frame a lovely view. Lunch-time dishes can be prepared in the morning, and there are such wonderful things in tins that meals can be exciting without any cooking at all. I have found that village bakers in Scotland usually have a splendid selection of good fare. Many times, from some small baker's shop, or travelling shop halted by a cottage, I have got sausage rolls, meat pies, or bridies—bridies being succulent triangles of pastry filled with meat—hot from the oven and so delicious that they just melted in the mouth. Then in many lovely old market towns I have found cooked-meat shops which have supplied delectable food all ready for the table.

Yet on tour in wilder country I find meals so entirely different that even when cooking is necessary the variety of food is a tonic: trout, fresh caught from a burn flowing past our door; that delicious middle cut of salmon from the gamekeeper; a brace of grouse or a cock pheasant from the laird; a chicken or duckling from the farmer's wife; venison from the forester; lobsters from the lobster-fisher—they all come our way, as well as honey, eggs, butter, and crowdie. We often make crowdie ourselves when near a farm. It is like cottage cheese and made from souring full-cream milk (not pasteurized milk). Here is the way to make it:

Stand two pints of milk in a warm place by the cooker until it is quite thick, then add a teaspoonful salt, stirring well. Turn into a butter muslin bag and hang up to strain overnight, or press out the whey. Add cream or creamed butter to taste and form into a small cheese. It is excellent cut or as a spread.

Then there are the fish which we have caught, coated with batter, egg and bread crumbs, or oatmeal, and fried. Herring or mackerel we often pot (souse) in vinegar with sliced onion. But white fish can be poached in a little milk and eaten with butter, a white sauce, or tartare sauce, or I sometimes steam filleted white fish with layers of sliced lemon and sliced tomato. On colder days I often make fish soup.

And while on the subject of caravan fare, I find a good store of flour, meal and tinned milk make us independent of shops for many days at a time when feather-light girdle scones and wafer-thin oatcakes take the place of bread; and if you have never made scones with tinned milk you would be surprised how tasty they can be. Scones are quickly made and my recipe is a simple one I once got from a farmer's wife in Galloway. Here it is:

> 2 teacupfuls ($\frac{1}{2}$ lb.) self-raising flour
> pinch salt and $\frac{1}{2}$-teaspoonful sugar.

Mix together. Break a small egg into cup and fill up with milk, mix, then mix into flour quickly. A soft dough, quickly mixed, makes the best scone. Turn on to the hot girdle, flatten out with a well-floured hand, then neaten round the edges with the knife,

2

no rolling required. Cook for about eight minutes, turn and cook other side. Cool on a wire tray and cut into wedges or slice. The thing to avoid when cooking girdle scones is a draught.

For treacle scones omit the egg, add black treacle and a half-teaspoonful ground ginger. For fancy scones rub 2 oz. margarine into flour, add a handful raisins or mixed dried fruit and egg and milk. Those are as good as fruit cake. Half sour milk and half fresh can be used omitting the egg or, better still if procurable from a farm that makes its own butter, use butter-milk. Dropped scones are also easily made and consist of a batter of flour, milk and egg dropped in spoonfuls on to the hot, greased girdle. Turn when the bubbles begin to rise.

In the caravan cooking can be reduced to a minimum. But I love cooking, and on wet or stormy days it comes into its own. Then there are wash days which can be ones too windy for the boat. I have a splendid enamelled, sparred extending frame, specially designed for caravan use, which I hook on outside my kitchen window. This is essential in Ross-shire where there are no trees. I use a more conventional clothes line when there are trees to tie it to. There is no need to bleach or boil linen beside the western shore, the clear, ozone-laden air whitens it.

But often those windy days with rollicking clouds are good photographic ones, especially after a spell of heavy rain when the air seems washed clear. So it's into the car and away on the job.

Those are happy, interesting days. Sometimes David can take an hour or more to get the sun, clouds and shadows just right for his photograph so I walk on, often for miles, to be picked up later. It is then I talk with roadmen, tree-fellers, farmers, game-keepers and other knowledgeable people I meet by the way. I glean a tremendous amount of interesting local matter and folk-tales. Perhaps at the next halt I shall sit in the car and write up my notes.

We rarely bother about lunch; time is too precious, so biscuits, fruit, sweets and milk suffice till a grand evening meal when we return to 'Golden Eagle'. By that time, as often happens, the wind has fallen and a calm sea or loch lures us afloat, and with a successful day's work in the bag we enjoy those evening hours.

Many a time I have been helped in research work by being given a loan of priceless old books from lairds and from librarians in small towns. What treasures those old books are. I love history, but not everyone does so I have to be careful not to incorporate too much in my writing. There was one little town, actually a cathedral city, where everyone I spoke to, in shops or by the way, told me I should get a certain book. In each case I asked did they have it and could they lend it to me, but the answer was always the same, they had given their copy to someone at some time to read and had never got it back. In desperation I tried the local library. The librarian had the old book but prized it and would not let it out of the library. However, after a chat on many subjects, he decided to let me have it for a few days. I appreciated his trust. That precious book was back in his safe keeping within two days, and I was the richer not only for the wealth of history I had obtained from it but for the happy friendship of that librarian.

A friend in a Morayshire town lent me a wonderful old book on local history which was out of print many years ago. It had been gifted to her father, when he was provost, by the author, and bore the author's signature. What a gem of a book that was. It seems a pity that such old books are never reprinted. I love books; books that describe things and places. Our tier of book-shelves in 'Golden Eagle' is packed with books on birds, wild flowers—especially prized is a recent addition on wild flowers of the Highlands—fruits of the wild, mushrooms, semi-precious gem stones and rock formations, sea- and fresh-water fish, sea-weeds and shells, butterflies, ferns, fishing books, books on bridle-paths through the hills, 'Highways and Byways' books of every section of Scotland and many more. They are all books to refer to, to pick up and enjoy at any odd moment and there are also many guide-books and maps.

We love maps, particularly Bartholomew's which show hills and rivers so plainly. Maps are essential to our touring and ex-ploring, and it often surprises me that many caravanners and motorists have such poor ones or an inadequate supply. Half-inch we find the best, because they give better name coverage and define many small roads not shown on smaller scale maps. But sometimes for local work inch size is preferred for local coverage. These maps are fascinating, showing many hill tracks and old drove or peat roads. The drove roads were those through the hill passes used by the drovers taking their cattle from the Islands or northern pastures to southern markets. The peat roads penetrate into the hills and are the tracks which crofters used, and often still use, to the peat hags where they dig out the peat with their sharp-bladed tools in the month of May, stacking them roughly to dry in the summer suns and the warm winds. When the time comes to transport this winter fuel supply to their crofts the peats have dried out and are much lighter to handle.

On large-scale maps one sometimes finds postman's tracks through the hills. Those were usually more direct and shorter than the present-day roads, and, of course, those were the tracks used to carry the coffins from remote townships for burial at some central place; the cairns, which grew as each mourner placed a stone where the coffin was laid down when they rested, are still there. I have always found those old hill routes interesting because they were so much shorter, and it was usual to ferry across the mouth of a sea loch or inlet and so continue through the next barrier of hills.

From time to time we are given priceless old maps from country people. How we treasure them. I have found names of islands and castles on them which even local people have never heard of. But one very modern one, which is a splendid asset to anyone exploring the north-west of Scotland is Bartholomew's Cape Wrath map. It takes in the whole western seaboard from below Ullapool to Cape Wrath.

So, with the larder and cupboards stocked, the lounge book-case filled with the books and magazines, the invaluable radio and all the personal things which make it homely, we travel the open road. And the more we tour the more I realize that this is the only way to explore the country thoroughly, because there are no accommodation reservations to tie our movements, we travel to the mood of the countryside and the whim of the weather, perhaps a few miles or a few hundred in a day, and each can be full of engrossing interest. We like to get up early to catch some of that clear fresh air which follows dawn into the morning, then, to the first song of the birds, we are coupled-up and away with the lark.

2

We Bundle and Go:
Springtime and the Journey to Galloway

It is a shining spring morning, the wind in the north, a scurry of snow like gossamer wings softly swirling earthwards, lit by the sun and sparkling, melting as they land. The cloud passes and the sun warms us in the car as we draw away from our home at the foot of the Pentland Hills with 'Golden Eagle' on tow.

For several days my heart has been singing "Bundle and go, Bundle and go," and now we are off. I look back to see 'Golden Eagle' following steadily and settle into my corner with a contented sigh. The winter is over, spring is here, and again we are free to roam; no bookings, no one expecting us, we know where we are going, but we can change our minds to a moment's whim.

At present we are taking the corkscrew bends on the old Lanark Road. The early sun is slanting through the still leafless trees, making me almost dizzy with the swift alternating change from glare to shadow. We clear the wood. A plough behind a tractor is turning the brown earth, hurrying, working early and, no doubt, late to make up for time lost through bad weather. We are into the lovely beech avenue now; there are fat buds on the trees, a brown leaf carpet is spread at their feet, and between their thick trunks we see the shaggy forms of golden-brown Highland cattle. They are peering at us through heavy fringes of hair. That is one of the lovely things about travelling in a leisurely way with the caravan; there is time to see things, just all the time there is, because we can stop and call it a day when and where we like.

We climb the snappy brae I call the magic hill, for over its brow the beauty of Harperrig Reservoir is suddenly spread before us. We draw off the road at the quarry and feel the wind bite into us as we leave the car and lean on the fence. The wind is bending the coarse grass in long rippling eddies, and I think, what a cold welcome for the lambs down there nearer the loch. A boat is putting off from Cairns Castle, the sun tempting anglers to brave the cold wind and try their luck on the rippling water. And over the loch and about its edges are the gulls which never leave this inland water although its elevation is about a thousand feet.

Old Cairns Castle, that sturdy old keep where in olden times the warden of the Cauldstaneslap lived, is easier seen today through the leafless trees. There, backing the loch, are the East and West Cairns and, between those comely peaks, the Slap; the old drove road through the long range of the Pentland Hills to Linton Roderick—now less musically called West Linton. Great cattle markets were held at Linton, and between 1631 and 1856 Linton was Scotland's chief market.

The Slap was the road used by the Highland drovers bringing cattle from the north. After selling them they bought sheep, driving them over the Shap, northwards to the Highlands to be fattened and driven back again for the two-day sheep sale in June, when as many as 30,000 sheep passed to new owners each year. The Linton sheep were a hardy breed with black faces and legs, and in great demand.

But those were lawless days when the old road was frequented by robbers, mosstroopers, freebooters, Border raiders and rievers, and became known as Thieves' Road where fierce battles raged and much blood was spilt. Knowing that the Pass required a keeper the owner of Cairns Castle, Sir George Crichton, appointed himself the Warden of the Slap. Sir George was High Admiral of Scotland, Earl of Caithness, and, besides having a castle and lands here, was the builder of Blackness Castle nearer the Firth of Forth, and also held the lands of Harehope on the other side of the pass. But being warden was no sinecure because the Armstrongs and Liddells, Border rievers, made off with his whole stock of wedders (ewes) from Harehope in 1582. In 1600 another band of raiders came through the Slap to his lands at Harperrig and stole fourscore oxen and many horses.

The wild glens and caves around the Cairn Hills were sheltering places for persecuted Presbyterians in Covenant times, and many meetings and conventicles took place in those lonely ravines. But today it is a lovely old road, just a stony track, but peopled with interesting characters of long ago who were real and not legends. Many a time I have walked it, crossing the baby Water of Leith, which rises here but is a beautiful river by the time it passes our home, far below in the valley.

We continue along the Lang Whang. The real name of this road is the Old Lanark Road but it is always called, even today, the Lang Whang as it cleaves its way over the desolate moorland—and a lang whang, or long way, it must have been to weary feet when it was rough and more hilly with terribly twisted little bridges. At the beginning of last century three stage-coaches a week left Edinburgh for Lanark by the Lang Whang. In those days there were many toll-houses and wayside inns, and at the one called 'Half-way House', a mile or two past Cairns Castle Inn, the first change of horses was made. There were highway robbers with fast horses and the close sanctuary of the hills for quick cover. The most picturesque was 'Gentleman Gipsy', Captain Baillie of Biggar, who rode with his sword by his side and his fine pack of greyhounds behind him. It is said he could act the gallant or robber at will.

In the days when the physicians of Edinburgh Royal Infirmary were paying for dead bodies on which to carry out research work, there was a brisk business in corpses, body snatchers lifting them from churchyards in Lanark and bringing them over the Lang Whang to the Capital. There are stories of the thieves dressing an exhumed body and propping it up on the seat between them, then driving over the Lang Whang in their gig behind a spanking horse. Of course, they were often caught, as was the man who passed westward through the village of Currie one morning with an empty cart. It puzzled the locals why a cart should come from Edinburgh making for Lanark empty, so they informed Mr. Cairns, the owner of Balerno Bank Paper Mills. He and friends lay in wait during that pitch-black night until they heard the cart rumbling back. Fierce was the mêlée but they captured the man and the straw-covered bodies which the cart contained.

Those were menacing, wild days but the old road does not slumber. It is a busy main road, except when blocked by snow because it rarely dips below the 1,000-foot mark, but in summer at the weekends it is thronged along its whole moorland length with cars and happy picnic groups from Edinburgh.

Peewits are starting up from the moorland as we pass, crying

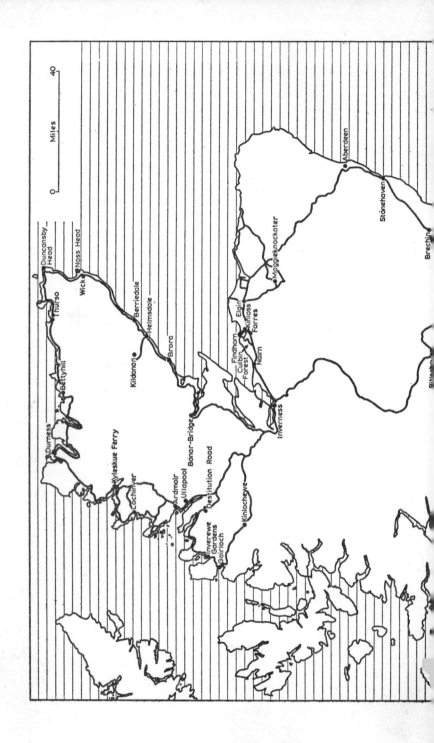

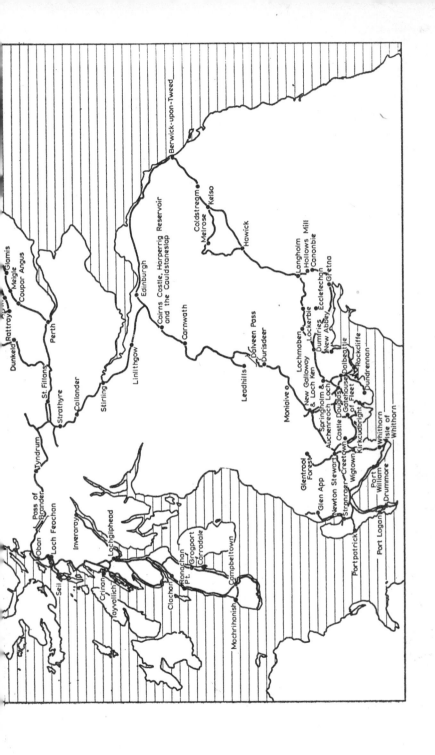

shrilly as they sweep in staggering flight away from their nesting-places. Below us the North Medwin, no more than a narrow, silver ribbon, is weaving a curving pattern through the moor, and wide are our views beyond it to distant hills.

Another avenue of stately trees with a bend or two brings us past one of the old toll-houses where we need neither stop nor pay, and so to Carnwath. We post those last-minute letters, for here is our first post office in the twenty miles from home, and fill our cake tins at that pleasant baker's shop, which has such a vast van-service around the countryside that they put little in the window to give an indication of the delectable fare to be had within.

Then on again, curving down and round the parish church, and remembering that over on our right lies lovely White Loch, though its beauty is entirely hidden to the passer-through who will not tarry and seek it out. Our road cuts the golf course in two and we stop for a chat with old, wayside friends, the Marshalls, who have their gipsy encampment in the bield (shelter) of close-fitting hillocks. The Marshalls are linoleum and hardware merchants serving a need of outlying farms and villages. Their two little daughters are a picture of health and high spirits, yet dainty in tartan kilts with their golden, curly hair tied with bright ribbons.

The next village, Carstairs, brings us to a land of glass, but we are too early for tomatoes. We leave the Lanark road here and pass a row of trim, modern crofts on our way to the River Clyde, which we cross by the many arched and ancient Hyndford Bridge. From here we have a choice of two roads, and for a moment are tempted to go by the lovely way of Douglas Water, but instead we turn left; and now we are in the thick of heavy traffic making to or from the Clyde industrial belt. From this wide, straight road we look down on the pretty village of Thankerton and across to Tinto, a mountain so much alone that it naturally has its legends and rhymes, perhaps the best known being the cynical saying that, no matter how ill-favoured a lass might be, if she has a pickle siller (a little money), "Set her on Tinto tap and the wind a lad will blaw til her."

Below us in the green valley flows a very young Clyde, yet, having already absorbed some eight or nine lusty burns, it is no weakling sprite. A long train, with two locomotives, is climbing towards the Beattock Summit. And so are we as we by-pass Abington and Crawford: but we never reach that summit for at Elvanfoot we leave the arterial road, but go on climbing gently right up and through the Lead Hills.

We pass the road-end to Leadhills Village. This is rather a fabulous place, which, with its neighbouring village of Wanlock-head, is set in a district which used to be called Scotland's Treasure House. Gold was mined in the hills here as far back as the six-teenth century and the crown of Scotland was made from this leadhills gold, and studded with River Tay pearls. Lead mining was already in operation and this gave the hills their second name of the Leadhills, although their real name is the Lowther Hills, the highest part of which is Green Lowther. It is 2,403 feet high, but does not look like a mountain because those beautiful hills are not rugged like most mountains, but rounded and green, like green velvet, friendly-looking hills on the boundary between Lanarkshire and Dumfriesshire.

Those hilltop villages, which are between 1,300 and 1,350 feet and the highest villages in Scotland, grew up around the mines. The first well-organized gold venture in the sixteenth century was by a man called Bevis Bulmer, and he had a staff of over 300. The place where he started operations became known as Bul-mer's Moss, and it is called that to this day; a fine memorial to that enterprising mining engineer.

Although lead mining started in the thirteenth century, it was in the late seventeenth century and early eighteenth century that it became big business, and continued to be so on and off until 1950 when the price of lead fell making lead mining no longer profitable. Now the Leadhills Village is developing the area as a sports centre for ski-ing, and the South of Scotland Ski Club has its headquarters in the fine Hopetown Arms Hotel. This hotel has the distinction of being at the highest altitude of any in Scotland. Ski-ing is only done during the winter, because these friendly hills rarely keep their snow-caps into the spring.

There have been many illustrious sons of Leadhills Village, among them Alan Ramsay, the poet, whose father, Robert Ramsay, was manager of the mines. It was Alan Ramsay who gave his native village a circulating library. The first of its kind in Scotland. Then there was William Symington who was born in the village in 1764; a long way from the sea, yet he built the first practical steam boat. The house he was born in is still in the village street which bears his name. But the local man who interests me most is John Taylor, a mining surveyor in the Leadhills. He was born in the village in the year 1637 and died there in May 1770, a span of 133 years. His tombstone can still be seen in Leadhills. One would imagine that life in this lofty village, although austere at times, must be very healthy, so little wonder that so many native people, retired from their busy life in the world, return, content to rest here for the remainder of their days.

Not unnaturally Leadhills, with its old mine workings, was a haunt of the Covenanters, and many secret conventicles were held there. But even fugitive Jacobites made Leadhills a place of sanctuary. James Stirling, a mine manager at that time, sheltered a wanted Jacobite for several years after the '45 in the mansion house which was his home. James Stirling was himself a keen Jacobite, but he had very advanced ideas for his time and was a brilliant mathematician.

Naturally sheep farming plays a big part in the economy of those green hills today. Their herds are the hardy black-face type and Cheviots. There is a railway station at Wanlockhead, but trains ceased to operate here many years ago.

The last time we visited those two villages was in January. The road we chose was from Abington, which gives a fairly easy climb into the hills. Those hills were white, but the road itself was clear and dry. A lone hiker was trudging his way steadily downhill in the cold, icy air, and at the ski-slopes many cars were parked with hardy skiers standing in groups looking speculatively at the hills.

The tremendous size of Leadhills Village always amazes me. It stretches a long way, and the road runs right through its full length. The houses and cottages are beautiful and well-kept. There is a post office, a general store, a lovely little country church at its western end, and the good hotel. We, and the friends who were with us on this New Year outing, had hoped to get some good photographs, but the strong wind was so cutting, like barbs of ice, that we were glad, as we left the car, to get straight into the hotel for a good hot lunch.

After our sojourn in our prosperous, roof-top village we go on our way. There are many wilder passes than the Dalveen, yet it is fierce enough, with the road clinging precariously to the steep hillside, as it tops the rise and zigzags steeply down. Far below lies the green, fertile floor with a ribbon-like river threaded through it and its green mountain walls rising sheer to the skies: Green Lowther, Lowther Hill and Ballencleuch Law.

We meet little on the descent, sheep and lambs scurry off the road to make way for us. We cross the twisted bridge where a waterfall thunders down through a steep, narrow, rocky chasm to join the river far below, and, with about a third of the descent to make, run on to a quarried wayside strip for a luncheon halt. We comment on the changed atmosphere, the barrier of hills has cut us off from the strong north wind and the sun is warm.

In strange contrast to the green hills opposite, the precipitous slope beside us is grey scree; which is why it would be used by roadmen as a wayside quarry for repair work in the days, not so long ago, when this was a narrow road without tar.

Near the foot of the Dalveen Pass a fascinating little road invites one to explore. It dips to cross the Carron Water then climbs to the ancient village of Durisdeer, which is only glimpsed in the distance from the main road where it is tucked in at the foot of the green Lowther Hills. It is a village full of character, history and local story, and set like a jewel in this section of peaceful, fair Nithsdale.

Although so quiet now, it was a weaver's village with a hand-loom in every cottage in the days when the main road from Edinburgh to the south-west ran through it. That ancient highway, called the Well Path, still climbs beyond the village beside the musical Kirkburn, to cut through the Lowthers by a narrow pass between the Well Hill and the Durisdeer Hill, and joins the main road near the head of the Dalveen Pass.

Before the Dalveen Pass was cut, the stage-coach from Edinburgh to Dumfries used the Well Path, stopping for refreshments and to change horses at the busy hostelry in Durisdeer. How thankful travellers were to reach that safe haven, after coming through that narrow pass of winter storms and highwaymen, and down the Lang Glen. Robbie Burns, knowing this way so well and tramping down-along one day, composed that most sprightly song:

> Last May a braw wooer cam' doon the Lang Glen,
> And sair wi' his love did he deave me.

But the lady's scorn was turned to anger and jealousy when her braw wooer went up the Lang Glen to her cousin, black Bess! However, a week later, the song tells, she "gaed to the tryst o' Dalgarnock", and finishes:

> He begged, for guidsake, I wad be his wife,
>   Or else I wad kill him wi' sorrow;
> Sae e'en to preserve the puir body his life,
>   I think I maun wed him tomorrow.

It was down this Lang Glen too that William Wallace and his men rode furiously, after relieving Sanquhar Castle, and chased the English right through Durisdeer; as Blind Harry recounted:

> Through Durisdeer he took the gainest gate,
> Right fain he would with Southern make debate.

But they were not the only warriors to use the Lang Glen, for long before their day Roman legionaries made this their road when a Roman camp was in the hills a few miles above the village and another a short way to the south.

That was a glorious day when we took the road which douce Nithsdale folk, Dumfries folk, Edinburgh folk, and countless more, have traversed through the centuries. The corn was turning to gold and the red sandstone of the little new bridge over the Carron Water stood out brightly in the sunshine; and so we came to the village on the foothills 550 feet above sea-level. A village fit to charm the heart away, with its white-walled cottages built in friendly fashion round a level square, while the overflow slips steeply downhill. How quiet it was. Gone were the hostelry and the once busy smiddy (smithy) and the only remaining shop is the post office-cum-general store.

So we came to the church, an immense building, out of all proportion to the size of the village today. But we found there was more to it than that, for part is not the church but was the old parochial school built in the times when the church made itself responsible for the education of the children. Now this grand old stone building has its windows built up and is unused. Many another church would give a lot for just such a building to convert into a hall.

The church is said to date from the thirteenth century, but the date on the sundial built into the wall above the South door is 1699. However, it is inside the church that most interest lies, for in the north transept are the famous Queensberry Marbles which date back 150 years. They, more than anything else, keep the name of this quiet little backwater alive and draw visitors from near and far.

The effigies are those of James, second duke of Queensberry and first duke of Dover, and his wife, Mary Boyle, daughter of Lord Clifford. Although the Marbles are to both, it was the duke, in love and sorrow, who envisaged this exquisite memorial and sought the skill of the finest sculptor of his day, Van Nost, to bring his dream to fruition. The figure of the duchess shows her asleep in her last sleep, while that of the duke pictures him alive, reclining on a cushion beside his beloved lady. But less than two years later his own ashes were mingled with those of his duchess in this same tomb.

In course of time, through marriage, the Queensberrys and the Buccleuchs became one family, and today it is in Durisdeer Church that the Duke and Duchess of Buccleuch worship when in residence in nearby Drumlanrig Castle.

In the church one is carried back to old descriptions and pictures of a century and more ago, because here are many square pews with seats round them, and a table in the centre which takes the place of bookboards and more naturally resembles the table of the Last Supper in the Upper Room. For communion too the ordinary pews have adaptable bookboards which are hinged. Two of the beautiful old communion cups were made in 1620 by James Robertson of Edinburgh, who also made the Scottish Capital's Mace. In 1874 the Duke of Buccleuch gifted another two cups as near as possible in workmanship to the ones which were even then 250 years old. Also preserved in this wonderful old kirk are two examples of sixteenth-century wrought-iron work, one a baptismal bracket and the other a holder for an hour-glass. This was used in the days when sermons lasted a long, long time; when all the sand had run through the minister knew that he had preached for an hour, and, turning the glass, probably gave his congregation another hour for good measure.

A curious custom, which has come down from earlier times, is for the kirk bell to ring at 10 a.m. every Sabbath to remind parishioners to get ready for the service. It rings again just before midday, as the service starts at twelve o'clock. In previous times the bell used to be rung at 8 a.m. as well, so that no one had any excuse for sleeping-in and so being late for church.

When the Well Path through the Lang Glen was a dusty high-way, and worshippers arrived tired and, in hot weather, thirsty, a pail of fresh-drawn water and a tumbler were placed just inside the West door. This door is no longer used, but still the old custom prevails, and fresh drinking-water is there for anyone requiring it.

The name of this village has a sweet sound and is thought to have come from either Duris, a door, and deer, a forest, meaning the door of the forest, or the door of the Daer, taking its name from the nearby Daer Water. But however the ancients coined its name, Durisdeer today symbolizes a place of peace and quiet charm in its glorious hill setting.

But we are still journeying to Galloway, so we go on through rich, rolling country of wide farmlands. Thornhill on the Nith, beloved by the salmon anglers, is slightly by-passed on a con-venient short cut, unless we require any shopping. We cross the wide River Nith where its shallow banks make a happy play-ground for Thornhill children; and there are always one or two anglers thigh-deep in the swift-flowing river. A few more easy miles and we are running through Penpont; a long village and where I first saw post-war Swedish timber houses. These have weathered to a pretty grey and blend well with the sturdy stone cottages.

We have to halt at the little bridge with the S-bend over the Shinnel Water, because of its charm: just a small river like many another, with a rocky bed, green banks and low trees, deep, shady pools, a man with a rod and a fat trout jumping, and sun-light sparkling the water where it runs fast and broken over the rocks. Close by the steep hillside is well-clothed with juniper trees; and this surely was a halt worth-while, because the man who runs the nearby farm told us that his juniper wood is one of the finest in Scotland. For the next few miles field gates, inter-secting the neat hedges, are pale apple-green, and a pheasant, a horse and other animals and birds of topiary art greet us at inter-vals, which shows what an artistic landowner can do to beautify the Queen's highway.

Kirkland, with its beautiful church, is our next village, then pretty Moniaive which is at its loveliest in June when roses cover the cottage walls and scent the air. Below us now are wide pas-tures, a tall belt of pines, a river and low hills; a tranquil scene in

'Golden Eagle' beside Loch Earn

the bright afternoon sunshine. But it changes as we climb to the long stretch of undulating moorland, a lovely way with sharp little bends, bridges over brawling burns and occasionally a clump of birch trees. But what pleases me most are the birds: curlews, with their long curved bills and sweet mating call; peewits, with their shining coats of iridescent green and purple; pheasants, arrogant and stately in their glorious spring plumage; and fat red grouse, with their guttural cry, "Go back, go back, go back", at our approach.

The moor ends. A winding, dipping little road takes us across the tree-bowered Garpel Burn, and we remember that in that deep dell, in Covenanting times, many a conventicle was held.

We pass the hilltop village of Balmaclellan, once the home of Robert Paterson, the prototype of Sir Walter Scott's 'Old Mortality', a sculptor who dedicated his life to keeping the names of the martyrs alive by carving them on headstones wherever a covenanter was buried. He travelled all over Galloway doing this self-appointed work without payment, and his wife took up teaching to earn enough to keep their home together and bring up their children.

Soon we were crossing Rennie's beautiful bridge over the wide River Ken. Rennie, the famous bridge builder, brought masons from Aberdeen to build this bridge, as they were accustomed to working in granite. Many of those masons never returned to Aberdeen, but married local Gallovidians and settled here. There was plenty of work for them in Galloway, because bridging the many rivers in stone instead of wood was the order of the day. There are descendants of those masons in New Galloway to this day.

But now my heart is lilting as we pass through little New Galloway, Scotland's smallest royal burgh, because another two miles and we'll be at Loch Ken; where the primrose bank is embroidered with thousands of yellow flowers, and silver birches are putting on gowns of green; where waterfalls cascade over red and silver granite rock, smudged with the green of moss, and willow catkins dance in the breeze; where countless birds nest, slow-worms sun themselves on the warm rock, and red squirrels claim us as their friends; where our own little slipway runs down through the trees to the loch and . . . we'll be afloat with the breakfast caught before the sunset gilds the Carsphairn Hills.

3

The lounge-cum-bedroom of 'Golden Eagle'
The author with a 19-pound pike caught in Loch Ken

3

Happy Days at Loch Ken:
Boating, Fishing, Talking and Exploring

Loch Ken, Galloway's largest loch and our best-loved inland water, we know in every season and every mood; fishing in the river and the labyrinth of backwaters which head the loch, until the early autumn dusk merges into starry night, and the stars in turn die as the great orb of the harvest moon sails high in the sky, then dipping the oars softly as we row homewards in a world of peacefulness and enchantment. An otter, like a black shadow, slips from the bank into the water scarcely rippling it; the peace is momentarily shattered by deer belling on Cairn Edward or the Bennan, and again by the hooting of an owl. The campfire of the old gipsy basket-maker gleams but feebly in the moon's radiance. We draw in to give him a fish for his supper, and the music of the mountain burn beside which he camps adds to the night's charm.

Storms long ago swept an enormous tree down the loch to become embedded in the centre, and on the tips of its up-rearing limbs a pair of cormorants poise watchfully earlier than we ever go fishing. Around that old tree the fishing is good, but care is needed not to entangle lines with submerged branches. In summer, as lilies and reeds grow, the fish move inshore among them, which makes fishing more difficult and exciting.

In its ten miles the loch is fed by innumerable burns, as well as the two great rivers, Ken and Dee, and at the mouths of the larger burns we fish carefully. The Lowran Burn is the nearest and a favourite spot, not so much for the fish we catch as for the beauty of that wild, joyous mountain burn leaping and roaring over its falls and under Mary Hamilton's bridge, to helter-skelter into the loch. A gnarled gean (wild cherry) tree by the bridge showers snowy petals on its amber waters; if it could speak it would tell us lively tales of Mary Hamilton who used to bide here, using her little cottage as a shebeen,[1] for in olden times travellers liked something stronger than Lowran's waters to wash the dust of the roads from their throats.

Long before Mary Hamilton's day, a Highland soldier drank gratefully of Lowran's mountain flood. Wounded and weary, he was making his difficult way homewards, but lying down to rest in the birches' shade beside the burn he fell asleep for ever. An old ballad paints the scene:

> He sank to repose where the red heaths are blended,
>   One dream of his childhood his fancy passed o'er;
> But his battles are fought, and his march it is ended,
>   The sound of the bagpipes shall wake him no more.

The hill slopes here are State forest, the trees tall and dense, but a section up by Lowran's glorious falls has been left to heather, bracken, and bog-myrtle and on it is a cross, clearly seen from the loch, standing out against its background of dark green conifers. It is to the memory of another soldier who lost his life in the First World War, and was erected here by his father, then minister of Balmaclellan, because his son had dearly loved this beautiful and sequestered Lowran Glen. In olden times it was a Kenmure retreat, and near the cross is a granite boulder shaped like a chair. Robert, fourth viscount, like all his family, was a staunch supporter of the Stuart cause, and when he heard of Cromwell's approach he fled to the Lowran Glen, and, sitting here, in sorrow and anger watched his historic castle burn at Cromwell's hands.

Kenmure Castle and its lands were owned by the Lords of Galloway, but at an even earlier day it was the residence of Dervorgilla who built Sweetheart Abbey near Dumfries in memory of her husband, John Baliol. It was in the fifteenth century that the Gordons became the owners of Kenmure, and Sir John Gordon of Lochinvar secured the charter from Charles I to make New Galloway a royal burgh. This little town, smaller than most villages, is extremely proud of being a royal burgh and the smallest in Scotland.

Sir John Gordon of Lochinvar was raised to the peerage by Charles I, with the titles of Viscount Kenmure and Lord Lochinvar. A descendant, William, sixth viscount, who supported the

---

[1] A shebeen sold illicit whisky made in nearby hills where water was suitable, as would be the case high up on the Bennan hill at the Lowran Burn.

Pretender in 1715, was captured at Preston and executed on Tower Hill. His estates and titles were forfeited, but by Act of Parliament they were restored to a descendant, John Gordon, in 1824. However, in 1847, the titles became dormant on the death of Adam Gordon, eighth viscount.

Kenmure Castle stands on a great knoll high above the loch's head, parts of it more ancient than records show, and parts of various periods because of several burnings and some rebuilding. It was here about 1760 that Viscount Kenmure, unsuccessful in his fishing, petulantly said to his gamekeeper that Loch Ken contained only minnows. Next day his keeper, John Murray, was amazed to see several duck on the water disappearing one after the other; so, taking a strong line and hook, he baited it with a duckling and caught a 72-pound pike, measuring over 7 feet long. Killing this mammoth fish he trailed it up to the castle, and, casting it down before his astonished master growled, "Ye can catch the next minnow yoursel'." That remains the largest pike on record caught in British waters.

When Kenmure Castle was recently being demolished, and the roof and interior timbers had all been stripped, Mr. G. H. Gordon, a descendant of the Gordons of Kenmure, had the demolition stopped. He bought the castle shell and grounds and has now come from abroad to make the former gamekeeper's house beside the kennels his home. He has started a company called Kenmure Fisheries Ltd., turned the backwaters of Loch Ken into a fish farm and aims at producing 200,000 rainbow trout (45 tons) a year. There are tanks in the hatchery building fitted with self-feeders. To help him Mr. Gordon has Mr. Paul Jensen, a fourth generation fish farmer from Denmark.

On the loch our catch used to be mostly pike and perch, but in the last two years the loch has been fairly cleared of pike, and now fat brown trout and perch are our usual catches. We miss the pike, for they were great sport varying in size from 1 to 20 pounds.

With our spinning reels, fine tackle, and artificial, or preserved, minnows, fishing for pike in Loch Ken was an art requiring the utmost casting skill and ingenuity. As the season advanced, and the reeds and water lilies grew round the loch's edges, the pike came in from the deeper water amongst them. Then, with the boat just the correct distance out, we cast in towards the shore, a tricky business, choosing narrow, clear spaces, perhaps only a foot wide, between the reeds and lilies, and dropping the lure gently and accurately between them.

If we were in luck, a pike would take the minnow at lightning speed, the water and reeds swirling at the lash of its powerful tail. Then the trouble was to get it speedily into deep water, because it is difficult to play a heavy pike on fine tackle among reeds and water lilies; and pike put up a terrific fight when lightly hooked in their hard mouths, often leaping out of the water just like big trout or salmon. Being accidentally hooked-up among tough water lily stems or reeds, and sometimes deeply submerged tree-branches, can at any time be trying, but with a good fish on the line it is terrifying. In each case we used to use our anchor to ease off and pull up the root or branch to which the line or lure had become attached, or to disturb and frighten out the sulking fish, a manœuvre which required good team work.

Pike from the clear, fresh waters of our Scottish lochs make good eating, and the monks of old knew a big pike's food value when they stocked our lochs with them. In the wide River Ken there are good trout of a fair size, but the tremendous volume of water from the Earlstone and Glenlee Power Stations often causes the river to run faster than a millrace.

In spring the Knocknarling Burn, which reaches the loch via one of the loch-head backwaters, often tempts us, and we row far up it, holding back willow branches to pass, while catkin pollen shakes over us; a way edged by the gold of kingcups, with the banks topped by wild hyacinths, and made more enchanting by birdsong. In the maze of beautiful, canal-like channels, or backwaters, which are formed by reed and grass banks, there is the chance of a good-sized trout. Here swans, goosanders, eider duck, and many other wild fowl nest, and scores of grey-lag geese return each autumn from their northern sojourn. Whooper swans also make this their winter home, soaring or gliding down the loch to the wild accompaniment of raucous trumpeting.

Half-a-mile below the Lowran Burn the loch narrows as the land juts out, and the road leaves the lochside. Offshore here are two islands; one, called Green Island, of natural rock, on which only Guelder Rose trees grow, beautiful but poisonous. The other called Burned Island is at least partly artificial, composed of innumerable small boulders and stones, and amongst a tangle of non-poisonous wild fruits (brambles, sloes, plums and apples) are the ruins of a very small building with rounded ends, possibly a tower. From this island shorewards runs a submerged reef of rock, which catches our hooks; or could it be partly a submerged causeway such as used by lake dwellers? Loch Ken's level was raised considerably when it became a hydro-electric power reservoir and originally this was the loch's foot, a usual place for lake dwellers.

Sea Mew, our boat, makes this island orchard ours in autumn, and helps to fill our winter store cupboard. Fishing is usually good around the islands, but sometimes we go across to the mouth of Shirmers' Burn where there is a chance of a salmon. May spreads a hyacinth carpet beneath the beech trees of Shirmers' Wood, but later queen-of-the-meadow throws a broad, wavy scarf along the shore-edge, like the cream froth of spume, and intermingled are splashes of mauve-pink where great valerian rises through it on long stalks.

Covering the steep slopes of the Bennan and Cairn Edward Hills is a vast forest. This stretches south and west for many, many miles, because forestry is a great industry in Kirkcudbrightshire. It makes me think of the primeval days when Scotland was covered by the Caledonian Forest. Perhaps it is the swing of the pendulum that is clothing our barren hills and moors once more with dense forests.

Trees are a joy to me, and Galloway and Perthshire have the most and best. Our old pitch in the lovely, disused lochside quarry became obsolete when the foresters began felling and taking the trees out, because they brought their forest roads down both sides, and now use the quarry as a loading station. From our quarry pitch we used to see deer coming down from the hills in the mornings to drink at the lochside. Those were pretty little roe deer, but high on the Bennan are herds of red deer. The roe deer invade the foresters' gardens, given the opportunity, and cause great havoc. One also caused a nasty accident on our road early one morning when a motor cyclist was going to work. It jumped down from the forest in front of him. The animal was killed, and the cyclist was in hospital a long time before being sufficiently patched up to resume normal living. Periodically there are shoots to keep their numbers down and to prevent disease spreading among them. There are foxes too in the hills, and the farmers also have shooting times to keep their numbers in check. One friend of ours is proud of her two beautiful fox furs made from pelts of foxes shot by her husband on the Bennan.

Recently our friend, the head forester, told us that golden eagles were nesting on the Bennan, but he and his men were telling no one where so that they would not be molested.

When we lost our quarry pitch we were fortunate in getting an even better site on a friend's farmland. It is well away from the now busy road, and is on the loch's edge, right opposite the islands.

Our views up and across the loch are superb, we get far more sunshine than we did on our old pitch, and it is better for our boat. To add interest there are many more boats on the water now. At the head of the loch the local Anglers Association has their fleet of boats, and down the loch from us there is a yacht club, and an occasional speed boat appears with water skiers. But the most amazing boat we have seen recently was one that berthed beside our own when its two intrepid voyagers crossed the loch in it. Those lads had made the boat in three weeks, and it consisted of a hollowed-out log, incredibly narrow, but they had outriders to hold its balance and a sail as power unit. The two boys were camped on the opposite shore in an improvised shack built against a hillock.

The other big 'industry' here, besides forestry and farming, is the hydro-electric scheme. The first in Scotland was the Galloway one which covers an immense area. The lochs which are reservoirs are magnificent and the power stations are set in glorious scenery. There is no shortage of water in Galloway, and every town has its own river, which makes them attractive and a delight to explore, which we do from our lovely Kenside pitch.

It may be that loving a roving life ourselves, David and I take unusual interest in gipsies and others we meet by the way. Gipsies are a fascinating and, we find, a friendly people.

Friendliness and a sort of effervescent, happy laughter was the spirit of a gipsy camp near Crossmichael. Turning off the Castle Douglas road, we were attracted to it by smoke rising from behind tall hedges, and saw, in a clearing, three gispsy caravans neatly lined up in a row, and sheltered behind and on each side by natural woods of beech, birch, oak and ash. These caravans were of the old covered-wagon type, with highly-varnished woodwork and ornate carving, high off the ground, with a wide flight of steps between the shafts. Inside each was a glittering, black coal stove, simple furniture, and furnishings with bright curtains. There was not much room, but a gipsy's 'van is more for sleeping in than anything else, so it is not surprising that the curtained bed at the rear end takes up most of the space. This bed is high, giving room for the children to sleep snugly underneath.

Everything was clean and tidy, yet many are inclined to think of gipsies as a slovenly, unkempt people. There was nothing either slovenly or unkempt about this family on the Sunday when we visited them. The young men's clothes were good and, although unpressed, not untidy. Their young wives were neatly and well dressed, only their hair in some cases showed a lack of care, or perhaps it would be more correct to say, a careless disregard to the entangling winds, the drying sun, and the soaking rains—yet did anyone ever see a gipsy with grey hair? They needed no artificial make-up, for the kiss of the sun had put roses in their cheeks, and their good, open-air life, away from the soot of towns, had given them robust health, putting a sparkle in their eyes and rippling laughter on their lips.

Their food is simple, yet richly flavoured and nourishing, mostly from the wilds. Their meat includes rabbits and hedgehogs, the latter a greatly loved delicacy; their vegetables, among other things, young nettle tops which they cook like spinach; spikes of the butterbur, which are like asparagus; and the young leaves of burdock, which are rather like cabbage. There are roots and nuts, wild fruits and mushrooms, all of which the gipsies use freely. From wild flowers and berries they make delicious wines; and from wild herbs and very old recipes, they make cures for all ailments.

Treated like a queen in that high-spirited camp was mother, but now she was sad and thoughtful, because only a month before her husband had died. She was proud of her sons and daughters and of their wives and husbands, and how she brightened up when they brought forward their pretty children; but how pleased and smiling she was when one of her sons led a beautiful black horse, her late husband's own, from the wood and lifted one of her little granddaughters on to its back for David to photograph. That was the signal for other sleek, beautifully groomed horses to be led forward.

I returned to the car guessing that David would be some time talking with the men and taking photographs, and shortly I was joined by one of the young women, carrying a very small and lovely baby wearing a daintily smocked silk dress. I opened the car door and she settled herself comfortably beside me; the baby, she said, was three weeks old, but one of the other girl's youngest child was only six days old and asleep in one of the 'vans—six days and the mother *running* about the camp! They are a hardy people, and, incidentally, all passionately fond of their children.

When she left me, two of the young men strolled across the road for a chat, talking in Romany to each other but in English to me. Mischievously I said that I also lived in a vardo, and was amused at their surprise that I should know any Romany. They looked so prosperous, I was curious to know what they did for a living. They told me that they were decorators by trade, doing painting work, mostly at farms. How did they transport their gear? I asked. They hired a motor lorry when necessary, at other times their light carts were sufficient. For a while they had had trailer caravans, they said, but had reverted to the old horse-drawn covered-wagons because they preferred horses. That was not surprising, for there is no better judge of a horse than a gipsy.

Undoubtedly gipsies are industrious, and when they feel like it they work hard and long, then, carefree, down go the tents, the horses are hitched-up, and, with their pockets well-lined, they are on the move again. But gipsies also love to bargain, so, when the snows melt, many of them, tired of being dug-in, take to the open road as hawkers. So it was with the Marshalls we met in that tiny valley with low, rounded green hillocks sheltering it on all sides. They carried a remarkable selection of goods, but linoleum was their big line, and neat rolls of it peeped from under tarpaulins or lay about. The haphazard layout of their camp made a pretty and colourful picture; a gay covered-wagon against a small, tussore-coloured marquee, ornate carts contrasting with their duller coverings, and a playful collie and happy, kilted children frolicking and making the most of their sunny corner. In the more remote farms and cottages throughout the country they find their best customers, and they seem really to be a help to country people; although their wares may not always be all that they would have their customers believe.

Thinking of hawkers reminds me of a very good-looking young gipsy couple, with a tiny baby, who passed our caravan several times. They were always on their way back to their little beehive tent in a disused quarry on that narrow road between Dalry and Balmaclellan; that enchanted road of leafy trees, splashing river, and a wealth of wild flowers and bird life. They were always seated on the front of a beautifully-sprung, light cart, behind a spanking chestnut mare. Halting one evening, we learned that they were china merchants—or at least pot, pan, and crockery hawkers—and that they sold all they carried every day; gipsies who revelled in a life which was systematically taking them all over Scotland.

We found another extremely colourful gipsy camp down off the road at Boat o' Rhone, where the railway bridge crosses what used to be the old foot of Loch Ken proper. Here there used to be a ferryboat, hence the name, Boat o' Rhone. This was a big camp of several beautifully-painted and varnished covered-wagons, and lovely ponies and horses, some prettily dappled black and white. Obviously the imperial head of this band was a very lovely and sweet-faced lady who looked every inch a queen in her regal bearing; tall, slim, beautifully dressed and graceful.

David had a splendid time with his camera here because the setting was superb under the sun-dappled trees with the blue loch as background; but he was utterly dismayed at one instant of clicking the shutter to hear a gurgle at his feet, and, looking down, found a tiny baby lying happily in the grass—one step back and he would have trodden on that little gipsy. When we passed that way again next day, the gipsies had gone without a trace of their ever having been there at all.

Gipsies have a wonderful imagination, and, although their home life is retired, in business they delight in the spectacular. A family who passed us twice at this same place certainly startled me so much with their bizarre appearance that they had disappeared before I could collect my wits. Their chariot was like a tractor, with a cab in which the several occupants all seemed to be standing, as they whirled past at an astonishing speed. The whole outfit was painted in vivid red and greens, and this brightness seemed to be repeated in the gipsies' costumes—but we were unable to find out anything about them; they may have made a practice of hiring out themselves and their outfit to farmers.

This same gift of imagination makes them perhaps the most successful of showmen, fortune-tellers, and trick artists; then, in contrast, their love of animals brings to the country folk the much-loved circus. It was our good fortune to watch a troupe pass our caravan very early on the morning following their performance in New Galloway. Down by that quiet, winding road beside Loch Ken they came; first the great, lumbering elephant, and last, a very long time after that slow-moving vanguard, the beautiful prancing ponies, surely the darlings of every circus. This cavalcade of animals and caravans was a gay advertisement of their next performance to be given that night in Dalbeattie. We wondered how long it would take that elephant and the gipsy escorting it on foot to reach their destination, but the gipsy was not worrying because, he said, the 'big top' would be up and everything ready when he arrived.

However, not only the gipsies roam Scotland, there are other nomads without either animal or mechanical transport, and one is our old friend, the basket-maker, whom we met again in Galloway after not having seen him for over seven years. For four days he camped beside the old boathouse about five minutes' walk from our quarry pitch. On this western side of Loch Ken the willows are plentiful, and these withes he cut and gathered in great bundles, stripping and bleaching them and weaving his lovely baskets. The evening we touched in beside his camp to give him two pike of a likeable size, between 4 and 5 pounds each, our old friend came half-way down to meet us, doffing his hat, which was of an indescribable colour and shape yet weathered to perfection, and in the dusk the light from his fire lit his shaggy red head and beard and silhouetted his tall, spare figure. When he spoke, his voice was as sweetly musical as the wimpling burn at our feet. Fish, he said, was a luxury and, with a courtly bow, added that he would eat it to our very good health.

We spoke of many places as the moon rose higher and his fire dimmed in its radiance; of the Borders, of Sutherlandshire, and many places in between, all of which he takes in his stride, a circuit of years. He said he would make me a basket, and what shape would I like? He had several designs, he said, but the most fashionable at the moment was the long-shaped oval, with the handle from end to end. What about the one he had been making earlier in evening, we asked, "Oh!" he said, "I sold that one. Two people passing on bicycles. I can sell all I make as soon as they are finished." Two days later he was gone; he was seen passing down New Galloway's main street with his bundle on his back and a great bundle of withes too, and there was nothing left to show that he had camped by the burn except a patch strewn with the soft green bark of the withes.

Another interesting rover who camped for a night here was a little man who repaired and sold umbrellas. As he ambled along the road with his strangely assorted bundle of umbrellas, his bearing reminded us of two others we used to see in these parts; one was the saw-sharpener who travelled the road with his wife, both fairly young, camping by the way; the other was the old oyster-pearl fisher who used to frequent the River Ðee above Stroan Loch when summer suns made the water warm.

In his flat-bottomed coracle, made from tree branches and old tarpaulin, with a glass 'window' in the 'floor', he spied the oysters and brought them up with a cleek (bent wire fastened to a stick). When winter came he sold his hoard of lovely oyster pearls to a jeweller in one of the local towns, and made sufficient money to live in comparative comfort through the cold, stormy months.

Gipsies were of Hindu origin, a wandering tribe who came by way of Egypt round the Mediterranean, scattering through Europe and in Britain in the sixteenth century. They are not tinkers. Tinkers were originally outcasts from certain Scottish clans who took to the hills, a vagrant type who speak Gaelic. Many play the bagpipes at popular stopping places for tourists in the Highlands, some sell white heather and also the paper flowers which the women make. They are itinerant, mending pans and kettles, tinsmiths in a rough-and-ready way, sometimes making milk cans and containers, and charging whatever they can get for them. When the raspberries are ripe many assist in the picking, particularly in Perthshire and Angus, and again when the potatoes are ready for lifting.

They are expert poachers, and, although many are decent, most are cadgers, begging from everyone they come in contact with, especially around the country cottages and outlying farms, they pick up anything, particularly in the food line, a hen or duck for example.

During our stay at Loch Ken we get drinking water, milk and eggs from the farm about a mile along the farm road. This water comes from a spring, cold and fresh with never a shortage even in a drought. At one time the highway passed the farm, with stage-coaches rumbling by, but now it is over two miles from the main road, and a tractor takes the milk to the road-end each morning for collection for the creamery at Kirkcudbright.

Three miles along this road is Mossdale, a clachan (hamlet) which grew up around the railway, because here, five miles from the royal burgh, is New Galloway Station. However, passenger trains no longer run on this line and the station house is empty, though the porter still lives in Mossdale, and has a thriving business as a general merchant with post office and petrol pumps.

But our chief shopping centre is Castle Douglas, ten miles from our site. Those are beautiful miles past Woodhall Loch to the pretty village of Laurieston, where we turn left to go across country to the Castle Douglas road. Until the middle of the eighteenth century, Woodhall Loch went by the beautiful Gallovidian name of Grenoch, meaning the sunny loch, and Laurieston village was Clachanpluck. An Englishman called Lawrie bought the estate and changed the names of loch and village. He built a beautiful mansion between Laurieston village and Woodhall Loch which he called Laurieston Hall. Today this fine old house with its magnificent Adam fireplace is a hospital for incurables.

Castle Douglas is a most delightful town, and a very busy one because it is the market town for the wide, surrounding farming district. The shops are first class and the shopkeepers so friendly that it is a pleasure to shop there. If they do not stock what one wants they go out of their way to say where it can be got, or, if necessary, will order anything required. The main shopping street is King Street, a long, wide street where parking is allowed on one side only, but that is changed to the opposite next day so that all the shops benefit on alternate days of each week.

When this rule came into force a few years ago, a zealous young lady police constable had just been drafted to work in the town, and finding a car parked on the wrong side waited until the owner appeared from a shop. With her notebook ready she asked his name, but the man expostulated that he was a county councillor so surely could park where he liked. Our lady P.C. would have none of that. She 'booked' him, and, in spite of his County status, the offender appeared in court and was fined.

There are several first-class hotels in Castle Douglas, and it is a sheer delight to lunch or dine in the 'Douglas Arms'; the cooking and service are superb.

One wild, stormy day in Castle Douglas my only desire was for a cup of tea in that hotel lounge. After shopping I battled my way in the gale-force wind to the garage at the town foot where David had said he would be. But there was no car.

Back I struggled to the corner where we turn out of King Street to leave the town, but seeing our lady P.C., I hurried across to her, and asked if she had seen a Vanden Plas Princess.

"No," said she crisply. "Have you lost one?"

"Yes," I answered, "and my husband, too." I told her where I was supposed to meet him.

"Shelter in that café doorway," she said, and off she went to the garage, to return and inform me that David could not get what he wanted there, and had been advised to try a garage at the head of the town.

"Stay where you are," she said, "I am going up the street and may find him."

David was belting down the long street when the lady P.C. dashed out and stopped him. He wondered what was wrong, but was relieved to learn that his only misdemeanor was leaving a frozen, storm-battered wife in a café doorway!

On spring market days hundreds of boxes of bedding plants are displayed for sale on a grassy bank at the head of the town. They are a real temptation, but being so far from my home garden I have to resist. However, there is a garden shop in King Street which is a delight to browse in.

Behind King Street lies Carlingwark Loch, and on one bank is the charming caravan park, although it can become crowded in July and August. It is in a garden of flowers, tall trees, and young spring-blossoming trees. There are little boats for fishing and pleasure on the beautiful loch with its pretty islands where swans and moorhens nest. This loch, of considerable size, was formed by springs filling old marl mines, marl being a calcarious clay used as manure in fields.

Before the eighteenth century, Castle Douglas was a village of about twenty cottages, called Causewayend from an old causeway crossing the morass at the loch's foot. But, as the village grew with the growth of the marl industry, the name was changed to Carlingwark. In 1789 a merchant and manufacturer, William Douglas (afterwards Sir William Douglas of Gelston), bought the land. Again the village grew, this time into a town which he got made into a burgh of barony, and changed the name again, this time to Castle Douglas. It soon became a cattle market and has remained one of great importance.

Two miles from Castle Douglas stands Thrieve Castle on an island of twenty acres in the sullen Black Water of Dee. This is now National Trust of Scotland property, and is a place beloved by ornithologists for the water birds whose habitat it is.

Another Douglas figured here, Archibald the Grim, who built Thrieve Castle in the fourteenth century when David II appointed him to govern Galloway. Before that he was a Sheriff of Edinburgh, Constable of Edinburgh Castle and Warden of the West Marches. Three years later, in 1372, he induced Thomas Fleming, Earl of Wigton, to convey to him the lands and superiority of the shire along with his title for the sum of £500—probably a reasonable fortune then.

The Douglas chiefs waxed strong, and their story makes grand reading for a lover of Scottish history, but suffice it to say that by the fifteenth century the fifth Douglas chief was Earl of Douglas, Earl of Wigton, Lord of Galloway, Lord of Bothwell, Lord of Annandale, Lord of Eskdale, Duke of Turaine (because he took ten thousand men to France to help the French to fight the English), Lord of Longuebille, and Marshal of France.

Although Castle Douglas is the principal town in the Stewartry of Kirkcudbright it is not the county town. That is Kirkcudbright, which is ancient, with a tremendous amount of history, and a delightful place to explore. The town and the surrounding countryside is an artist's paradise, and for many years innumerable arstists have made their home here. Many live in old, modernized houses down quaint little pends (alleyways). These are gaily painted, with bright tubs of geraniums and other flowers on their cobbled entrance ways.

One such inhabitant is Mr. Jeff, who has a hand loom, and among other activities does scroll-writing and lectures up and down the country. I said that, being a journalist, I was interested in his work; so we got on to the topic of writing when he suddenly said,

"There was one writer I loved but, I don't see so many of her articles these days. She used to write a lot about Galloway. Agnes Innes was her name. I don't know what's become of her."

I just smiled, but the friend who was with me said, "Well, she isn't far away! She is standing grinning at you now!"

Mr. Jeff hugged me, and, although I pointed out to him that other customers were awaiting his attention, he armed me out to the car as if he wouldn't let me go. The car in front of ours he said was his. It had suddenly arrived one day, new from Coventry, and the driver handed him all the documents and receipt of purchase in his name; but he has never been able to discover who the kind friend was who made him this magnificent gift.

Kirkcudbright is on the estuary of the River Dee, and at the harbour the National Trust for Scotland has made a splendid job of restoring and modernizing the little fishermen's houses. The spectacular old castle close by dates from 1582 and was built by Sir Thomas Maclellan of Bombie, a nearby estate.

The old Tolbooth, of which the burgers are proud, was built in the sixteenth century. This edifice of unhappy memories is pleasing with its little tower and projecting parapet, supported on corbels with tiny arches between. At least part of the Tolbooth is thought to have been built from stone removed from Dundrennan Abbey, which for a long time was used in this district as an easy quarry. The market cross was removed from the High Street a century ago and placed on a platform at the head of the Tolbooth's outside stair.

Among the many imprisoned in the Tolbooth was Janet Corbie in 1697. She was accused of abusing her neighbours with scandalous words, and, when those pious people were at the kirk, of stealing vegetables from their gardens and selling them in the country. She was to remain in the Tolbooth until the Monday after her imprisonment, at 10 a.m., then she was expelled for all time by transportation across the estuary by ferry-boat.

Fifty years later another prisoner did not escape so lightly. Henry Grieg was a tinker and found guilty of "theft, robbery and house-breaking". He was taken from the Tolbooth "to the

Loch Ken from the roadside

ordinary place of execution, and there hanged by the neck on a gibbet until he should be dead." His two lady companions were not exiled across the estuary, but transported to His Majesty's plantations somewhere abroad, never to return.

There is a fine museum in St. Mary Street. Among the interesting things there is an old kirk bell which bears the inscription: "Awake thou that Sleepest and Christ Shall give thee Life". The very old church beside the castle is St. Cuthbert's, and is also interesting in that there has been a church on this site since time immemorial, and it was from this ancient kirk that the town and shire derived its name, Kirkcudbright, the 'cudbright' being from Cuthbert. The pronunciation of Kirkcudbright can cause strangers from the south some confusion. It is pronounced 'Kirkcoobrie'.

Six miles south-east is the village of Dundrennan with the remains of the once beautiful Dundrennan Abbey. It lies far below the road in a peaceful valley surrounded by glorious trees. It was here that Mary Queen of Scots, fleeing after the Battle of Langside, spent her last night in Scotland before embarking in a fishing-boat to cross the Solway to Cumberland.

But two of the most delightful villages to visit from Kirkcudbright are Kippford and Rockcliff. They are near each other. Kippford is a place of boats and yachts, a real holiday, sea-shore village. Rockcliff is built in and on the red cliffs which here fringe the shore. The houses are beautiful and some of the gardens are made on the rocks, with brilliant flowers planted in every little cleft and spilling over the red rocks.

Also near Kirkcudbright is the place where Paul Jones was born in 1747. He was the gardener's son from Arbigland. He later became the founder of the American Navy, but his services were also given to Russia and to France, and he died in Paris when he was only 44. However, the Americans are very proud of their Paul Jones, and they took his body back to America in 1913.

To reach the old granite town of Dalbeattie, the road skirts round Craignair Hill, where the famous granite quarries are. Quarrying was first started in the first quarter of the nineteenth century, when the granite blocks were required to build Liverpool docks. From then it was sent all over the world, and among some of the enduring projects made from Dalbeattie granite are the Thames Embankment, the Birkenhead and Manchester town

Galloway gipsies with their 'vardo' or covered wagon

4

halls, many insurance buildings in London, Liverpool and Leeds, the lower part of the Eddystone Lighthouse, and the lighthouses in Ceylon called the Great Basser and Little Basser. In this sturdy old town are many good hotels, and we sometimes lunch here when exploring its beautiful surroundings. It lies in the valley of the River Urr, and three miles to the north is the Moat of Urr, one of the finest earthworks in Scotland. It is said to have been the judgement seat of the Kings when Galloway was a country on its own. It consists of a citadel, base court, and moat.

Now I must take you by my favourite route to another old town, Gatehouse-of-Fleet. This road starts at the cross-roads in Laurieston village and climbs right up through the forest and on to the moors. The road is narrow but good, and it is a glorious way, especially on a spring day when the larks are in full song, and the road-bordering hawthorns, as we drop downhill towards Gatehouse, are like drifts of snow on either side.

Gatehouse is a grand holiday town with its own caravan park and another one among the sand-dunes on its sunny shore. Many of its old houses are the homes of foresters and farm workers. As its name implies, in turnpike days a gate across the entrance halted travellers, as they thundered down the long hill into and through the town, and gave time to collect the toll money.

It was a busy road then, with stage-coaches and mail-coaches, because this was the straight way to Port Patrick in the west, which connected Donaghdee in Ireland by packet-boat, the shortest sea route. Travellers came from every part of the country, even from London, by this route, because the terrors of highwaymen were nothing to the terrors of the Irish Sea under sail.

Looking at the quiet town now, it is difficult to imagine it as a busy little industrial town, but behind the prosperous-looking main street are the crumbling, ivy-grown ruins of its once busy factories. In its heyday there were six cotton mills manufacturing that useful fabric, but another mill turned out lovely muslins, from which the ladies of that period fashioned their many-flounced crinolines. A soap factory produced good, plain soap, lacking the present-day glamour of delicate perfumes and enchanting names. Water, which was plentiful, was suitable for making beer and fine ales, so, from the local brewery, the inns and hotels of the town were stocked. A tannery kept local saddlers, bootmakers and cobblers supplied, while several pirn (bobbin or reel) and bark mills were kept busy by the many factories.

The River Fleet ran too low to turn the mill-wheels, so the mill owners utilized the waters of Loch Whinyeon in the hills three miles away. Stopping its outlet to the River Dee a tunnel was blasted through a hill, and the water brought by means of an aqueduct. Then a canal of 14,000 yards was constructed to enable ships to navigate the Fleet right up into the town, and at the same time reclaimed 170 acres of valuable, fertile land. Shipbuilding and ship-repairing became another industry, allied with their trades of sail-making, ship-chandling, etc.

So their merchandise was exported by way of the River Fleet, and when money flowed in a bank became necessary, so the Paisley Bank, one of the first in Scotland, opened a branch.

Gatehouse also had its own trade token depicting the mill and name of the largest manufacturer, and known as the Gatehouse halfpenny, the only coin of its kind ever used in the south-west of Scotland. Had the roads and road transport been then as they are today this little industrial town would have continued to thrive and grow, but larger steamships replacing sail could not navigate the Fleet estuary, then later, when railways arrived, Gatehouse station was built high in the hills six miles from the town and reached by a wild hill road, which many a time must be snow-blocked in winter. So larger industrial centres took their trade.

A relic of those prosperous days is the beautiful granite clock tower in the square. But to me the most beautiful thing here is, crossing the bridge, to see the thick, trim hedge which edges the Anwoth Hotel, in bloom, a mass of tiny roses. This beautiful garden has green lawns sloping to the River Fleet, below beautiful trees and bushes. Anwoth Hotel is one of the very old ones, but is delightful. More famous, but now a ruin, is Anwoth Church on a little back road. Built in 1626 its minister was Covenanting divine Samuel Rutherford, and so powerful a preacher that even after 300 years Anwoth and Rutherford are still thought of together.

Just outside the town, going westward, the road climbs past the hill where gaunt Cardoness Castle stands high. Its empty windows gaze far over the Fleet's estuary and its low-tide golden sands, across the restless Solway, to Cumberland's faint blue coast, as they gazed long ago when a little sick girl found herself alone with her nurse, the sole survivor of her large family. The story goes that the laird, an old Border ruffian, who had married to secure an heir and perpetuate his name, had nine daughters. With his pride in the dust he was so irate that he swore if his wife presented him with another girl he would drown the lot, and his wife, too, in the hill-loch above the castle. However, the next baby was a boy, so in jovial mood, and it being midwinter, he ordered a great feast to be prepared on the frozen loch. Here friends and family assembled, even the wife and precious baby, and fun and feasting were at their height when the ice cracked and the whole company sank below the icy, black waters. The little heiress grew up and married, changing her name to Mac-Culloch, so the rascal's name was lost for ever.

The main road runs for twelve glorious miles high above the shore all the way to Creetown. At the estate of Ravenshall, far below, are wild rocks and cliffs which occur in Sir Walter Scott's *Guy Mannering*. It is here that Dirk Hatteraick's cave is; and, in hiking days, a friend and I scrambled six miles along the shore rocks from Creetown to find it. It is a narrow slit, high up on the cliff face. From inside the cave I dug out a tiny heart's tongue fern and it is still growing strongly in our garden.

In an old Gallovidian book, which I prize, the author asked a friend which road in Scotland he considered the most beautiful. The answer was the twelve miles from Gatehouse to Creetown. And which was the second best, he was asked, and his reply was the twelve miles from Creetown to Gatehouse. But there is another, more ancient highway westward bound, an old military one, the Carse o' Slates (the crossing of the passes), which takes to the hills by old Anwoth Church, and, fringing old lead workings, comes down into Creetown.

In the last century there was a man, an engineer and millwright, who lived at Barley Mill, half a mile from Gatehouse. He had three sons. I wonder if he was disappointed that none of them followed him in his business, or was he justly proud of them? Those were the celebrated artists James, John, and Thomas Faed, probably the first to do justice to this beautiful district. Many of their wonderful paintings are still to be seen in houses and halls throughout the Stewartry.

And so, after unavoidable dallying by the way, we come to

Creetown, or, to give it its old, lovely name, the Ferrytown of Cree (because from here a ferry used to go across the Cree to Wigtownshire). This little town also has a granite clock tower in its square and a hotel which is called The Ellengowan after the *Guy Mannering* story. It was in this hotel that Dorothy L. Sayers stayed when she wrote the thriller, *Five Red Herrings*, which is set in the locality.

I cannot leave the Stewartry without a word about their own novelist, S. R. Crockett, who was the well-loved minister of Laurieston. He was born here in 1860 and died in 1914. His writing was all about his native Galloway, especially Glen Trool and the mountainous region there. The best known of his thrilling tales was *The Raiders*, but they are all good reading. He was buried in Laurieston Churchyard, and a fine granite memorial can be seen as we enter the village from our Kenside pitch.

4

Westward to Wigtownshire:
Robert the Bruce, Smugglers and Covenanters

To explore the other half of Galloway from our Kenside pitch means going farther afield, and entails many whole day outings. We could tour it all with 'Golden Eagle', stopping at various caravan parks, but we prefer quick travelling and returning to the comfort of the caravan, the beauty of Loch Ken and the pleasure of being afloat on the loch at the end of a day out and about.

From the little royal burgh of New Galloway there are five ways to choose. We came in with our caravan across the River Ken by Rennie's beautiful bridge. Even at the other end of the bridge there are three roads: the main road to Castle Douglas, the main road to Dumfries and the road north to Dalry, or, to give it its old name, St. John's town of Dalry. Its name came from the saint, and its church is St. John's. It is a beautiful village on the banks of the River Ken, with its old market cross reminding us that a weekly meal market was held here before all markets became centred on Castle Douglas.

But a road from the head of New Galloway's main street also goes to Dalry, climbing steeply past the Kells Parish Church, a fine old church with a beautiful organ. A little road, steep and narrow, known as the West Port, climbs out of the centre of the main street and eventually joins up with the main road.

But we have not looked much at the little royal burgh itself yet. In New Galloway are the homes of many foresters. There are several shops and three good hotels, but apart from that there is no industry. Yet it is a delightful centre for a holiday from which every part of Galloway can easily be visited. There is also a regular bus service to Castle Douglas and to Ayr, but for real enjoyment in Galloway a car is necessary.

The road signposted Newton Stewart is the one we take west,

and it is a beautiful road. It climbs high on to the moors, it dips and twists, the peewits and the curlews cry, the larks sing and the wind is fresh with the sweet smell of hill-land, moorland and river, because we are wending our way by the Knocknarling Burn. This old road was known as the Old Edinburgh Road because originally this was the way through the hills for travellers from the east.

Shortly we are looking down on and far out across the great expanse of Clatteringshaws' Reservoir. This valley was flooded during the hydro-electricity scheme, to bring the waters from Loch Doon, which is a storage reservoir, and feed them through tunnels to the power stations at Kendoon, Carsfad, Earlston and Tongland. A great dam stretches across the foot of Clattering-shaws close to the road, which was a new section of road when the dam was built. The Forestry Commission has not yet reached Clatteringshaws, but they are approaching it. When its banks are clothed in trees it will appear less windswept and bleak.

Higher in the hills, Loch Doon is even more windswept. It originally discharged its waters by the River Doon to the Clyde, but, by the construction of a dam and a tunnel, its waters are diverted into the Ken Valley. An interesting feature of Loch Doon was the island on which Loch Doon Castle stood. This was a stronghold of Robert the Bruce and, instead of just submerging the lot, the walls of the ruin were carefully photographed, every stone was numbered, then it was demolished and rebuilt exactly as before on the west bank of the loch under the supervision of the Ministry of Works. This was in 1935–36 when the actual scheme came into operation. This colossal project cost £3,000,000.

Our westward road descends and brings us to a little bridge, where the Grey Mare's Tail thunders down from the heights, foaming white as it dashes on jagged rocks, spume flung high. This is a beautiful waterfall and many are tempted to picnic here. In this extremely rugged country there are innumerable numbers of wild goats, and by the waterfall is a favourite centre for them to congregate. We have watched family parties of all ages of goats here. Also those high cliffs attract a great number of buzzards, which sail out high in the sky with their lovely mewing cry.

Our next stop, only a short way beyond the waterfall, is beside Murray's Monument. There is no dearth of monuments to

illustrious sons in Galloway, but this obelisk on top of a hill by
the roadside is a rather special one. Alexander Murray was born
in a shepherd's cottage here in 1775. His father was a shepherd,
and, while tending the sheep on the hills around his home, the
boy must have dreamed of a very different life. He wanted to
learn but schooling was difficult. First he attended intermit-
tently the school at New Galloway, then one at Minnigaff, near
Newton Stewart. But they were too far away, and the shepherd
and his family were very poor and required his help. However,
it was then that Alexander realized that all languages were easily
learned. His clever Minnigaff master encouraged him, teaching
him French, Latin, Greek and a little Hebrew. From that small
beginning he went on himself and added Arabic. It was the parish
church minister of Minnigaff and the laird of Orchardton who
got him to Edinburgh University, where he mastered every
European language, including the Icelandic and Slavonic languages. From there he added Abyssinian, Tamil, Sanscrit and
Persian.

Through the help of various professors, and a bursary, he was
able to continue his studies. He then became editor of that fine
old magazine, *The Scots Magazine*, which started publication in
1739 and still goes strong. The culmination of that brilliant
career came in 1812 when he was appointed to the Chair of
Oriental Languages at Edinburgh University.

It was then that the War Office in Whitehall received a dispatch
which nobody could read. They sent it to Alexander Murray,
who quickly returned it with the translation, saying it was in
ordinary Abyssinian! He died shortly after that at the early age of
37, cut off in his prime with tuberculosis, the terrible scourge of
that period.

A little beyond Murray's Monument there is a wayside
cottage. It is now disused, except as a farm store. Someone must
have lived there who loved trees. That would be before the great
forests were planted all around, and when there was moorland
and bare hills. Little trees were planted on the opposite side of
the road (it may have been in their garden), and every one is
different. There is a cypress, a Scotch pine, a holly, a sycamore, a
beech and several others, all beautiful, anything from 10 to
20 feet high now, and a real joy to me as I pass that way.

The road climbs through dense forest, and at its peak the

The harbour, Isle of Whithorn
Newton-Stewart from across the River Cree
The Water of Luce framed by an arch of the Stranraer railway viaduct

Forestry Commission have made a view point, with room to park and a seat. This looks down a deep, narrow valley or gorge, completely covered in forest trees, one of the wildest, most spectacular views I know.

For many miles we continue through deep forest land, dropping down all the way to the Cree valley, until we join the main road from Creetown to Newton Stewart, and about a mile farther we are crossing the wide river right into the town.

This is a fine old market town set cosily around the River Cree and backed by the great Cairnsmore rampart of well over 2,000 feet. The town dates back to the early seventeenth century and was first started by William Stewart, third son of the Earl of Galloway, who owned the Castle Stewart estate here. In many ways it does not look like a Scottish town, with so many of its houses and green lawns dipping into the river.

It is still a market town, and a very busy one for the vast county of Wigtown. There are several good hotels and excellent shops, so, whether it is browsing in the art dealer's among modern paintings of the countryside, buying tweeds and other delightful merchandise in the tweed shop, or delicious hand-made bread in the baker's, quite a while is always spent in Newton Stewart. It is a place beloved by anglers and a wonderful tourist centre, with roads connecting every part of Galloway; main roads and leafy by-ways, by river, loch and mountain, by wild rocky coast or quiet friendly little hills. Being on the border of Wigtownshire it gives a warm welcome to all who visit it. But the pride of it all for scenery and story is Glen Trool.

> Land of brown heath and shaggy wood,
> Land of the mountain and the flood,
> Land of my sires, what mortal hand
> Can e'er untie the filial band
> That knits me to thy rugged strand?

This quotation, carved more than a century ago on the little stone bridge over the Buchan Burn, near the head of Glen Trool, symbolized what I felt as I looked down on it from the eminence of the Bruce's Stone knoll and far beyond it to where the Gairland Burn toppled over its mountain to fall in white foam, looking like a slash of white marble down its face.

That was on my first visit to Glen Trool in hiking-days. We

Portpatrick on the Rhinns of Galloway
Glen Trool showing The Bruce's Stone and the
   battleground below Muldonnach Hill

had walked every mile from Newton Stewart, leaving its bustle to go through the dewy morning, by the sweet serenity of the Silver Cree, with its green meadows, dappled with placid cattle, its harvest fields awaiting the reapers, all made homely by white farms and the peace of an old kirk.

But almost imperceptibly the scene grew wilder. We crossed the rushing Minnoch Water and the mountains crowded in; we were in the glen, and ever wilder, more rugged and untamed grew our way. Gradually the wondrous beauty of the mountain-walled loch unfolded before us as our track climbed high along it . . . and that day Glen Trool laid a spell on me which has drawn me back countless times.

Across the glen from the Bruce's Stone rises Mulldonach, where his handful of men toiled all night to lever granite boulders into position along its summit. King Robert had word that the Earl of Pembroke was on his way from Carlisle to capture him, with a much larger force than his own. Near where his Stone stands now, he lay concealed, but with a full view down the glen, and when he saw the English soldiers leave their horses and creep single file along the narrow track under Mulldonach, he sent his bugle signal reverberating among the mountains. The boulders hurtling down Mulldonach's precipitous face crushed many, and swept the remainder over the brink to drown in Loch Trool. At the loch's head a green strip of meadow, where many of the soldiers were buried, is called the Soldiers' Holm.

The story of the Bruce in Glen Trool has many recorded incidents, but perhaps the most far-reaching that describing how he sat frustrated in his cave, and found new heart and courage to turn Scotland's tide as he watched the perseverance of the spider.

Coming forward in history to the 'killing time' we find another monument, lying south-west of the loch, on which 'Old Mortality' chiselled the names of six Covenanters from four families of this glen, who were surprised at worship and cruelly murdered.

The hills around Loch Trool, and by the wild, tumbling Minnoch Water, as well as by the Silver Cree, were once all deep in trees as part of the great Buchan Forest. The old forest disappeared long ago, but when the Forestry Commission took over they turned Glen Trool into a National Forest Park. They bridged the Water of Trool, and there turned a beautiful forest clearing into a fine caravan and camping site, so that people can live awhile in, and explore that wonderful glen. Those who can climb the mountains at its head will find other amazing lochs, like huge mountain tarns; the Long and the Round Lochs of Glenhead, Loch Valley, the Dungeon Lochs, Loch Enoch and Loch Neldricken with its Murder Hole. S. R. Crockett, in *The Raiders*, makes grand use of this wild mountain terrain, and for John Buchan it was indeed *No Man's Land*.

Loch Enoch has several interesting features. It is said to be the highest loch in Scotland, yet its inner loch, a lochan separated by islands and called Loch-in-loch, has a surface some sixteen feet higher than Loch Enoch. The fine, white granite sand of Loch Enoch's beaches used to be prized for sharpening scythes, but it must have taken a stout heart to carry sacks of sand from that elevated loch in the shadow of Merrick.

The magnificent mountain panorama rising from the Trool and Cree valleys, and terminated by Cairnsmore of Fleet, can best be seen from the summit of the road climbing from Wigtown. It was a May evening, after a day of sleet and hail, that, coming over the brow of the hill, we were spellbound by their beauty as the setting sun turned those snow-covered mountains rosy pink; and far below the iridescent, gleaming, silvery Cree stretched lazily from Newton Stewart.

Wigtownshire is fascinating. Its land borders extend for some thirty miles, but its coastal boundaries measure over a hundred miles, comprising one side of Wigtown Bay, both sides of Luce Bay, the long edge of the Rhinns Peninsula, and both sides of Loch Ryan. Its towns are few, old and peaceful, and its villages are gems spangling that golden chain of coastline. Its heart is arable and grass-land.

Wigtownshire farmers are justly proud of the beef and milk they produce. Their beef herds are mostly of the local all Black Galloways, Galloway Belties, so named because of the broad white band right round the middle of their black bodies, and Dun Galloways, which are a soft mink colour. The dairy cattle are mostly Ayrshires and Friesians. It is interesting that the Galloway cattle are a native breed, a sturdy one said to have evolved to withstand the rather wet and often boisterous climate. They have a thick, shaggy outer coat which throws off the rain, and a soft, very thick under coat which keeps out the cold. They can safely be wintered out.

Being isolated from industrial areas, large creameries absorb the milk from their splendid dairy herds. After sterilization it is sent in bulk to the large towns and cities, or turned into farm butter, delicious cheese, or dried milk powder.

In springtime Wigtownshire's rocky shores gleam where whins and broom capture the golden sunshine, and wild hyacinths spread carpets of heavenly blue. But the sun does not always shine here; there are days of rain and fierce gales which sweep in from the Atlantic to batter the narrow Rhinns Peninsula. Those winter storms stopped Portpatrick from being the most popular port for Ireland, twenty-one miles from Donaghadee on Belfast Lough, for when steam replaced sail, from sheltered Stranraer to Larne became the route.

In the days of sail, Portpatrick was to Ireland what Gretna Green was to England for runaway, or rather sailaway, eloping couples, until the practice was stopped in 1862. Recorded during the fifty years before that, thirteen noblemen, 200 gentlemen, and fifteen naval and army officers were among those who risked the stormy passage with their brides.

Cattle and horses too came by this route in 1790, its heyday, 1,800 being imported to start their long trek to Glasgow, or south to Liverpool and even to London. In 1662 a weekly post between Scotland and Ireland was started via Portpatrick, and English mail too went by this route. In 1774 the post office built the first pier, in 1790 the daily post came into force, and in 1820 the Government began improving the harbour and building protecting piers for its regular mail service. It was intended to use the south pier for hauling out the sailing packets until sufficiently clear to catch the wind, but by the time work was completed steam had come into use. Sheltered Stranraer, useless in the days of sail, became the ideal port for steamboats, and Portpatrick, with its splendid, horseshoe-shaped harbour which Rennie built, its railway and huge, cliff-top hotel, lost its importance. Today, however, it is a busy fishing port and a yachting centre.

Farther south lie the incredible Logan Gardens. A former owner, as at Inverewe in Ross-shire, proved that the western Scottish seaboard, favoured by the warm airs of the Gulf Stream, can grow tropical plants and trees. Here are fantastic avenues of palm trees, a sunken pond with gigantic goldfish, some over a foot long, rock gardens edging lovely pools, quiet walks edged by exotic trees and flowers, and over all a feeling as if our magic carpet had transported us from this most southerly part of Scotland to some Eastern clime.

The most southerly village of any size on the Rhinns is Drummore; the name means great ridge, yet it is right down on its own bay in the wide Luce Bay. There is a beautiful stretch of sand, a wonderful place for bathing, and a small harbour. Just a delightful holiday place, yet remote and quiet with a coastguard station, some fishing boats, and friendly people.

Its church, which perches on the hill-top half a mile away, is known as the Kirk Covenant, because it was built in 1639 which was the year when the National Covenant was signed throughout our land.

Behind Drummore there is a ridge, however, which is part of the spine of that long peninsula, and all over this parish of Kirkmaiden is a maze of small roads. I remember once, a few years ago, when David and I were exploring this section, a heavy sea-mist suddenly descended. We decided to retrace our way as quickly as possible to Portpatrick. We left Drummore heading north, but four times we landed back in Drummore! Once a momentary lifting of the mist revealed the sea on our left hand when it should have been on our right, and once we landed in a farmyard, where a ghostly man welcomed us with, "Well I'm blest! You passed me miles back! If I'd known you were coming here I'd have dumped my bike and come with you." He proceeded to recount all sorts of weird local tales to us and insisted that all the people there were queer! However, he directed us—back to Drummore! The Drummore brownies just would not let us go! (A brownie is a type of sprite who haunts houses by night and does the housework while the inhabitants sleep, for which the housewife always leaves a bowl of milk and a bite to eat as payment, but never money which would be an insult.)

Five miles south of Drummore village, at the very tip, stands the Mull of Galloway lighthouse, and even on the calmest day this place is wild with surging seas and screaming gulls. It is good to have some 270 feet between those swirling currents and the lighthouse balcony. On a clear day the views from this lofty balcony are wonderful; far north lies Kintyre, nearer are the Ayrshire and the Stewartry peaks, west looms the Irish coast, south the Isle of Man, and across the Solway the Cumberland coast and fells. This wild, rocky coast, with its deep fissures and sea-washed caves, renowned in olden days for smugglers, is a paradise for sea-birds. At the foot of rugged cliffs lie remote and lovely little coves, while on the cliff-tops the vivid green turf is spangled with the delicate pink of thrift.

Smuggling has always been a characteristic of people of Britain. We are an island, and there are always those willing to lead a hazardous life with the added spice of going against restricting laws, and enjoying the game to the full. The fact that caves were plentiful and transport restricted to single horse-power per unit, makes it all the more romantic, and often laughable.

About seventy years ago some workmen discovered a secret cellar in a cave and in it a store of brandy. The men, with the help of friends, transported their treasure trove to more convenient hiding places, one concealing his cask in a field on his farm. But rumour of that ploy leaked, and an excise officer from Dumfries came to investigate. The farmer had made a daily trek to his cask, and a well-trodden path across the field had resulted. His only way to keep this secret was to plough the field, which he did, and a year earlier than his lease stipulated!

Early one morning a big lugger, heavily laden with rich contraband from the Isle of Man, was surprised off the Mull of Galloway by the Revenue cutter. They disregarded an order to heave to and, setting every bit of canvas, raced away. The cutter followed suit, and with a fair wind blowing their speed was tremendous. It was dangerous to attempt rounding Burrow Head with its jagged rocks in such a storm but the lugger did, on the crest of the wave one minute and lost in the trough the next, but by expert seamanship she made it. When the Revenue cutter observed their prey making for the Isle of Whithorn they guessed that they were giving up the struggle. So the cutter shortened sail and in a leisurely way sailed into the Isle harbour to tie up and look around for the lugger. But the lugger had vanished! She had made an impossible attempt and pulled it off. At that time there was another very small inlet to the harbour which little craft could use at high tide. But the tide was exceptionally high that day, the following wind fierce so they raced their big boat through those narrows and when the Excise men got to view-point she was heading for the English coast under full sail. In her passage the keel of the lugger had scraped along the gravelly bed for fully a hundred yards and dislodged several stones on either side.

But best of all I like the story of the smugglers' accomplice, Maggie McConnell. In a creek on a lonely stretch of shore smug-glers had just completed the unshipping of a tremendous cargo of wines, brandies, gorgeous silks, tea from the East, tobacco from the West, and fine Hollands, when they were pounced on by a custom-house officer and a stalwart comrade from Stranraer. The smugglers fled, and the officer sent his man off to get trans-port for the booty. Seating himself on one of the cases to wait, he looked carefully to the priming of his pistols.

Presently a well-favoured, sonsy dame came strolling by; she was fair to look on, and the customs man, in high good humour over his coup, thought a chat would while away the time, so offered her the hand of friendship. Maggie gripped his hand but at the same time her other arm encircled his waist and he was flat on the ground with Maggie sitting on top. She tied her apron over his eyes, removed his pistol and cocked it. Nothing the poor man could say or promise would make her relent, so he was glad when he heard footsteps and horses draw near. He shouted for help in the King's name, but still Maggie held him. After a while she relaxed and, kindly kissing him, untied the apron. But the contraband had disappeared and all that could be seen was a few cows peacefully grazing and Maggie strolling away. It is said that he kept quiet about being held up in his duty by an unarmed woman and in due course was anonymously rewarded for his silence!

Between Glenluce and Stranraer other beautiful gardens which always draw us back again are those of Lochinch, home of the Earl of Stair, by the old Kennedy Castle. We always endeavour to make our visits coincide with rhododendron-time, when the masses, variety and beauty of these exotic flowers, and of the azaleas, make the walks a way of enchantment.

About two miles up the glen from Glenluce stands the old abbey, in its beautiful setting of low hills and trees and sur-rounded by the greenest of turf, said to be the result of the monks, centuries ago, riddling the soil. The abbey was founded in 1190 by Roland, Lord of Galloway, for Cistercian monks from Melrose.

There is a great deal of ancient history in Wigtownshire, but for the antiquarian this surprising shire has rather more than its share of standing stones, stone circles, old sculptured crosses, holed stones, a moat and earthworks.

The road south from Glenluce verges a stony shore and going through Port William circles the Machers. On the east of this peninsula we find the ancient town of Whithorn, which claims the distinction of being the place where the first stone church was built in Scotland. This was erected by St. Ninian in 397 and dedicated to St. Martin of Tours. Here are some ancient ruins of the priory, notably the supporting pillars of a pend, which are decorated with oak leaves and shields, and a richly carved Norman doorway. Many kings and queens made pilgrimage to the shrine at Whithorn, among them James IV, who often journeyed on foot from Edinburgh or from Linlithgow, twice a year.

South on its own little peninsula is the Isle of Whithorn—not a true island, in spite of its name—and the villagers declare that here was St. Ninian's kirk. But on a summer's day this is such a lovely little jewel-village set in blue waters with dancing boats that its present-day appearance makes us forget such far-off things. They are brought sharply to mind again in the old county town of Wigtown with its sad tales of Covenanting days and martyrs. In the churchyard are the graves of the two Margarets, one old, one young, who were tied to stakes in the Water of Bladenoch and drowned by the rising tide. But to me Wigtown is a sunny place of white houses round a huge square with enticing by-roads off.

The Covenanting years were bad and lasted a great number of years. Charles II was on the throne and he would have bishops in our Scottish kirks and turn them into Episcopalian. But here the Scots were Presbyterian and were willing to fight to preserve their own form of worship. They got up a tremendous army and many battles ensued, but the unfortunate thing was that so many Scots, in the old tradition, insisted on being loyal to the King. So Scots even fought their own countrymen.

The whole thing was vicious and terribly cruel. The persecution of our preachers and of those who would not, even at the point of death, sign away their freedom to worship as they

Sheep-shearing in the old style

wanted, was dastardly. It all made history and helped to impoverish Scotland, but it seems such a waste from beginning to end. Galloway was one part of Scotland where the adherents of the Presbyterian Church were strong and therefore the more persecuted.

5

Bagging the rolled fleeces

5

Clipping Time in Galloway:
Day at a Hill Farm

One fine evening, when we dropped in to see some farmer friends near Balmaclellan, we found their talk mainly of the clipping to be done on the morrow, a dry day being essential for that job. This was a dairy-farm as well as a hill sheep-farm, and after the milking they were for the far hills to gather in the sheep to the lower pastures ready for the morning.

"It'll be a big day," said the farmer, and his wife smiled. For her, too, it would be a big day, for the many helpers as well as her own folk would have to be fed.

After tea we left them to their tasks and returned to 'Golden Eagle' by the side of Loch Ken. How wonderful it always is to return to the quiet peace of that lovely place. But there was a ploy afoot; we were going to have a whole day at the clipping, and find out all there was to know about it.

Next morning saw us up betimes, and, armed with some of the fish we had caught from the loch the night before, we set off for the farm. There all was bustle. The milking had been got over early, and only the dairy-maid was left clattering in the dairy, outside which stood a row of milk-churns awaiting collection. The farmer's wife parked their red saloon car ahead of us, and a long-legged farmer uncurled himself from the seat beside her. She had been to fetch him from his farm several miles away, because his car had broken down. He was only one of several farmers and shepherds who were coming to lend a hand, for, of all trades, surely farming is the most generous in lending man-power when necessary to those of a like calling.

We caught snatches of their greetings to each other and to the farmer.

"A grand morning, Jim. Looks like keeping fair."

"Aye, there's mist ower there on the hills, but it cleared early here."

And above their talk came the bang-banging away of the tractor, and the clatter of gear being loaded on to the heavy truck it was to pull. Some of it strange gear, too, to the uninitiated, especially the long clipping-stools, just a comfortable height and width to sit astride, with sufficient length in front to accommodate a sheep. Then there were the branding-irons, and a pot of black indelible branding-fluid, because branding a sheep is not now a barbarous, searing business. Bundles of sacks were thrown in— huge sacks, six feet by three feet, into which the wool would be packed—then long posts, the use of which was a mystery to me until later, an odd assortment of tools and, last but not least, bottles of liquid refreshment.

Then into the truck climbed some of the older men, preferring to brave rattled bones on the circuitous, rough track rather than face the stiff, straight climb up the hill. For, although the sheep had been brought down from the heights, the clipping pens were still high in the hills above the farm. As we climbed to them, a wonderful view unrolled before our eyes; beyond the green valley of the Water of Ken lay the Rinns of Kells, with sunshine and cloud-shadow chasing each other across the face of Meikle Millyea; and farther away, but rearing higher still in blue shadows, was Corserine. We crossed an amber-coloured burn and passed the Ayrshire cows, *and* bull, peacefully grazing. Overhead the larks were singing, beneath our feet was soft, springy turf and the air was filled with that indefinable hill perfume; the wafted scent of hay and thyme, of clover, and the dozen other things which are its ingredients.

I would have lingered on that sunny hillside but our desire was to be at the pens when the tractor arrived. Round it came, with the trailer bumping behind, its ploughman-driver quite unconcerned—and who would believe that this man, with his happy laugh, his alert eyes, and quick answers, was deaf?

The trailer was quickly unloaded, and the posts which had so intrigued me were erected, two upright, about 9 feet high, with one horizontal across the top from which the wool-sacks would be suspended. They were called the packing-posts, and a shepherd later told me that 12 feet was a better height, allowing more freedom of movement for the packer.

A sheltered spot against the wall of the pens was chosen for the clipping-stools, for the wind was keen up there in the hills. The stools were firmly fixed and levelled by setting the legs into four holes made with a machete, then sacks were thrown over as padding.

Meantime the shepherds were skilfully engaged in penning the sheep. They were black-faced sheep, a very hardy breed producing a strong wool. The bleating of the bewildered lambs on being separated from their mothers was tremendous. However, in the close-herded flock, an occasional lamb escaped the vigilance of both shepherds and collies and had to be lifted and dropped into another pen. The same evicting procedure was employed on any strays from neighbouring farms.

Now the clippers were settled on the stools and busily touching-up their shears on oilstones, for they kept those gleaming blades razor-sharp, handling them with almost loving care and touching them up at meal-times and during any break. As soon as they were ready, the first unwilling sheep was dragged from the fold, and with one swift, upward movement was heaved on its back on to the stool in front of a waiting clipper. With one skilled hand he quietened the sheep's struggles, while with the other hand, dexterously wielding the shears, he started to clip. Smoothly, evenly, the fleece slipped from the neck and down off one side like the unrolling of a blanket. Then like a flash the sheep was turned over and clip, clip went the shears until the last of the fleece unrolled itself, and a shout from the clipper as the fleece dropped to the ground brought the ploughman running with the branding-iron to stamp a large black *H* on the back of the animal.

While the work was going on, swiftly, smoothly, steadily, I had time to look at the men taking part. There was twenty-year-old Jimmie, strong, willing and seemingly tireless, who played a heavy part in that day's work. His main task was to keep the clippers supplied with sheep, and so fast did the clippers work that Jimmie sweated at his job.

When the ploughman, with quick, watchful eyes, saw Jimmie being too hard pressed, he would leave his own job of branding and rolling the fleeces to give Jimmie a hand. Then the old farmer, with his twinkling eyes, would seize his chance to show that he could still take an active part in the day's work, in spite of his 83 years and the rheumatics, by grasping the branding-iron and hurriedly limping to the sheep that was ready for it. His son, Jim, the farmer now, was like his father, not over-tall but of a strong, heavy build.

The row of clippers were all lean men, some well on in years, some in their prime. The older men with greying hair had hard, weather-beaten faces, while the younger men's showed the ruddy tan of many an hour's exposure to the summer's sun. As I watched them, bent over their task, I saw that they did more than clip; the tails and trotters of the sheep were trimmed, the teeth examined, any blemishes noted, and where an animal appeared to be out of condition medicine in the form of a capsule was expertly pushed down its throat.

There was dexterity, too, in the rolling of the fleeces. As soon as a fleece dropped to the ground the ploughman whisked it aside and, as it was dry, it was rolled wool inwards and tied with a pulled-out end of itself, then thrown on to the ever-growing pile. Here, from time to time, a few of the bleating lambs would come searching for their lost mothers, almost burying themselves as they hunted among the cut fleeces. As a sheep, white, thin and forlorn-looking, left a clipper's hands—yet usually with a happy skip and jump as if glad to be rid of its burdensome weight of wool—it went in search of its offspring, bleating hopefully and running hither and thither to be met everywhere by disdainful youngsters who would not think of taking up with such a disreputable skeleton!

As the forenoon wore on I left my husband busy with his camera and went back down the hillside, giving the bull, who was eyeing me malevolently, a very wide berth! In the farm kitchen a white flour-sack, now only quarter full, stood on a chair, and one white scrubbed table was piled with great batches of floury girdle scones, dropped scones, fruit-cakes, gingerbread, and rhubarb tarts. At the other table spreading was going on; then the big, square baskets were packed, the pitchers were filled with scalding tea, and off we went up the hill again, with Mrs. Jim, flushed from her baking, and looking, in her short blue dress, as bonny as a summer's day, to personally superintend the feeding of that hungry band of workers. During the meal there was a complete relaxation from the job, time for much badinage and 'cracks' between farmers on the state of crops and prices and the latest foibles of the Government.

In the afternoon two newcomers arrived and had to stand much banter about having slept in. But even as they were explaining how it had been a morning of rain and hill-mist at their distant farms, so that they did not think the fleeces would be dry enough to cut before the afternoon, off came their coats, their shears were unwrapped and Jimmie was heaving sheep on to their stools.

Then back once more to the big, airy kitchen, with its snowy muslin curtains and scarlet geraniums at the two windows which framed such entrancing hill-scenes, and its Esse cooker radiating heat. And now there were hard-boiled eggs to mix with butter as a spread for thick sandwiches, great wedges of cake to cut, and more making of tea; then another long climb with the laden baskets and heavy pitchers when the tea-break was due.

As the day wore on, and the pile of fleeces grew, bagging was started. A big sack was suspended from the posts, and a few bundles of fleeces were thrown in; then into the sack climbed the farmer himself to tramp down the wool. So to the very last fleece and the very last sack and to the loading of the truck. Already the sheep and lambs were dispersing about the hills, following their own little tracks, and their bleating was dying away. Down the hill the men came striding, and perched on the truck the old farmer rode in state, as game now as at the start of that long day.

Mrs. Jim had already taken the hill-farmer home in time for his milking and, returning, had cooked a hot meal ready for the men coming in. Then the table was groaning with the best that the farm could offer, and the room was filled with the jovial talk and deep laughter of men who had the satisfaction of a good day's work done.

6

On Tour from Galloway:
the Borders, a Meal Mill and a Tweed Mill

Now our faces are set for other places. We are always sorry to leave our beloved Bonnie Galloway, yet there is so much of Scotland and we love it all.

We choose different routes. One winter's day, when we had dallied longer than usual and it was now cold and frosty, we took the coast road by Gatehouse, Creetown and Stranraer. The early dusk caused us to halt for the night in a disused wayside quarry near Glenluce, and next morning the sun flooded into 'Golden Eagle' across the dazzling waters of Luce Bay. Every leaf, branch and blade of grass was glistening white with hoar frost.

We did some Christmas shopping in Stranraer, and as we sat at lunch in the caravan we watched the Irish steamer sail off for Larne. The sea had only a gentle ripple, so crossing would not be difficult. Then we continued by Loch Ryan, climbing steadily, and were soon into Glen App. Here the rock walls of the pass were festooned with icicles and very beautiful.

It was in this pass, the story (surely an Irish one) goes, that St. Patrick fought a battle in which his head was chopped off. But, nothing daunted, he made his way to Portpatrick and, no boat being handy, he swam the channel to Ireland carrying his head in his teeth!

At Ballantrae we crossed the River Stinchar and continued by the wild, rocky shore. What tales there are here; of a bandit family in a cave who were cannibals, so no human was safe from them. They were eventually captured, taken to Leith and there burned.

Then there was the bluebeard who amassed wealth by courting and marrying heiresses, then throwing them into the sea over those fearsome rocks. But the eighth lady, May Colean, was a match for him, because she threw him over the cliff to drown far below. And that was the end of the false Sir John. There are twelve verses to that old ballad and when the wretch cried for help May Colean called down to him:

> Nae help, nae help, thou fause Sir John,
> Nae help nor pity to thee;
> Ye lie not in a caulder bed
> Than the ane ye meant for me.

Ailsa Craig dominates our seaward view here. From that massive, craggy, cone-shaped island comes the wonderful rock from which beautiful curling stones are made.

But a homeward route we like is through the Borders, so one lovely autumn day we left our Kenside pitch. We had had a busy summer with glorious weather for about six weeks, touring with 'Golden Eagle' in Wales, but we experienced severe storms for the remainder of our stay in Galloway.

In Castle Douglas we shopped, and then, on our way to Dumfries, passed through the little village of Springholm and stopped beside Auchenreoch Loch for lunch. The day had clouded over, and soon rain was once more falling heavily, so we decided to stop on a more suitable pitch lower down beside a boathouse.

Early morning was showery, but by breakfast time the sun was shining and the loch calm and very lovely. We waited until after lunch and found a bush of delicious brambles to add its fruits to our sweet course.

It was 1.40 p.m. when we left that delightful pitch under a golden oak tree. Traffic was brisk, but there were no heavy vehicles, and even the circus and showmen's cavalcade, which had passed our pitch early on, had disappeared. From Dumfries we took a new way, the one to Lochmaben, instead of going by Annan. It was more hilly than the way nearer the shore, but a delightful road through undulating country, with wide views over golden harvest fields and rich grazing land with large herds of dairy cows.

We passed through the pretty village of Torthowald and came to Lochmaben, which was a larger town than we expected. The lochs here, which are much fished and are famous for their own particular fish found nowhere else, looked pleasant but not beautiful as we know lochs.

A few more miles brought us to Lockerbie and the Carlisle road, with heavy commercial traffic, but still quite a few caravans heading north. We had a fancy to take a by-road from Echelfechan to Canonbie, but the garage proprietor where we got petrol advised us against it, as there was a bad turn into Canobie that way. Echelfechan brings to mind an Englishman and his wife lunching at our table in the Ellangown in Creetown. He was enthusiastic about this, their first, holiday in Scotland, and said he hoped all hotels would be as good as the one of the night before. I asked where that was, but ruefully he replied, "I can't pronounce it!" and drawing his hotel receipt from his pocket, pointed out Echelfechan to me.

We continued on to Gretna Green. I always find this placarded, commercialized marrying haunt irksome; it never looks romantic to me. We crossed the imperceptible frontier into England, but only for a few miles for the road took us back into Scotland at Scotch Dyke station. Soon we reached a story-book village with an old coaching inn, which knew all the bustle of the London to Edinburgh stage-coach. Here were white cottages glinting in the sunshine, and high on the hill overlooking the village stood its grey stone kirk. Below, holding the village in its crook, flowed the River Esk, wide and deep with its steep banks clothed with spun gold spilled from the tall trees which climbed to the sky-line. Canonbie was the village and on its lea there was racing and chasing when Young Lochinvar came out of the west and spirited away his bride from Netherby, on the English side of the Esk as near Scotch Dyke, on the eve of her forced marriage to an unwanted suitor. They were the forbears of the Gordons of Kenmure Castle at Loch Ken.

Our lovely way took us climbing up above the River Esk until we crossed it at Gilnockie Bridge, which is now usually called Hollows Bridge, with Hollows Mill beside it. There is a ruined tower near here called Hollows Tower, part of Johnny Armstrong's stronghold, although his real residence was Glenockie Castle, none of which remains, its stones having been used, it is thought, to build Gilnockie Bridge. So the bridge takes both its names from the nearby towers.

Approaching Hollows Bridge, the beauty of the River Esk flowing wide and turbulent far below, captivated us, making David halt the caravan. Then our eyes were drawn to the old yet strangely new-looking mill lying in a twist of the river. In the brilliant sunshine, with glinting water half circling it, the mill seemed to sparkle invitingly.

The miller was friendly and bade us enter, saying that he would like to show us around, but he was hard pressed to get deliveries out, so he would have to let us find our own way about. We did this and got ourselves completely lost in a maze of rooms and passages, and ladders up and ladders down. In this way we found ourselves in a room in the very depths of the mill; before us were the giant spokes of the semi-enclosed water-wheel and the huge pinions and shaft which extended upwards to the grinding mills. It was, however, not those which impressed me most, but the sensation of power, and the roar and spray from the pounding water.

Up on the main floor we found four meal mills all in a row. As we examined them the miller's son, who was following in his father's footsteps and would be the sixth generation to work Hollow's Mill, came over and explained their uses. All four mills worked on the same principle, each having a bottom stone which was stationary and a top stone which revolved and could be adjusted up or down, so grinding the grain coarse or fine. In the centre above each mill was a hopper fed from a large container in the room above. This hopper dropped the grain into a spreader which was agitated by flats on the grinding stone spindle, giving an even spread and flow to the grinding surfaces.

Number one mill was principally used to remove the husk from the whole grain; to do this the top grinding stone had long, narrow, spoke-like grooves cut on its surface. Number two mill ground the kernel into meal. For this purpose the top grindstone had short, narrow grooves radiating from its centre, and its whole surface was of a porous nature. The grain was fed by the spreader to the grinding edges; then the small grooves carried it in between the stones, from which it emerged at the edges as meal mixed with husks. It then dropped through chutes to the shifter, which separated the meal from the husks by means of a vibrating sieve. The meal dropped straight into a container and the husks fell from a spout on the right into a sack.

Number three mill was used to grind the husks and meal seeds for animal feeding. The fibrous nature of the husks required different treatment, and a flat, porous grinding stone was used.

The offal, which flowed from a chute into a sack on the floor below, looked quite palatable when compared with the shells entering the mill on the floor above.

Number four mill was not used much nowadays, because it was for grinding Indian corn or maize. This very hard grain requires a grindstone like the second mill, but in this case a very hard stone was used, called French burr. As the maize meal was used for animal feeding it was not necessary to sift it, so it was bagged as it fell from the mill chute.

Alongside the mills was a winnowing machine which graded the grain, both for seed and milling purposes. This winnowing machine was fed from a large container in the room above and could be described as a special type of bolting mill, as it sifted the grain in a most efficient manner.

Next to catch our attention was a rolling mill. This was somewhat similar to those seen on most large farms, its working parts being two power-driven rollers of rough-faced steel which gripped, bruised and flattened whole, unshelled oats, making them suitable for horses and cattle to digest. This was necessary as, of course, cattle are unable to digest whole grain.

The kiln behind the mills was a large room where the oats were roasted before being ground. The whole of its floor was perforated with quarter-inch holes through which passed the heated air from a furnace below. On this floor stood a large number of sacks of oats, all well spaced out to allow good circulation and easy passage of hot air from the floor.

The rattle of chains drew us away from this sweet-smelling roasting chamber, and we found that sacks of grain were being lifted from floor to floor through a series of self-closing trap doors. Through these trap doors, from a power-driven winch above, passed a chain with a hook which caught the neck of the sack and quickly lifted it to the appropriate floor.

We were back on the floor on which were the grinding mills. As these had stopped working the soft, white dust was settling over everything, its dancing motes lit by shafts of sunlight slanting through the deep-set windows in the enormously thick walls. One small, square window was open, and in and out flitted a robin; it flew about inside, perching on the handrail of the wooden stairway and on various parts of the mills, putting its head on one side and eyeing us inquiringly. Quite obviously it regarded us as strangers, but the robin itself was entirely at home.

We came down again to the floor with the bolting mill; here stood the tall scales for weighing the sacks of meal as they left the mill. But what interested us now was that on the wall behind the scales was a fair-sized switchboard with many knobs, switches, glistening white fuses and glass-fronted meters sticking out from its glossy black base. Whatever was this for? Except for a few lights and a fan I had seen no electrical apparatus. The answer came from the miller's wife, who explained that the switchboard controlled a 3 Kw. generator which charged a battery of accumulators. The electricity was used for the milking machine on their farm, which adjoined the mill, and for all other farm requirements as well as for all lighting and domestic uses. The generator being driven by the waterwheel gave the farm cheap power for all purposes.

I asked how old this fascinating mill was, but the miller did not know. He could only say that it was very, very old and that at some time it was burned down and rebuilt. We were unable to see a lade leading to the mill, which seemed extraordinary. But the miller enlightened us; the water which drove the mill-wheel had a subterranean passage for fully half a mile, and the tunnelled lade was cut out of solid rock. This amazing piece of tunnelling was, according to legend, done by a man and his wife, and one wonders why the first miller decided to build his mill at just that spot on the Esk, which meant putting the great wheel into the very depths of the mill and then having to lead the water with which to drive it by so difficult a passage. Hearsay has it that the subterranean passage for the lade was made as an escape tunnel for the Armstrong reivers of that district, and the mill so placed as a blind to the tunnel's real use. Johnny Armstrong was a famous Border reiver, very strong and powerful, loved by many but feared by others. He was particularly dreaded by King James V, who looked on Johnny Armstrong as a king in his own part of the country and resented and feared his power.

In 1530 several of the Border lairds came to the King seeking mercy and giving assurance of quiet behaviour, so Johnny did likewise. But he first made arrangements for a sumptuous banquet to be prepared at Gilnockie, in the hope that after his parley with King James at Caerlanrig he would be privileged to entertain him. He arrived at the meeting place in royal array with forty chosen vassals, but, unfortunately, this was only a ruse on the King's part to get the reiver into his clutches, and he hanged Johnny and all his brave company.

Before leaving Hollows, I had a chat with a dear old lady from one of the pretty cottages at the mill road end. She was wearing clogs and said they were so comfortable that she disliked going from home when she had to wear ordinary shoes; her clogs were nearly thirty years old and were made in Canonbie where there was still a clog-maker.

As we talked the air was suddenly full of tiny spiders, and we were becoming tangled in their gossamer silken webs. It was a strange experience, but the old lady declared that it was a sign of good weather. Then, saying she had been baking, she popped into her cottage and returned with some delicious scones and queen cakes for our tea.

Our road with its beautiful autumn trees remained a delight all the way to Langholm. We passed through this Muckle Toon at 6 p.m. when it was wrapped in Sunday quiet, and we came to the Kilngreen with the Ewes Water rushing by. As we sat at supper, Langholm's twinkling lights were reflected in the river and lit the bridges; quaint, beautiful, friendly, lovable Langholm, how happy we were to be here once again.

To paint a word-picture of this old Border town, I thought, would be easy, but the trouble is to know where to start, there is so much of it. And if you who know it don't believe me, just look at that word 'Muckle' and hark back a hundred years to the old man here who thought Edinburgh would be just another toon the same as the Langholm. They travelled little in those days; busy days of expansion when the cottage looms had given way to factory weaving and Langholmites felt justly important. It was about this time, too, that one of their tweed travellers called on an Edinburgh merchant, who, pleased with the samples shown, gave a big order, asking where the cloth was made. On being told Langholm, he said, "Never heard of it. Where is it?" Perhaps there was some excuse for him, because Langholm, behind its secluding barrier of hills, is the farthest south of all the Border towns and probably the least known.

But neither size nor importance can colour my word-picture so much as its setting. It is always evening when David and I come in from the west with 'Golden Eagle'. Approaching from the south-west we are always halted at Skipper's Bridge by our first glimpse of lovely Langholm. A mile or so away are five tall chimneys and a church spire. Under them is the grey compactness of the town broken by intervening trees, and the whole surrounded, cupped in green hills and lit by the brilliance of the evening sun.

The Ewes Water, high and brown after heavy rain, was surging past in gleeful haste to join the parent river, the Esk, a few yards away. And would it not be enough for any town to have two good rivers meeting in its heart; but lucky Langholm goes one better, for, a few more yards and the River Wauchope pours waters into the Esk as if saying, "Here you are, you need me to make you really big enough to pass through the Muckle Toon." (Muckle, of course, simply means 'big'.)

There, I think, lies the town's chief charm, it's beautiful rivers; nor in the olden days were Scots, as weavers, slow to realize their worth.

But the history of Langholm goes back before the days of the Scots; to the Roman occupation and even earlier, to the dim past when a battle was fought where Langholm now stands.

In later troublous days, when Border history was in the making, all this was Johnny Armstrong's territory, and on many a night must the cobbles of the High Street have rung to the hooves of galloping horses. In those days the whole town was huddled on the east bank of the river at the foot of Whita Hill. It was the Duke of Buccleuch, the Good Duke Henry, who saw that his people needed better homes than the clay biggins with thatched roofs and earthen floors of his time (about 1780). There was sandstone in Whita Hill and timber on the slopes; so, in a co-operative measure with his tenants—the Duke supplying stone, slate, timber, and lime, while the tenants gave their labour or paid others to labour—fine new cottages took shape.

As the tall chimneys grew, so the town's population increased, making expansion imperative. There were two difficult alternatives; to cross the rivers or to climb the hills. It chose both. It built bridges and planted its new toon on the flat on the other side —first the cottages, later superseded by long rows of sturdy, grey-stone, double-storied houses, flush with the thoroughfares or pavements and unrelieved by gardens. But they made the roads between the rows wide and straight and long.

There is something strangely fascinating about those long straight streets of grey houses, so independent of all colour to beautify them, as if stressing the fact that they were built for use and not for ornament, built solid and good to last and to house many generations of weavers. But that was in the days when the looms were turning out cloths of sober black and hodden grey, and a few lengths, maybe, of more frivolous shepherd's plaid— black and grey check—which originated in Langholm. Now the great looms turn out glorious tweeds of every hue, tartans, checks and every modern variation; and even blankets of peach, green, blue, or yellow, as this brighter age demands. So, while those grey houses have always interested me, I feel they have not moved with the times, and I would like some good fairy to wave a wand, so that on every window-sill a window-box would appear full of the brightness of flowers.

Now what did they do with the hillside which is so terribly steep?

Just for the moment let us go back to the other night when we stood on Skipper's Bridge—so called after the well-loved ferry-man who was relieved of his arduous job when the bridge was built—and high up the hillside above the town the sun lit to gold a beautiful house among the trees. This was the first of many that the mill-owners built for their homes, and up to them is the most amazing series of steep, narrow roads; up and up, forking here and there to a white gate and another house, but climbing all the time, slantingly, up along the hillside. A shelf was levelled for each house, with the gardens terraced higher and higher, and with flights of steps reaching dizzy heights. But those nineteenth-century mill-owners, whose sons and grandsons occupy those fine houses today, chose their sites well, for the views down over the town, up the dales and across to the farther hills are very lovely.

In olden days Langholmites had to climb a bit to their parish kirk, but as the New Town grew across the river, and bridge building was the order of the day, they put a new kirk at the junction of the Wauchope and Esk. Crossing from the Old Town at this point, there is a narrow chain bridge, but even the New Townsfolk have a river to cross to reach this rather aloof and beautiful kirk, for it is on the other side of the Wauchope, with a good, wide stone bridge all to itself.

Behind the kirk is a gift from the Duke of Buccleuch, Buccleuch Park, which also has its own bridge across the Wauchope, with the war memorial at the entrance, a winged figure of Victory and Peace. This park has a beautiful situation, edged on two sides by rivers and sheltered by Warbla Hill, an old peat hill with a track down which the townsfolk used to bring their fuel.

In our exploring we always come again to the High Street, and here we find—for it is rather tucked away behind other buildings—the plum of Langholm's architectural beauty in the Thomas Hope Hospital. Behind the fine wrought-iron gates this exquisitely designed building with its crow-stepped gables is far removed from any resemblance to the austere appearance of most hospitals. Inside is equally lovely and perfectly equipped; Langholm's own hospital, built in 1896 and endowed by a bequest of over £100,000 by Thomas Hope, a New York merchant and a native of Westerkirk, the adjoining parish. That was a lot of money in those days, and more than was required for the hospital; so the surplus was used to help the poor. This smaller portion the town managed to retain and administer in the usual way when the Government took over their lovely hospital and all its assets.

On the other side of the High Street is the very interesting Telford Library, founded by Thomas Telford, the famous bridge builder and civil engineer. Here was another 'lad o' pairts' who came from the little school of Westerkirk and started his apprenticeship on Langholm Bridge, which crosses the confluence of Ewes and Esk. The Langholm library was erected in 1872, and one of the town's manufacturers, Alexander Reid, gave £1,000 to assist in the building.

Outside the library there is a beautiful marble statue of Admiral Sir Pultney Malcolm, a friend of Telford, who served under Lord Nelson. He was one of four illustrious brothers who were knighted for their services to their country. On top of Whita Hill, a sandstone obelisk, 100 feet high, is to the memory of General Sir John Malcolm, a great Anglo-Indian statesman. Then there was Sir James, Colonel of the Royal Marines and a K.B.C., and Sir Charles the youngest, who was a Vice-Admiral of the Fleet. They were affectionately known as 'The Four Knights of Eskdale'. But the most surprising thing is that those

A tweed mill, passing the warp
Tweeds for export

four brothers were also educated at the little Westerkirk school. Their two cousins, James Little and Charles Pasley, Langholm lads, were also knighted; so no wonder the people of Langholm, the capital of Eskdale, called their town muckle.

We turned the car across Langholm Bridge at the sign pointing to Eskdalemuir. Up past the New Town, on and up, with the road closely shut in by trees and a wall, to the Buccleuch policies. Then suddenly trees and wall ended and we were winding over moorland into the dale, with wide views of hills, steep yet beautifully moulded, without a single sharp peak or point, green yet gold where the bracken was fading, and with the green patches liberally sprinkled with sheep. A thin belt of tall, old conifers, which ran down a little valley, were swaying gently in the strong north wind, which made me glad to have with me my lovely Innes-tartan scarf, woven in one of Langholm's mills, for that wind was bitter.

So, in about four miles, we came to the little village of Wester-kirk, so prettily set in a fold of the hills, with its fine kirk, its village hall, its smiddy (smithy), its contractors' business, its school, and its Telford's library. Yes, Thomas Telford endowed this one too, surely the finest token of his undying gratitude to the dominie who taught him and to the gracious lady of Lang-holm who gave him, as a lad, free access to her wonderful library.

By the side of the road, a short distance past the school, there is a bronze plaque of Telford's head set in granite, with two granite seats where, on a summer's day, one might rest a while.

Talking with a villager, who was hurrying up the road to the school to meet her five-year-old son, I thought what a proud record that little lad, Telford, had in the history of his school. Westerkirk must be a happy place to live in, for this lady smilingly told me that they were all a jolly family party, making their own amusements with dances, concerts, the Rural (Women's Rural Institute), a flower show and, of course, reading, and are well content. She also told me that there is white heather growing on the surrounding hills, although not a great deal, and every year a shepherd brings her down a bunch, some of which she sends to friends abroad.

However, there is one day in the year when even the people of Westerkirk come down the dale to the Muckle Toon, this is

6

Three old meal mills

the Common Riding Day, the last Friday of July. On this day the town is gay and packed to capacity with the influx of visitors from the surrounding districts, and even from overseas. Racing and chasing, Crying the Fair, Riding the Marches, processions, games and dancing; children with heather besoms, and the famous Town Band which dates back to 1813, bright in their scarlet coats, playing and playing on this day of the year, which starts at 5 a.m. and finishes with a dance in the town hall which begins at 10 p.m.

So by these old customs the memory of more lawless days is kept green; days when riding round the hills—from whence the peats were brought, and sheep, whose wool was their living as time went on, were grazed—and marking the marches was very necessary:

> Now, Gentlemen, we're gan' frae the toun,
> And first of a' the Kil-green we gang roun';
> It is an ancient place where clay is got,
> And it belangs to us by Right and Lot,
> And then frae there the Lang Wood we gang throu',
> Where every ane may breckens cut and pu';
> And last of a' we to the Moss do steer,
> To see gif a' oor Marches they be clear,
> And when unto the Castle Craigs we come,
> I'll cry the Langholm Fair, and beat the drum.

Now, Gentlemen, what you have heard this day concerning going round our Marches, it is expected that every one who has occasion for Peats, Breckens, Flacks, Stanes, or Clay, will go out in defence of their property, and they shall hear the Proclamation of the Langholm Fair upon the Castle Craig.

So the fair is cried, with the crier standing on horseback in time-honoured style.

But the gay day passes, and Langholm reverts to its own busy life. I like work-a-day Langholm. I like taking my basket and shopping in its High Street, for its shopkeepers have that charm of all those in country towns; they are unhurried; there is time for a chat and sufficient interest in the visitor; they are knowledgeable and prepared to answer questions. The summer hurries past, as summers always do, and bright September, when the heather is fading on the hills, but the bracken is turning to gold, brings the Flower Show with all its glory of cherished blooms, vegetables as beautiful as any seedsman's catalogue depicts, and preserves, cakes and handwork of the busy housewife, enough to make one's mouth water.

Then October, when the leaves are falling, brings the Cattle Show, and besides sleek and well-groomed beasties trampling the greensward of the football pitch, there are burly farmers and lean farmers and many visitors crowding the field. So life goes on today in the Muckle Toon o' the Langholm and—yes, I like Langholm.

As usual, when staying even for a few days in a place we wanted to know more about its main industry, which in Langholm was tweed manufacture, so I visited the town clerk. He took us to the largest mill in the town, the Buccleuch Mills, which does the complete job, from getting the wool straight from the sheep to producing the finished bales of tweed.

Undoubtedly the pioneers of Scotch tweed gave to this country a cloth and a name which endure, but their wildest dreams never envisaged this aristocrat of cloth penetrating to every corner of the world as it does today. Nor could they, in 1835, picture the modern giant carders, spinning mules, power looms, and the beautiful patterned and coloured tweeds of the modern mill.

Their mills were situated in the same delightful spots, in Border valleys, amidst rich sheep-rearing hill-lands, and fed with ample water to turn the wheels of their fulling stocks, carders and spinning machines.

These were days of great progress, the days when teasing and carding by hand and spinning on spindle and distaff had been left far behind—even the spinning-jenny was being displaced by the mule—but the art and craft of their forbears in turning out a cloth of great warmth, kindly to the touch and hard-wearing, remains today.

In the experimental room early looms and associated equipment were shown in working models of hand-and-foot-operated types. The flexibility of these small looms is of real value in trying out test pieces of new designs and effects. New effects are always being created, this being the life-blood of any industry. The Scotch tweed trade will also accept small orders for specials in colour and design which, although more expensive, are valuable because of their exclusiveness.

After this introduction, we entered a wool store crammed with bulging 'sheets' (sacks) of wool, mostly Cheviot but also white and silky merino, and warm, clinging curly lambs' wool from Australia, wool which would give character to any cloth.

Following a heavily loaded trolley, we entered the washing and dyeing section; here in mechanical washers wool was being tossed and forked about in rich soap, soda and softened water solution to emerge from rollers almost dry, and free from dirt and the natural oil which would prevent dyes from being absorbed. After watching the simple yet highly skilled dyeing processes, we followed the dyed and now clotted wool to a Willey machine where a spiked drum tore it apart. A teaser continued this work and re-oiled the wool to make it supple and assist processing.

The next stage is carding, which is carried out with almost incredible thoroughness, because on it depends the ultimate smoothness and evenness of the yarn. At the same time blending different coloured wools can assist matching and give a rare charm and glint to yarn which creates liveliness in the finished tweed.

A carder refines the wool by a complex system of drawing out the fibres on revolving wool-carrying cylinders, then stripping and replacing rollers, all covered with graded wire in brush formation. Wool is fed into the first section, the scribbler, by an ingenious automatic weighing device which ensures a level supply, and the output of wool fibres resembles balls of untwisted rope. A ball and bank feed passes these and any blending colours into the intermediate section. A broad ribbon of more refined wool leaves this by a Scotch feed, which passes the wool through the last section with its fibres at right angles to their previous direction, so ensuring that they are all mixed up—an essential feature from which Scotch tweed derives much of its warmth or loftiness (softness).

The wool leaves this condenser section in rows of rolled strands called 'slubbing'. These are wound on to spools and illustrate the first stage in the manufacture of yarn. At the spinning mules we watched long rows of slubbing spools unwind, the mule spindles drawing out the requisite length to the right thickness and tension, then starting to spin, the mule cleverly working closer as the wool strands shortened.

When spun the yarn is wound on to the cop at the base of each spindle, and the whole operation is repeated until the cops are full. These cops go to the winding room, where colours and plys are twisted together, shuttle bobbins are wound for the weft thread, and warp mill cheeses made. The actual start of making a piece of tweed is at the warp mill, which creates a build up of perfect yarn in the correct number, order, colour and length for the cloth to be woven; and when complete all these thousands of warp threads are wound simultaneously on to a warp beam which is over 6 feet long and holds all the yarn which stretches lengthwise in the cloth.

Then to the looms; but first there is the painstaking job of drawing, passing the many threads on the warp beam through the needle-eye loom healds, with never a mistake. In the loom these sets of healds guide the warp threads into position, where they are interlaced with the weft thread from fast-moving shuttles. So, amid the deafening clatter of flying shuttles, we watched alert girls, each operating two looms, and saw Scotch tweeds in their many beautiful patterns and colours grow before us.

Tweed, after leaving the loom, still has far to go. After inspection, thread repair, and washing, it is usually milled. This makes it more wind-resistant by means of slight or heavy felting, which thickening may reduce its length and width by a sixth. Next it is stretched on tenter hooks and dried in an oven-like machine. Conditioning follows, until it holds wool's natural amount of water. Now the tweed is either brushed, cropped to give it a smooth surface, or teasel-raised to produce a fluffy finish.

Shrinking comes next, to protect it against rain or the tailor's iron, then it is ironed in a Bailey finishing machine, which sets the material permanently and gives it a beautiful lustre and smoothness. A final inspection and moteing[1] follows, and the finished tweed goes to the warehouse.

In the warehouse we inspected roll after roll of lovely tweeds; fine suitings with delicate colours for town wear, and heavy tweeds of rich shades which spoke of the hills and heather. In the designer's office was explained the technique used in designing some of the tweeds, reversible overcoatings, rugs and tartans which we had seen, and the way in which such materials were adjusted to suit export demands large or small.

---

[1] Removing specks, bits of thread and other minor faults.

It is interesting that different countries require different weights of tweed. America likes 9 to 12-ounce per yard material for summer wear, up to 15-ounce for winter, and up to 24-ounce for overcoatings, while here and on the Continent summer weight is 15-ounce to 16-ounce, and for winter 20-ounce to 22-ounce. Canada and Europe take overcoatings up to 32-ounce. This is quite a problem when combined with each country's local taste, which in American cities demands reserved styles, while holiday clothes and sports wear go to the other extreme. But these are requirements which the Scotch tweed manufacturers are willing and determined always to meet.

The Scotch tweed industry is probably the only industry in the world which has a complete production unit attached to its technical college, so that training students, under mill conditions, are turning out, as a paying business, high-class marketable goods. The Scotch Woollen Technical College at Galashiels is operated by the manufacturers with aid from the Scottish Education Department. Its standard of education is very high, most students sitting the Wools and Worsted City and Guilds examinations. The college also demands a very high standard in examinations before awarding its diploma. This close combination of technical and practical training ensures a steady flow of capable young people to executive positions, and, for those taking a section of the whole course, a sure step towards the position of foreman or departmental manager. Day students are encouraged by financial assistance, bursaries and scholarships. There are also local centres run under the auspices of the college, such as at Langholm. Here promising pupils are tutored for the City and Guilds examination.

It was the following Christmas when I received the wonderful gift of my Innes tartan scarf which Mr. Bell, father of the present mill owner, wove specially for me on the beautiful little hand loom which he used mainly for trying out new patterns. I prize my scarf very much, not only for its smart appearance and its wonderful warmth, but also for the kindly thought and work that went into its designing and making.

A beautiful morning tempted us to continue our journey, and, as we went up the Ewes valley, we were steadily climbing between great, rounded green hills, the kind which to the Borderer means sheep, wool and industry. At first, where there were farmlands, our road was edged with low, compact hedges of rich, russet beech. But, as we climbed, the valley narrowed, edging the road with rough hill-grazings and tumbling waters.

Right in the heart of this upper valley we passed the old Moss-paul Inn, which looked particularly attractive with its white walls and scarlet woodwork against the green hills and blue sky with fluffy white clouds. Here we left the Ewes Water, but shortly, after crossing the watershed at 1,156 feet, we picked up a diminutive River Teviot and watched it grow all the way to Hawick.

Hawick is a busy town at any time but our passing through was at the lunch hour, and a lively, crowded picture it made as we edged between streams of cars, cycles and happy, racing girls; just a sudden wonderful stream of living colour flooding the main streets as the woollen factories opened their doors.

At Kalefoot, where the Kale Water joins the Teviot, we found a delightful wayside halt and, next day, leaving 'Golden Eagle' there, we renewed acquaintance with Kelso, four miles farther on. A gracious, old town, Kelso, with its wide rivers and beautiful Abbey ruins, and, lying at the gates of Floors Castle, the stately home of the Duke of Roxburgh.

From there we visited lovely Dryburgh Abbey, so peaceful and picturesque in its setting of old cedars of Lebanon; then took a lofty road through the hills, looking down on the River Tweed, which brought us into Melrose. From there we headed east again, through St. Boswells, where we lost the friendly Eildon Hills to run above the Tweed, passing the scanty ruins of Roxburgh Castle, and looked across to Floors Castle lying proudly in its green park. As daylight was fading we reached the warm comfort of 'Golden Eagle' and a delicious meal of trout caught in the Tweed that morning.

Next morning was another beautiful sunny one with a touch of frost, and the Tweed was flowing blue and clear under Kelso Bridge as we ran down the long, curving hill to the town. From the wide square we took the road to Coldstream. About 1659 General Monk raised the regiment, the Coldstream Guards, in this Border town. Crossing Coldstream Bridge into England brought to mind that here there used to be a ford which was crossed by many famous people, as well as many eloping couples, and Coldstream, so aptly named, took shape because travellers required lodgings when held up, often for days, by the Tweed in spate. In 1766 a much-needed bridge was built.

We were kept on the English side of the Border right to Berwick-on-Tweed; but even in this old ding-dong town we were still in England, although it was not always so. Was there ever another town that changed countries so often as Berwick? For a long time it belonged to neither country, and could anyone blame it for holding itself aloof. It had been invaded, pillaged and burned, and had witnessed so many cruel deeds that it must have been as sick as a town could be of both Scots and English.

From there it was the fast Great North Road to Edinburgh. Although our home is nearly seven miles west of the city this is really our home town, and as usual we felt a special pride as we slipped down to, and along Princes Street. There was Sir Walter Scott's monument in all its glorious tapering gracefulness and, behind it across the gardens, the old town of Edinburgh rising to the skies and culminating in the fine old castle high on its rocky crags.

The river mouth at Loch Awehead, Argyll
Oban from McCaig's Tower

Journeying up to Argyll:
Loch Awe, the String of Lorne and some Islands

Another part of Scotland which we find so full of interest and beauty is Argyll. Here was the foundation of Scotland when the first Scots came in after the Pictish era. Scotland could almost be sectioned off in eras of occupation, because so many seemed to think it a plum worth picking; Picts, Romans, Norsemen, they all came, left their mark, notably in place-names, speech and even customs, then disappeared, vanquished in the end by the Scots.

For anyone who finds old history engrossing, Argyll is a very happy hunting-ground. But for those who just want scenic beauty it is entrancing, with its seascapes which bring in islands and glorious mountains. And for those who just want this day and age, its people are friendly to the stranger and always helpful.

If we are travelling to Argyll from home our way is by Linlithgow. What a fine old town this is. So much of it is being pulled down to make room for modern houses, but nothing can take away the character of this place which was the home of kings and queens and the fine nobility of Scotland. In the Palace here, now a ruin, Mary Queen of Scots was born on 7th December 1542, and here the 'Bonny Earl o' Moray" who was regent, was murdered. It was the English dragoons under General Hawley, who, in 1746, destroyed this beautiful Palace.

The parish church, St. Michael's, was founded by David I, and is one of the few ancient ones in Scotland still in use. It was in an aisle of this church that James IV saw the strange apparition which warned him against his fatal expedition to Flodden Field. He ignored the warning, and on Flodden Field he was mortally wounded.

When the old houses were demolished, I hoped they might turn the ground into gardens, because here was the priceless asset of the town, their glorious loch. What a vision that would have

Clachan Bridge, designed by Thomas Telford
The slate pier at Ellenbeich, Seil Island
Inverary Castle

been for the tourist. But in this modern age there seems to be only one use for ground in a town centre and that is to cram it full of houses. Perhaps some future demolisher will see and appreciate the beauty those houses are hiding.

Falkirk is the next town we pass through; another ancient one but up-and-coming these days. Perhaps its houses were just old and of no historic value, but in their place have grown up palatial hotels and fine shops, and now there is a splendid college. I like Falkirk. We are often through it, and to me it is a delightful place to shop, and we can still stop the car in its main street. This is a one-way street, which has its uses. There are good town gardeners in Falkirk and some beautiful examples of their work around the town, especially in Dollar Park with its beautiful floral clock.

We pass through Bannockburn. There is little to show that here we 'licked' the English good and proper, unless we take the Glasgow road at the roundabout at St. Ninian's to the field of battle, where proudly stands the bronze equestrian statue of King Robert the Bruce which the Queen unveiled a few years ago. Here in the rotunda bronze plaques are let into the wall, giving details of that decisive battle. This all belongs to the National Trust for Scotland, and lately a hotel and restaurant have grown up here too.

At the roundabout we are into Stirling, another fine old town which has always known the coming and going of troops, even until today, when its grand old castle, perched high on a mighty rock, 340 feet above the town, is still garrisoned. In 1304 this old stronghold held out for three months against Edward I. It remained in English hands for ten years. But this strategic 'gate to the Highlands' was so important that, to keep the castle, Edward II mustered a great army and invaded Scotland, only to be completely beaten and routed at Bannockburn. The views from the castle battlements on a clear day are glorious; over the Vale of Menteith to the Highland mountains and across to the beautiful, 220-foot high Wallace Monument on the Abbey Craig, while below are the incredible windings of the River Forth. It was here that the Battle of Stirling took place, Wallace's first victory over the English.

Up from Stirling's main street is its residential area, with beautiful, square-built stone houses. The roads are flanked by lovely trees on high, sloping grass banks and it was here that a bit of modern history took place two or three years ago. A Dutchman spent a happy holiday in Stirling and on his return home he sent Stirling a present of thousands of daffodil bulbs. These were all planted on those grass banks so that in springtime they are now like banks of gold.

We had lingered long in these fascinating old towns, but were able to hurry on, because as we leave Stirling we are on to that astonishing road called The Drip (why, I have never been able to find out) which runs for many miles dead-straight and flat. There is never a bit of traffic on it because it clears itself so rapidly, and after the congestion of the towns it is absolutely exhilarating.

The next village of any size is Callander; a story-book village, because it is the centre for a fabulous bit of country. But at the moment we are not stopping, except momentarily to stock up from one of its three splendid baker's shops and one of its first-class butcher's shops. Then we are twisting by the turbulent River Leny, by lovely Loch Lubnaig, to go through Bonny Stratheyre. Beyond Lochearnhead we breast the long hill up Glen Ogle. At the top we are rewarded by a glorious view of Ben Lawers, and on the particular spring day I have in mind, it is still heavily streaked with snow.

Glen Dochart took us a-winding for many lovely miles until we came to a disused quarry which invited us in for tea; and having inveigled us off the road it held us for three wild days of storm. We were hostages while the inferno raged, gale-force winds and squalls of rain and sleet. We were right at the foot of Ben More, the glen's dominating but magnificent giant. He broke the clouds as they wreathed about his head, and from his snow-filled clefts came an icy wind to chill the air around us. Drinking-water was from a nearby mountain burn, which, being in spate, afforded David happy hours with rod and line and gave us speckled trout for evening meals. We were storm-bound but not starved. It took my largest pot to boil the 5-pound gammon which a Callander grocer had assured me was the finest on the market. With sour milk I baked scones, then used tinned milk. As our bread grew older, our feathered friends fared better, also the shepherd's collies when their masters stopped for a chat. The birds were tamer here than I have ever known them, particularly a cock chaffinch which only looked up and chirped his thanks as we went out and in. A pair of green linties (linnets), a fat little robin, a couple of wagtails all had no fear of us. When the sun shone between squalls, larks filled the air with music, while from the mountain came the sweet call of a curlew.

There were few wayfarers going by. Our two shepherds passed up and down, doggedly tending their flocks and rejoicing in the rain which they said had made the grass grow with new vigour on the hills and even faster than in the valley, sweet and succulent food for the ewes and lambs. And one day at teatime some gipsies plodded into the teeth of the storm. The young man left his father to go on with their hand-cart, and the woman with the pram, which may have held a baby under all the piled paraphernalia, and, grabbing his pipes, gave us a rousing rendering of 'The Road to the Isles'. A coin for the cheery rascal and rosy apples for the bairns, and I wondered where they would pitch their beehive tent in that night of storm.

It was a shining day when we continued our journey. The storm had spent itself and the air seemed washed clear and cold, but the sun grew warmer as we went through Crianlarich. At Tyndrum we forked left, climbing until over the top and dropping down into Glen Lochy. Well down the glen we found a lovely spot where we could get off the road and have a meal. But once again we were tempted to stay longer, so we spent the night there and David fished the river which gurgled and sang its way past our door.

That was a beautiful spot and I was sorry to leave it next morning, but soon we were on the long curving hill to Inverlochy, with, before us, a superb panorama; Ben Cruachan, 3,689 feet, at the head of Loch Awe, sharp of outline and intensely blue, and the whole valley between, vivid, rich green, with every hillock and clump of trees standing out with amazing clarity. At Inverlochy our trout river was a glorious, wild, deep, amber-coloured rush of water. Here it met the River Orchy for their last few rollicking miles before losing themselves in Loch Awe. Loch Awe has twenty-five miles of the rarest charm, bounded by mountains and leafy glens, spilling their grandeur and beauty to the water verges and over its many islands. Its lands are steeped in history of ancient Scots: MacDougalls, MacGregors and Campbells; yet a loch of sheer beauty from its wide and rugged head to its foot with quiet waters and lush meadows around Ford. At its head Kilchurn Castle adds a touch of ancient fierceness.

So through Dalmally, asleep in the sun, our road climbing round the end of the loch, with glorious vistas of blue waters and misty hills and with Kilchurn browsing on past glories. Then we were in the Pass of Brander, narrow, steep-walled, skirting the foot of Ben Cruachan, with the River Awe skirling through in a succession of mad rushes and deep pools; a river famed for salmon, and where, in the good old days, the same angler caught two, in different years, each weighing around 56 pounds. It was in this wild pass that a great battle was fought between Robert the Bruce and the Lord of Lorne, and in that narrow ravine fierce must have been the mêlée.

Here, at the foot of the loch (Loch Awe has a small foot here and a big foot at Ford) there has been, for the past few years, another scene of intense activity, as the 400,000-kilowatt Loch Awe–Cruachan power scheme has progressed. The Ben Cruachan power scheme is the North of Scotland Hydro Electric Board's largest, and the world's second largest, pump-storage power station, and the world's largest reversible-turbine type station. The storage reservoir has been created in a cirque on a shoulder of the mountain by a massive buttress dam, 153 feet high and 1,037 feet long. From here the water drops 1,200 feet, through concrete-lined shafts, to the underground power station. When the power-plant turbines are operated as pumps, water is drawn from Loch Awe through the tailrace tunnel, and moved up the 1,200 feet into the mountain reservoir.

So here is not only another loch, but also a mountain that have been harnessed to the use of man; but once the disfigurations of gigantic construction operations have disappeared, there will be less than usual evidence of a power scheme, because it is nearly all in and on the mountain.

A strange feature of Loch Awe is that its outlet, by the pass, is close to its head, only a short distance from the inflow of waters from Glens Lochy, Orchy and Strae. This is thought to date from the Ice Age, the passage having been forced by an ice stream pressing its way seawards. But originally its outlet would have been the valley of Kilmartin Burn and River Add. This valley, and the loch itself, are considered to be a continuation of the geological feature called the Great Fault.

On its western side we came to Loch Awe (without the caravan) by the wild and lovely way through the hills from Kilmel-
fort, and at the tail of it dropped down beside the turbulent
River Avich to Loch Awe. Here we had the choice of two roads:
one up the loch to Kilcrenan, or one down to Ford. The latter was
marked 'Closed to traffic', but, being told we could go through,
we chose that way. This road runs through a great forest, taken
over about ten years ago by the Forestry Commission. Some way
along we came on Dalavaich, a typical forest village of timber
houses for the 'men of trees' and their families.

From there the road was adventurous, as it climbed through the
thick forest; ten miles of short, steep hills and sharp bends, which
gave us little time to see anything but that narrow ribbon of
road. But on either side there was little to see but trees, with an
occasional alluring, tantalizing glimpse of Loch Awe far, far
below.

Still exploring Loch Awe, we brought 'Golden Eagle' back
through the Pass of Brander, and found a delightful pitch on the
lochside opposite Loch Awe Hotel, a massive pile with its grey
stone in keeping with the rugged grandeur of its splendid setting.
Next day we explored the eastern side of the loch, and the views
across it were enchanting; its pretty islands floating on a loch of
silver, which stretched deep into the Pass of Brander, guarded by
its sheer hill walls. At Chadich House we took the little lochside
road, narrow, winding, at parts hilly, but a lovable road with
a fresh picture round every bend. At Portsonachan we heard the
musical tinkle of cow-bells from among the hillside trees, a
necessary precaution for straying cattle on unfenced land.

Across the narrowing loch were the lovely hills with their old
roads known as the String of Lorn. Between us and Loch Fyne
to the east rose an even higher hill-barrier, and down through
its wooded foothills tumbled many brown burns, in places
glorious, foaming waterfalls.

Loch Awe's shores and islands have for so long been the
haunt of man that history and legend are as great themes as its
fabled beauty. On its many islands are the remains of castles,
chapels, ancient burying grounds, a convent, and subterranean
causeways. The ruined Castle of Ardchonnel on the little island
of Innis Chonaill near the loch's foot dates back as the oldest
stronghold of the Argyll family and inspired their battle-cry, "It's

a far cry to Loch Ow," while Kilchurn Castle at its head was built about 1440 by Sir John Campbell of Glenorchy, ancestor of the Breadalbanes.

In more modern times some of the islands have been transformed from rabbit warrens to island forests of coniferous trees. On some in autumn the gold of dying bracken colours them richly, but in spring the purer gold of daffodils, and the clear shining yellow of primroses hold sway on islands and shore-edge.

From here we journeyed on, through Taynuilt and, passing the Connell Ferry road bridge (the railway which used to cross the foot of Loch Etive here is now discontinued, which gives a much better and wider carriageway across), we shortly turned south on our way to Oban.

The lovely town of Oban makes a delightful centre from which to explore much of Argyll—and not only its county, because, for those who love sailing, it is the busy port from which Mac-Brayne's fine steamships sail; to Staffa and Iona, to Tobermory on Mull, to Loch Sunart, to Fort William, to Stornoway, and many other places near and far. Breakfast as well as lunch and tea can be had on board, which saves the caravan wife a morning hustle. For short sea trips there are motor-launch cruises to Lismore Island and its lighthouse, and to Port Appin, with time ashore for tea at Aird's Hotel—a tea to remember. It is all part of a West Highland holiday which makes it so different from others; and all cruise information and bookings can be made on the spot.

For caravanners there is the splendid municipal site at Ganavan Sands with an easy approach, and, although close to the golf course and with a wide, safe bathing beach, it is only about a mile from the town centre. The site has a cement base which makes it firm and clean, and there is a handy tearoom. But it is the view which makes this site something special, for off-shore are small green islands set like precious gems in the blue sea, and Kerrera, a green island too, sheltering this lovely place. Beyond are the blue mountains of Mull, and the whole is lit by that clear shine which only West Highland air gives. This is as near the perfect site in the perfect setting as any town could offer the tourist, but for that very reason it becomes over-crowded in the peak holiday months, and those who can choose May or June will be well repaid. Even September can be busy, but sunsets can be lovely then.

There are one or two farm sites near Oban and at Taynuilt which help out, and there are lovely wayside pitches by Loch Feochan, and on the machair (grassy foreshore) by Loch Melfort.

Oban is a vivid, glamorous town, crescent-shaped to the head of its sparkling blue bay, which is sprinkled with yachts and light craft. It climbs its green hills until the pillars of MacCaig's Tower are set like a crown on their top. This Colosseum-like circle of granite pillars was erected near the end of the nineteenth century by a banker, as a memorial to himself and his family, and, it is said, to give employment to masons who were out of work. It never was completed because the builder ran out of funds.

But the fairest view of the town is obtained from Pulpit Hill. A steep road leads to the summit, possible by car, with parking room at the top and seats to rest while admiring the magnificent panorama. A mountain indicator pinpoints the many peaks near and far which make a fitting background to the shore-edged town nestling on the fringe of their foothills.

Oban, so splendidly and solidly built, with its fine hotels and shops, looks as if it had been a town for a long time, yet it only dates from the latter half of the nineteenth century and the epoch of steamships and railways. Before that a tiny fishing village held all the glory and the wonder of that superb bay; and its lonely people, going about their tasks, little dreamed of the lovely holiday town which would supplant it. It is also a busy fishing port.

One clear, shining June morning with practically no wind we ran into Oban early from our pitch eight miles south of the town. We parked the car, obtained our booking on the S.S. *King George V*, watched her sail into her berth, and, along with a throng of holidaymakers, boarded her for the Iona cruise. We had promised ourselves this trip for a long time but the weather would never co-operate until this day, which remained perfect throughout.

As we cleared the bay we saw the fussy little steamer, the *Lochiel*, as she approached the Lady Rock. This small steamship, carrying mails, makes an inner circuit of nearby little islands every day and is a great blessing to the islanders.

Our first stop was at Tobermory the small capital of Mull, and when we left there David and I went to the dining saloon for the first lunch, which we enjoyed thoroughly as our breakfast had been early, and the sea air was making us hungry. By the time we were finished we were thrilled to see the great crags of

Suilven, the Sugar Loaf

Staffa looming ahead. Our ship anchored off the island and two large ferry boats, into which the passengers clambered, drew alongside. It was a shuttle service because, like ourselves, a few hundred more had awaited this perfect day. If it is too rough passengers are not allowed to land on Staffa.

The island landing is a flat rock and not difficult, but it is a considerable distance to Fingal's Cave along a rocky shelf, which is fairly rough going. Another rough track, higher up but parallel, with a light rail for safety, brings the passengers back along to the ferryboat.

Fingal's Cave is a poem in stone. It is edged by gigantic, fluted, ribbed pillars of basalt, and roofed in the same way. The cave is 70 feet in height and around 230 feet in length, and we were able to go inside for a considerable distance on a narrow rock-ledge path. To me the most beautiful aspect of the cave was looking from deep inside, out, past the magnificent columnar entrance, to the blue sea and the soft, downy clouds of the sky. Not for me the deep sombre darkness of caves, but the clean, sweet air and sunshine which I love.

Staffa lies in the same longitude as the Giant's Causeway on the Irish north coast, which probably accounts for its shore rocks being in the same block formation, as if chiselled and shaped by hand. Once all the passengers had re-embarked it took no time at all for us to get under way again. The ferryboats raced off ahead, but were awaiting to ferry us ashore by the time we dropped anchor off the Island of Iona.

"Fifteen minutes only," we were sternly told, which, of course, was quite impossible for Iona, and I am afraid we were in the first boat over and the last boat off. I was surprised at the size of the village; no one had ever told me that there was a village, but here was a row of beautiful white cottages and pretty gardens, colourful with many flowers. One can stay on the island for a holiday and many do. Given good weather, I could imagine nothing better than a few days on this peaceful green island. In one of the shops, when I said we weren't allowed nearly long enough here, the shopkeeper suggested that I come again and stay awhile.

Most of our time ashore was spent in the abbey, which has been so greatly restored by the Iona community under the guidance of Dr. Macleod. We were conducted through its precincts in

7

Ullapool viewed from the pier
Fisher girls topping-up the barrels of herring
  before the coopers fit on the lids

groups, by young students, and shown much of the work that had been accomplished.

Here were the tombs of many kings as well as many saintly men, and our guides were very proud of a walk from the pier to the abbey which had just been found and uncovered and was the path of the dead kings, up which their coffins were borne for burial in the tomb of their ancestors. The path was composed of boulders, rounded on top and most difficult to walk on, but they were all laid flush with one another, and, although the path itself was steep, were level.

The nunnery of St. Mary had withstood the pressure of time better than most parts, and was embellished with tufts of a beautiful, wild red flower, growing in clefts on its gable wall. The flower looked like a squat, sturdy version of great valerian, but actually I did not recognize it at all.

Once safely back on the *King George V*, we found that the sea air had given us a grand appetite for the fish-tea which the ship's galley provided. It took very little time after that to sail serenely back to Oban at the end of a wonderful day.

8

Loch Feochan's Shores :
Fishing, History and Birds

When David brought 'Golden Eagle' to rest near the mouth of Loch Feochan, it was late afternoon and raining in intermittent, downpours, and, although it would shortly be the longest day of the year, the keen north wind had ice in it. Yet, in spite of all that I loved this place, and immediately fell under its spell. The pitch was a flattish piece of ground, gravelled with granite chips, and starred with daisies, silverweed, and tiny, deep pink geraniums. From the tide-washed golden tangle on the rocks below us was wafted a powerful ozone scent; beyond the loch lay calm, green where reflecting the hills, but with the sheen of silver satin where it mirrored the sky, and only the cry of sea-birds broke the sweet peace.

In the days that passed the gossamer threads of first impressions turned into stout chains of interest, beauty and friendliness to hold us well beyond the time we meant to stay. As we got to know the people of Kilninver, a mile along the road, we learned that we had halted in no ordinary place and that the black and gold-encrusted rock below was no ordinary rock. It has a name, Creag na Marbh (Rock of the Dead.) From here, when they died, the kings of Dalriada were taken to Iona for burial.

Off the rocks the channel is deep and narrow; beyond are sand-banks, which may have been there 1,400 years ago; perhaps the heap of stones, so obviously purposely gathered, and which puzzled us so much at first, could have been part of their formation. This stone cairn is now only covered during high spring-tides, so how massive it must have been when it was built so many centuries ago. It is called Carn Alpin, and Alpin was king of the Scots and father of Kenneth, who conquered the Picts and made one united country of Scotland. It may be that Kenneth on his return from burying his father on the Sacred Isle had this sea-bedded cairn raised in his memory. If only that black rock below us could speak; but its secrets are held and we can only draw our pictures from imagination.

I wonder if it could have been such a night as this one in which I write, when, at the end of the long journey on foot from Kilmartin, with the stones growing in number on the cairns at every halt, those stalwarts bearing the coffin with their dead king laid it on the black rock to await embarkation for Iona. Round the rim and over the top of massed black clouds spilled the setting sun in flaming gold. The tide was almost full, leaving only a small strip of uncovered sandbank edging the channel, and, as I watched, it took the shape of a galley, and the gold of clouds reflected in the channel took the form of golden sails. It looked so real that I was wafted back through time to a scene such as the old rock must have witnessed, and words from Tennyson's beautiful hymn came unbidden to mind:

> Sunset and evening star,
>   And one clear call for me!
> And may there be no moaning of the bar,
>   When I put to sea,
> But such a tide as, moving, seems asleep
>   Too full for sound and foam,
> When that which drew from out the boundless deep
>   Turns again home.

And so my galley sailed away carrying the King of Dalriada on his last voyage—was he old or was he young; had he fallen in battle, as more than one must have done when the Picts from their Loch Etive fortress attacked? There was no one to tell us.

However, that was not the end of the usefulness of this convenient rock edging the deep channel between shore and sandbank. Later sailing ships loaded timber here; and one theory is that they discharged the stones carried as ballast which form the sea-cairn; but that does not explain its age-old name of Carn Alpin.

Still later puffers from the Clyde used the rock when unloading coal. Each boat carried 120 tons, and each house in the district was allowed five tons a year. For days after the coal was discharged the scene here must have been a busy one, as every available farm cart was put to the job of carrying it away. The track which they used down to the shore is grass-grown but still good, although it is over twenty years since the improvements in roads and road transport put a stop to the coal boats coming.

Those 'Para Handy' (coastal cargo) boats had a tricky job at this port of call; coming in on high tide, they depended on the turn of full tide to let them down the channel again. But occasionally the sandbank got them; then we can imagine the skipper's shout: "All hands on deck. Come up baith o' ye!" But sometimes a week would pass before a spring-tide came to refloat them.

Perhaps they ran aground when crossing the loch to pick up a return cargo from the slate quarry which was directly opposite us. This deep quarry stopped working in 1926, but still there were stacks of roofing slates forlornly awaiting a puffer to transport them. The quarry became flooded and later the owner, whose house was on the point of the peninsula, breached the sea wall, making the quarry basin a safe winter anchorage for his own yacht and that of his neighbour. Those two yachts, swinging at their summer moorings, added to the beauty which our caravan windows framed; the one boat, green, slim and graceful, the other, white, larger, sturdy and serviceable looking.

The sandbanks added their own interest. Once at low tide we crossed the channel by boat and, landing, explored one. It was covered thickly with a smooth, fine gravel, quite dry and pleasant to walk on. Here and there, among the scattered small rocks, were many large shells and the rocks themselves were festooned with a golden tangle which floats on the water long after the sandbanks are submerged until, on the flood-tide, it too disappears. Under the tangle the rocks were encrusted with mussels and buckies (cockles, whelks), and swathes of soft, vivid green seaweed.

It was because of those sandbanks and the splendid feeding they afforded, that the bird life at the foot of Loch Feochan was abnormal. And it was the bird life which held us there longer than the two nights we had originally intended. Swans were always in the picture; we counted over forty at a time. Sometimes after feeding they lay asleep on the soft tangle—cushions on the sandbanks until the rising tide floated them off. Sometimes they floated down the loch on the ebb tide, and came awake when they hit the tangle which halted their progress; and, no matter how many were in the party, there was always one awake as if on guard.

While swan-life made a fascinating study, there were many other interesting birds. Never, for instance, had we seen so many oyster catchers; when we were passing in our boat close to the shore at the loch's foot, dozens of pairs rose to skim low over the water, circling us and shrilly scolding. In about the same place we raised over thirty herons at a time. Their heronry was in the tall trees on the cliff-face of the peninsula opposite us. In the spring eight pairs had nested there, each bringing out seven or eight chicks; so they were always to be seen, sometimes in groups but more often singly, on shore-edge, rock or sandbank, awaiting the sudden appearance of small eels from under stones, or pouncing on unwary crabs and small fish.

A great northern diver with its chicks often swam and dived in the channel and small bays around our rocks; then, too, as if in company, we usually saw a white-throated diver with three very fluffy chicks. A pair of mergansers dipped and splashed, then preened and sunned themselves on the rock, and mallards were frequent visitors.

Gulls use the rock for dropping shells on so that after breaking them they can get at the fish; there were parts of our black rock white with shells, but without a whole one among them. Often in the picture were great black-backed gulls, and terns larger than any we had ever seen before. Less beautiful, and growing more numerous with fewer gamekeepers to keep them down, were the grey crows, or hoodies. Then above the crags of the peninsula we saw eight ravens flying together; possibly a pair, as they mate for life, and six of their chicks fully grown, because they often hatch as early as February. Curlews we heard frequently, their sweet, trilling mating call coming from the hills beside us, and early each morning, when the tide was suitable, we watched one on the rock searching for his breakfast. Flocks of whimbrels, whose name so aptly describes their cry, also haunted the rock; and from high above the hills came the soft mewing cry of buzzards making us strain our eyes to watch the graceful, playful flight of four or five of those huge birds at a time.

Small birds were too numerous for individual mention, yet they added their links to the chain which held us; among them were yellow hammers, green linnets, mavises, dabchicks and sandpipers. Our neighbour across the loch told us that a pair of sandpipers insisted against all his protests in building their nest in the roll of his yacht's sail. There they brought out six chicks and these went to sea in the nest, the mother bird leaving them at the mouth of the loch and rejoining them there on their return. During the voyage the yachtsman fed the chicks on breadcrumbs, and until the young birds finally left the nest the sail was not used.

Here at the mouth of the loch, as in various parts farther up, salmon fishers were busy netting the salmon and sea-trout as they came in on the flood-tide. When keen eyes detected the movement of fish and the cry went out, "They are coming!", a rush was made for the boat. The next few moments were tense, as with great sweeping strokes, and with the help of the swift-flowing tide, the boat streaked round, while the net, loaded on the stern, paid itself out. An instant more and the boat grated on the pebbles, the oarsman leaped ashore, and all hands were carefully drawing in the heavy net. Only at the last were the silver beauties seen, struggling as they were drawn from the sea on to the grass.

Loch Feochan lies at right angles to its narrow mouth, and the rush of water at the flow and ebb is something to wonder at. We discovered, too, that the higher loch kept on pouring out its water for about two hours after the tide in the Firth of Lorne was running in. The clash of these waters threw a bar of churned water across the mouth until the outrush ceased and the terrific tide-rush gained supremacy. When fishing beyond the mouth, we found it more comfortable, even with our 3 horse-power outboard motor, to wait until the turmoil abated before attempting our return; but what joy it was to row with the flood-tide on a passage so swift that the land appeared to be racing past.

The small glen roads of Lorne are to me an irresistible lure, and the charm of their hidden lochs a prize worth seeking. Near the head of Loch Feochan a narrow, winding road to Loch Nell and Loch Lonan starts. At first it meanders through green fields and by the River Nell with no indication of what is in store. Here a little road branches for Glen Feochan, and, passing it, we come shortly to our first view of Loch Nell; and whatever the season we will never forget it.

Its pretty islands are like gems in this lovely setting. Those islands, like so many on our fresh-water lochs, were artificially built by lake dwellers, and had submerged, and often crooked, causeways to the shore, so preventing enemies and wild beasts from reaching their primitive dwellings. There are many other interesting indications of man's early connection with this district and the foot of Loch Nell. Close by is a serpent mound, like an elongated letter *S* and about 80 yards long. When the head of this relic of serpent worship was excavated, flint instruments and an urn containing ashes were discovered, and these are now in the Edinburgh Museum. Great standing stones are also to be seen and a cromlech supposed to be the burial place of Cuchullin, an Ossian hero.

In the Gaelic this is Loch nan Eala—Loch of the Swans; it is also the home of many water birds and waders, even herons and gulls invading its waters. In the spring its shores are a paradise of flowers and song.

The narrow road winds by the loch, then, climbing high above it, re-displays the vivid scene now set in an array of wild hills and mountains. And stretching out from the green valley is Loch Feochan, with, beyond, the Firth of Lorne and the mountains of Mull towering high above its wild, storm-beaten shores. Onwards the narrow road lures us, steep in parts, rough, becoming little more than a track, without a straight yard to it, winding through the hills. We verge, and cross wimpling, brown burns, open and shut gates, and stop now and then for sheep and for horses wandering along the road, or for a timber wagon, and to watch the wood-cutters with axe and saw.

Such is the unhurried and exquisite prelude to the enchanting scene awaiting us as we come up Glen Lonan to Loch Lonan. This very lovely glen was well populated before the Clearances, and beside an almost obliterated village are the ruins of an old distillery. Loch Lonan is an artificial loch for fishing, yet loses no charm for that. The supreme beauty of the loch is its background; mighty Ben Cruachan, draped in palest mauve and pink.

In the past those old drove roads through the hills were the only ones connecting Oban with the immediate country southwards, and, taking their natural way between the hills, they still link by bridle-paths the glen roads, so that to the hiker there are no dead-ends. One such old way was up Glen Feochan and through the hills connecting the head of Glen Euchar, then on by the String of Lorn to the road by Loch Avich and down to Loch Awe, and so on, by ferry and hill-track to Loch Fyne and the south.

However, we take the easier way up Glen Euchar from Glen Collan, which rises sharply from Kilninver at the foot of Loch Feochan, to find another of the lochs of Lorne, Loch Scamadale. Our road runs by the River Euchar, which tumbles over rocky falls and under an old bridge entwined in honeysuckle. Loch Scamadale is surrounded by steep, high, velvety-green hills, and the road, winding onwards, discloses white farms and shepherds' cottages nestling in every fold, where tiny, deep glens split the hills.

Such is the peace that we let time go, as if it stood still and nothing mattered beyond the quiet and loveliness of this fair place. Yet, a little over a century ago, this glen road was the main route between Netherlorn and the Lowlands, and, after the Roads and Bridges Act was passed in 1803, it was proposed to put a main road through here; but the advent of steamers serving the western shores, and, later, trains to Oban put a stop to any such idea.

At the head of Loch Scamadale stands the old house of Bragleen, where it is supposed the famous Brooch of Lorne was secretly held for 170 years after the siege of Gylen Castle, a MacDougall stronghold on the island of Kerrera, before being restored to the MacDougall chief at Dunolly Castle in 1826.

To seek lovely Loch Avich, set so deep in the hills, we climb the steep, narrow road up past Kilmelford's parish church; a harum-scarum road with a terrific hair-pin in the centre, and a glorious backward view down across the village and low green hills to blue Loch Melfort, before it goes on soaring right into the hills.

High in the hills we pass a little, hill-edged lochan where anglers in one of the Culfail Hotel's boats add life to a pretty picture. Then the road drops to a little stone bridge, and a short way beyond the tarmac gives out, and we are bumping onwards on the old rocky road of boulders, sand, loose stones, ruts and potholes. In winding, dipping and twisting, we are given a succession of dainty vignettes: an old gate and wood-railed bridge, a clump of small trees, a pretty cottage, some beautiful old Scotch pines, while the road is edged by moss, rock and bog-land, by fragrant bog-myrtle with its rusty-looking flowers, by lavender scabious, which in some parts is known as Queen Mary's pin-cushions, by tormentil and purple heather. A road of delight to carry us by the side of Loch Avich, Ossian's Loch Launa.

Our pitch at the foot of Loch Feochan was close to the village of Kilninver—pronounced Kil-inver. Here was the post office and the church, and the bridge over the foaming Euchar River where we stood with the gamekeeper as he pointed out to us the salmon, lying in the deep brown pools. Beyond the bridge was a very steep hill, at least so it seemed the first time we came that way on bicycles when petrol rationing still precluded much touring by car. But we have always loved this wayward road which leads to Seil Island and little Easdale.

Seil and Easdale; there is music in those names, the sweet, soft music of the west, such as was coming from the open door of the little Easdale Island post office. The music was one of the lilting tunes of the Isles, played superbly on an accordion, with all the pathos and love, tears and laughter of the Gael, and this island player would be in great demand that night at the ceilidh, which between times was being so animatedly discussed. David and I were seated at a little table outside the post office over an alfresco cup of tea with delicious home-baked scones and cream tarts. From our corner in a scattered half-square of age-old cottages we looked past cattle grazing contentedly on the overgrown green which separated us from the harbour; a pleasant spot, sheltered from the keen north wind, where, relaxing, we enjoyed the beauty and peace pervading that little island.

It had been a day of exploration, from the moment we topped the hill and rounded the bend at the little road-edging farm with its enviable view up and down Clachan Sound. Here we looked down on Clachan Bridge with its enormous sweeping arch which adds grace to the beautiful shores and joins Seil Island to the mainland. It was designed by Thomas Telford to allow small cargo boats to slip through Clachan Sound instead of taking the more perilous detour round Seil Island. But could the detour possibly be more perilous than going through that narrow, sheer, rock-edged channel, where the tide-race is sometimes so terrific that the bunched waters from the Firth of Lorne sweep every-thing before them? The skippers of those little puffers must have timed the tides to a nicety, and probably got as big a thrill out of steering a straight course as they were swept through as a canoeist gets shooting the rapids, or a racing motorist in covering the track.

From the bridge-hump we gazed down into the channel which looked so like a fast-flowing river that it seemed incongruous to see golden tangle streaming in the swift current. A little way up channel a boat put out from the shore and was swiftly borne under the bridge on the rush of the tide. A fisher was getting his trolling rods ready while his companion dipped his oars, and the boat slipped out into the widening channel where the sea was blue with a radiant sheen on it. The small boat reminded us of a yachtsman's paradise hereabout, but, before seeking it, we went down to have a better look at the bridge, and found that nature too had played her part by adorning this great arch, cramming every crevice with maidenhair spleenwort ferns, their rich green and black like a pattern in mosaic against the old grey stone.

Crossing the bridge, we followed a track by a white cottage and up the steep hill, but left it to gain the high tops, and were soon scrambling up over dykes and through birch, hazel and bracken. Breathlessly we reached top after top, until at last an amazing view of mountain-peaked lands and islanded-spangled sea lay before us. The islands of Kerrera and Lismore almost filled the inner Firth of Lorne, which, curving outwards round the great barrier rocks of mountainous Mull, carried our eyes to a limitless Atlantic. Offshore the sea was wild and foam-capped in the wind which blasted us, yet below us was peace in a mile-long lagoon guarded by little islands and wicked, tooth-edged rocks, now white with spume. And, to complete this haven, which might have been stolen from the far Pacific, were the little boats and, by the mouth of Clachan Sound, a sheltered entrance.

Skirting the lagoon as far as we could, we then descended the hill by a more sedate route, where the freshness of sea air mingled with the scents of wild thyme and bog-myrtle, and, as we approached the hotel by the bridge, the wafted scent of woodsmoke. Tigh-an-Truish, meaning kilt and trousers, is the name of this old hostelry, because here, in Scotland's troubled days after the '45, the islanders used to change from their tartan kilts to trousers, before crossing to the mainland where the wearing of the kilt was banned.

Our road wound onwards through Clachan village. On we went past boats and a smart yacht in a sheltered cove, and by pretty Obanseil farm with its busy folk gathering in the harvest in the fields below—an interesting way, with, over the Sound, the green slopes of Ardmaddy, and beyond them the high lands of Kilbrandon and Kilchattan. Here the narrowing water appears bridged by the long slate headland of Balvicar Bay, its very darkness making brighter the rows of white cottages forming the old slate-quarrying village of Balvicar, a place now given over to old folks, holiday homes, and a few slate quarriers who remain.

A retired quarry engineman showed us the way through disused workings to the quarry. The rock had been blasted, and great slabs were being levered out and split into convenient blocks, which were then loaded into little trucks and hand-propelled through a narrow rock-cutting to the men in the 'dressing' sheds. There we watched them being deftly split and 'dressed' (shaped) into roofing slates, and neatly stacked ready for transport.

So our morning hours were flying; but yet another forking road lured us down to Cuan Ferry, where a ferryboat large enough to take lorries operated between the islands of Luing and Seil; for Luing is a busy island, rich in agriculture, slate and lobsters.

Back we went to the road fork and to the 'main' road, which took us climbing, until before us lay the glorious panorama of Easdale and Ellenbeich. Far below us sheltered waters gently lapped a rocky shore at the foot of Dun Mor and Ellenbeich's white cottages. Beyond lay Easdale with its great quarry-gashed hill black against the sky, and beyond that a dancing sea reached to the cliffs of Mull, whose riven faces were blue with indigo shadows, but golden where sunlight touched them.

Down we went into the village nestling below its lofty crag, Dun Mor, to wander among its neat rows of whitewashed stone cottages which, with their black slated roofs, are sturdy enough to withstand winter's ferocious onslaught from the Atlantic. It is a beflowered village of charm, with many pretty corners, and even in the little windows, set deep in thick walls, beautiful geraniums added splashes of vivid colour. The narrow road and most of the little gardens were sheltered by tall drystone dykes of slate, and there was a fine old slate pier which will still be there when the wooden one has disappeared.

Eilean-a-beithich, meaning the island of birches, is the real name of this surf-beaten village, an appropriate name too, because it is built on the rocky edge of this almost forgotten birch-clad island, and over the filled-in channel between it and the great crag. It makes a thrilling story, for was there ever another island engulfed by both land and sea, out of which grew a village? For more years than anyone knows the tiny island was excavated, 7 to 9 million of the finest roofing slates being taken out of it annually, and the waste rock and debris was flung into the channel separating it from Seil until Eilean-a-beithich was no longer an island in its own right. So the blasting and levering out of slate-rock continued until the quarry was worked to a depth of 250 feet below the sea, with only a shell of rock around it. Then in 1881, on a November night of unprecedented storm, the force of a terrific sea broke the fragile sea-wall and flooded all but the shell; a disaster, as 240 men and boys were thrown idle and Easdale lost its best slate quarry.

On the old pier we twirled a handle which sent the blare of a klaxon out across the narrow sound and summoned the ferryboat from Easdale, an island where everything is slate: roads, dykes, harbour, breakwater, houses, sheds and even hen-houses.

The hill, which looks so massive from Seil, has been quarried on both sides until nothing is left but a straight narrow wall of rock. Perched high up on the almost stepped, hewn end of it, I marvelled at the labour of men which had through the centuries removed its two solid sides. No one knows when quarrying started here, but it was from this hill that the slates came which roofed Castle Stalker on Loch Linnhe in the fifteenth century. Below us lay the island village, and from my lofty height I counted over fifty of the white cottages which appeared to be still occupied, although quarrying stopped here many years ago. High above me on the rock David patiently awaited the removal of a black cloud shadow from Dun Mor on Seil. Neither of us was impatient, for ours was the peace that only a small island knows. There was the warmth of the sun and the coolness of the breeze, and wide views with sea and dancing waves between us and the little islands of Belnahua, Garbh Eileach, Eilean Dubh Mor and Lunga.

Coming down from the hill, an islander told us that he and another were still turning out Easdale slates, and, directed by him, we climbed and scrambled over rocks until we found his mate, splitting slate rock, on the island's northern shore. Those two old-hands, both over 70, were justly proud of their effort in keeping the island's tradition for good roofing slates alive. Once a year, at the highest spring tide, when the sea recedes far enough to let them get at it, they drill the rock, using a pneumatic drill, and set their charge far below the usual low water mark. Then their herculean task is to lever out the blasted rock and lift it all clear in the short time this high spring tide allows them. The annual highest spring tide happened just two days before our visit, and we looked down through the clear water to where the rock had been so newly blasted out that even the drill markings were still visible, and, by the pile of rock slates taken out of it, it looked as if the old quarriers would be kept busy splitting and dressing slates for some time.

At other times of the year they split and dress slates, of not quite such superlative quality, from a small quarry in the slate hill, while in June, July and part of August they give up quarrying for salmon fishing. As we left them to retrace our steps to the island post office and that welcome cup of tea, they gave us a pressing invitation to join them in their exciting salmon net-fishing adventures when that time comes round again.

9

Down Kintyre's Long Peninsula: Campbeltown, Crinan and Tayvalich

It was well into autumn the first time we left our Feochan pitch to continue our touring and exploring down the long peninsula of Kintyre. We climbed high and through the Pass of Melfort, famous for its beauty of scenery, where we look over trees to Loch Melfort opening out between hills. Below runs a very old road which one day we walked along and found so lovely. It is edged by sheer rock on one side, and winds high above the wild River Ouda, which tumbles in short, sparkling falls into deep, chocolate-coloured pools. The small dyke (dry-stone wall), which separates the little road from the brink, is moss-covered and starred with tiny, pink, wild geraniums, while all along the road-edge gleam the delicate white flower of grass of Parnassus. What an exciting route this must have been when the old four-in-hands galloped along it! How many of the thrills we miss by modernizing the highways!

From the pass we dropped to the village of Kilmelford and lovely Loch Melfort. And now our way was wonderful with beautiful seascapes across the loch, sometimes losing it, sometimes high above it, crossing foaming mountain burns, then cutting inland across the green breadth of the Craignish peninsula and into the ancient parish of Kilmartin on our way to Lochgilphead.

Beyond Kilmartin, with its ancient church, a road branches for Crinan, a place with beautiful yachts and small cargo boats lying in its basin, because this is the north-western terminus of the canal from Ardrishaig on Loch Fyne. The whole length of this canal is full of interest, with its locks and boats all making fine pictures. From near Bellanoch, on the way to Crinan, a road goes south down Loch Sween, and half-way down is Tayvalich with its splendid, almost land-locked bay. A favourite holiday resort, especially for yachtsmen, with good accommodation and a caravan park. All this indented stretch of waterways forms a holiday retreat for those who seek peace and glorious seascapes.

But meantime we are on our way to Lochgilphead on Loch Fyne; a grand old town with a wide square, beautiful stone buildings, and good shops. It is a splendid centre for those interested in the astonishing collection of archaeological remains, particularly of the Bronze and New Stone Ages, in the surrounding district. At the head of Loch Gilp the town's views are open and wide down its three miles of Loch Fyne and beyond to Tarbert; and often clearly seen are Arran's high peaks with Goat Fell towering above all others. Like all Loch Fyne's towns, this was a busy fishing port. However, it had more to do with the sea than that, because it is famed for the number of master mariners bred here and now commanding ships sailing to every part of the world.

From childhood days Loch Fyne had always been a name symbolizing to me the largest and finest herring which the fishwife, with her creel, brought to our door. Glibly she called them "Loch Fyne herring", even if they were landed at Musselburgh, near Edinburgh, from where she hailed, or from Ullapool in Wester Ross! But only when our caravan brought us to this great sea loch did I realize how beautiful it was. Especially when we found a wayside pitch where we looked down into the loch and far across it to the Cowal shore.

Some five miles south brought us to Tarbert. Kintyre just missed being an island, and in spite of various attempts has continued to hang on to Knapdale by a mere mile-wide isthmus. At the head is Tarbert, and it was from the farmer there, who halted his milk-cart to fill my jug, that I learned that Tarbert means 'dragging boats'. Then a story, vaguely remembered from school history books, became real; Magnus, a wily Norse king, was promised by the Scots king all the western islands round which he could take his galley; so the crafty old warrior had his boat dragged across the isthmus between the West and East Lochs Tarbert, thus claiming the whole of Kintyre as his.

That narrow isthmus tempted others to make Kintyre into an island. A canal was first thought of from the Sound of Jura to save small cargo boats the long and often hazardous voyage round the wild Mull of Kintyre. But there was neither hill loch

The mountains around Loch Baddagyle

nor large river near enough to supply the necessary fresh water for the locks, so the canal, about six times the length it would have been here, was built between Ardrishaig and Crinan.

Tarbert, so entrancingly picturesque in its setting of sparkling water and sheltering hills, is a charming little holiday resort with many yachts gracing its wide bay; yet also a busy fishing port, with its quaysides lined with colourful fishing boats. High on the hill stands its ruined castle, built on this key position by King Robert the Bruce as a fortified watch-tower to guard both sides of the isthmus and the road to Kintyre's rich pastures.

The Clyde steamer arrives here about noon, and passengers for the Isles go westward uphill between sturdy stonebuilt houses and shops, then across the narrow isthmus to the pier on West Loch Tarbert. We arrived there to find the island steamer, the *Lochiel*, loading for her daily voyage to Gigha, Islay and Colonsay. Her cargo is always a varied one: mail and bread, boxes and hampers, kegs and casks, cattle and cars. The passengers made straight for the shelter of the cabin away from the strong wind which was tossing the waves. But the captain seemed to think little of the wild sea and said it was nothing to what it could be outside the loch; but he loved this island run and wouldn't change it for any other.

From there the road continued wild and lovely, edging the West Loch under rocky cliffs, then on through woods of oak and hazel. But soon its comparative flatness gave way to hills. The ups were steep and the downs were steeper, but the worst of all tumbles into Clachan, a charming village on the road's crook, of pretty cottages, beautiful flower-filled gardens, with a burn running through and a picturesque church.

Beyond Clachan the road curved right down to the shore, to the open sea where madly tossing waves smashed in a smother of foam on wild rocks. The seaward view was island-bounded, the lumpy Paps of Jura distinctive, Islay fainter with distance, and, close-in, sleek little Gigha.

Once past Ronachan Point the road ran flat for miles, and, bowling along this easy and delightful road, we soon realized that the narrow peninsula had more to it than sea-washed rock— for its centre is rich farmland. Few farms are visible from the road, being high in the hills with superb views. Only their road-ends tipped our road and edged it with milk-loading platforms.

8

The Old Man of Wick Castle
Wick on the day of the crowning of the Herring Queen

Then we passed through several small villages of individual charm; the cottage walls of Killean were built of stones of every size and shape, as if gathered from the beach, their roofs were red-tiled, the wide verandah portions being supported on ornamental pillars, a Dutch style of architecture favoured by a former laird of Killean House. Mausdale was a village of crags and old cottages, and, emphasizing its country character, a bunch of Kintyre tinkers, with all their worldly goods in hand-carts, were mouching their way through the village. Pretty Glenbar, at the foot of its green glen through which tumbled the Barr Water, specialized in gardens filled with the glory of flowers. Glenbar Abbey, in its beautiful setting on the river bank, is one of Kintyre's loveliest old houses, with mullioned windows and Gothic pinnacles.

Just beyond the next village, Bellochantuy, we found a delightful wayside pitch on the foreshore, fairly sheltered by high rock, but with a grandstand view of the great breakers smashing in white foam on that rocky shore. And to add to the real-life drama of the sea which our windows framed, we watched lobster-fishers, a short way off shore, putting down lobster-pots, one instant their boat riding high on the crest of a wave, the next lost to sight in the depths of a trough.

It was from a Bellochantuy woman, who was chasing her runaway billy goat, that we learned of a clear spring close by. She chatted while the goat calmly chewed his way through a bramble bush beside the caravan, the bramble thorns apparently having no terrors for him.

Making this our temporary base, we found the next few days exhilarating, bracing and filled with glorious scenery and interest as we explored southwards. As the peninsula's hilly spine flattened out, farms came lower down; fine, stonebuilt houses and steadings, with stack-yards full to overflowing with golden stacks, all beautifully thatched; and only here did I ever see a farmer shaving down his stacks with a scythe to make them trimmer still. Fields were immense, and, besides large dairy herds and herds of beef-cattle, there were horses and foals, and hundreds of farmyard fowls with whole fields to themselves.

And so we came to Kintyre's largest town, Campbeltown. Its old name, and what a wonderful one, was Kinloch-Kilkerran which carries us right back to the days of St. Kiaran; to his cave-cell in Kintyre, to St. Columba, his pupil, to Aiden, first Christian King of Scots, to the wild Macdonalds: Angus Oig, Lord of the Isles, and his strong castles, Dunaverty and Saddell where The Bruce found sanctuary, and which guarded Kintyre and the great loch and village of Kinloch-Kilkerran. Then, in blood and fire, came the Campbells, and left the prosaic name of Campbeltown.

With such a background, this modern town can be viewed from many angles. Visually from land, sea or air it has a look of serene beauty, as it nestles at the head of its glorious sea loch, which forms a large natural harbour between great headlands, with the green island of Davaar almost filling its mouth. I remember it best with its sheltered waters almost calm and vividly blue, and ringing with the raucous cries of gulls circling the many fishing boats unloading at the quays. At another pier a large foreign cargo boat was being unloaded and loaded again at speed; and at yet another, colliers were berthed, and being fed amid noise and clatter by a string of N.C.B. lorries, tipping their contents into the loading chute.

On those cold, autumn days the long esplanade, which gives a clear view of this beautiful waterfront, was almost deserted. How different from the holiday season when there is a daily steamer from Fairlie; a glorious sail by the Cumbraes, round Arran and down Kilbrennan Sound arriving at Campbeltown just three hours later; a splendid day trip allowing two hours ashore. Campbeltown's airways form an essential mainland link with the Isles, and also a speedy and spectacular way of getting from Renfrew in just half an hour. Then there is the daily Glasgow bus via Loch Lomond, Rest-and-be-Thankful and Inveraray. Three services which make this one of the most beloved resorts of the west.

At the library on the seafront is a museum showing the geology of the district: plant and animal fossils collected from an old coal pit and from fossil-bearing strata in the Tirfergus Glen and the Mackrihanish beach; cases of local shells of strange hermit and spider crabs, sea-urchins and queer starfish; of birds in realistic settings; every specimen to be found in the glens and on hills and shores of the peninsula; of dainty butterflies, some of them rare; and of models of ships of local fame to make us wonder at the patience and skill of their seafaring men.

And then, going right back in time through the long history of man's association with Kintyre, we found Neolithic and Bronze Age urns and Azilian flint implements. But of more recent origin was the 'penny-farthing' bicycle, which set me wondering how the people negotiated the town's hilly streets and Kintyre's steep roads on them.

As far back as the eighteenth century this was a busy fishing port with hundreds of fishing boats landing the famous Lochfyne herring. Much of the catch was salted and exported to the West Indies by local ships which brought back cargoes of sugar and rum; and, no doubt, "laces for my lady and baccy for the laird", because the wild cliffs and caves which surround Campbeltown's coast were a perfect haven for smuggled goods.

It was from here, too, in 1774, that Flora Macdonald and her family set sail from their native land for North Carolina in the good ship *Baliol*. And if we could ask for any more evidence that this old town had seafaring men with a love of trading in far places, we have just to look at the mural tablet on an old tenement in Argyll Street. This was the birthplace of Sir William Mackinnon, founder of the British India Steam Navigation Company and one of the splendid 'clan' of Empire builders of last century.

But not all its famous sons had sea-connections; in the old manse of the Highland Church, in Church Avenue, Dr. Norman Macleod, the famous divine, was born and attended the local grammar school. From this town also came the famous artist, William McTaggart, R.S.A., two of whose beautiful pictures hang in the museum. To find the work of another artist who started life here, we must cross to Daavar Island. This is possible by boat or, at low tide, on foot across the Dorlinn, a natural, shingle sandbank. On the wall of a cave Archibald Mackinnon painted the Crucifixion of Christ. This wonderful picture on bare rock draws many people to the island; but people go there too for picnics on its lovely turfed base, or to climb its 600-foot hill, climb and explore its eastern crags, or to go round to the northern tip where the lighthouse is perched on its rocky edge.

A road runs west from the town to Mackrihanish, a holiday resort with a lovely sandy beach and rocks, and a splendid golf course which was laid out by Tom Morris. But this sea-washed village also has two coal mines; and coal mining here dates back about 300 years. There are records of James IV sending a man, John Davidson, down the long peninsula in 1498 "to see if colys may be wonnyn there".

Near the village is the old church of Kilkivan, named after St. Kiven who founded the chapel whose broken walls çan still be seen. I liked the story we heard of his simple solution for those unhappily married. Once a year those unfortunates all came to St. Kiven, who had them blindfolded, then three times turned about, and at his word, "Seize quick", each man grabbed the nearest woman, who became his wife for at least the next year.

South by this shore are tremendous cliffs with wild, rock scenery; and here are three caves, from the roofs of which hang beautiful stalactites: in one they form a curtain like a sheet of frozen water, while others are like pillars. Farther south on this coast is the Mull lighthouse, and the road to it is a terror, dropping in its last three-quarters of a mile from over 1,000 feet to 300 feet, in a series of hairpin bends which, the chief lighthouse keeper told us, the postman cheerfully negotiated in his Land-Rover, thinking nothing of it even when covered with ice and snow. It was wild and windy during our visit, but nothing to what this exposed lighthouse on its 280-foot headland of jagged rock must experience in winter gales. It is one of our oldest lighthouses, built in 1787, but has always been kept abreast of the times, and has its fog signal and wireless beacon.

Southend, on the southern shore below Campbeltown, hides much of ancient history below its quiet appearance. From the village the road curves round to a glorious sandy bay which must have witnessed many a landing. In A.D. 82 Agricola's soldiers were stationed in Southend, it is thought as a jumping-off place for a proposed invasion of Ireland; but instead the Irish invaded Southend, which was equally handy for them (as St. Columba also found). This Irish prince was fleeing from his own land to St. Kiaran, a former teacher, already in Kintyre. St. Columba stayed two years here before continuing his journey to Iona in 563, and the ruins of the church he founded at Kiel, just round the bay, are still there in the ancient burying ground beside the sea.

Dunaverty, a stronghold on its headland near Kiel, was always in trouble. In 1250 the English stormed it, then Alexander III garrisoned it, but it fell to King Haco of Norway in his attempt to conquer Scotland from Kintyre about the time of his defeat at the Battle of Largs. In 1306 the English attacked this outpost again when they attempted, unsuccessfully, to capture The Bruce, who was sheltered here by Angus Oig, Lord of the Isles, after the battle of Methven Wood.

In 1558 the Earl of Sussex sailed in and burned Dunaverty on behalf of Queen Elizabeth. The Macdonalds rebuilt it, but their own atrocities at the burning of the House of Askomel in Kinloch-Kilkerran in 1598 directly resulted in the Earl of Argyll obtaining Royal consent to annex Kintyre. So began the Campbell invasion of this old MacDonald territory, and in 1647 Dunaverty was destroyed by the Covenanters, who cruelly massacred the garrison and their families.

On the green headland today there is little trace of the old castle which helped to shape Scotland's history; where Scotland united was cradled, and from whose early Scottish kings has come down the royal line to our own Queen Elizabeth.

We took 'Golden Eagle' back to West Loch Tarbert before exploring Kintyre's eastern coast, and got a delightful pitch beside a roadman's cottage, which had a gable completely smothered in a glorious, pink, ivy-leaved geranium.

The road on Kintyre's eastern side is hilly, winding through rich farmlands; through hazel groves, with the trees laden with nuts and golden leaves; twisting through little villages and over wild rivers deep in tree-fringed beds. A road of enchanting scenic views, with the Sound narrowing until Arran seems only a stone's throw away, and Ailsa Craig dominated the Ayrshire coast. Arran's hills rise mauve and grape-blue, while, below their beetling cliffs, lie yellow sands with white farms studding green and golden slopes. But to see this road at its best go, as we did recently, in June, when great stretches of it are lined with flowering rhododendrons; it is truly something out of this world.

At Saddell the hillsides are Forestry Commission land, a modern phase for this historical place with its fortress castle. The road topples from cliff-top to sea-level and curves past the gates of Torrisdale Castle, then through Dippen on the Carradale Water. Carradale, with its silver sands, lies at the end of a shore road, a place beloved by holidaymakers and artists; but nearby is a real storybook village, Waterfoot, which has wonderful views of

Arran's mountains. Its cottage gardens, in which grow palm trees, were masses of colour: of begonias and gladioli, with hedges of hydrangea and fuchsia, and gables covered in geraniums; and a sandbank alive with sea birds.

10

Ardmair on the Minch:
Northwards to Lochinvar and Kylesku Ferry

Very often high summer finds us at our best-loved sea haunt, Ardmair in Wester-Ross. There is no other place quite like Ardmair. On our return we are immediately drawn again into the tiny township's warm circle of friends; and nowhere else have we met and made such good caravanning friends. Our pitch used to be above the steep beach, on the top strip of shingle, which was grass covered. This strip, and the adjoining road, which was then very narrow, form a natural breakwater which at some time, during a terrific storm, or many storms, must have been thrown up by the fury of the seas. To the road's landward side, and deep below it, are the crofters' narrow-strip fields stretching to the steep-rising hill. Before the shingle-barrier excluded the sea it must have covered that ground, and the sheer hill would then be bare cliff; for rock-cliff it still is, and, although its ledges are patched with heather, coarse grass and bracken, still its red sandstone rock is whitened with salt from the spray with which winter storms lash it.

Now the green strip on which our caravan, and so many others, used to rest, has gone, swallowed up by the new road construction, but we found another pitch, in a crofter's field, more sheltered, and with our windows framing sea-views out across to green Isle Martin, beyond to the bulwark of Ben More Coigach and across Loch Kanaird to a white house nestling at the foot of green hills. We have also found a safer place for our boat by the crofter's pier, which has made voyaging and fishing much easier.

The present crofter's father was a boat builder with his building yard and sheds here. He built small but strong sea-going fishing boats, which, in his day, depended more on sail than engines. But long before that the sturdy, stone-built, two-storey house here

The gate of Mortlach Distillery
The old gateway of Glamis Castle
Whisky, being rolled into Mortlach's warehouses

was an inn, where many a time travellers must have rested rather than brave the stormy passage to Isle Martin when winds were shrieking and seas raging.

Before a road was made at all along the shingle-barrier, a rough track, which can still be traced, ran high through the hills some twenty miles from Ullapool to Achiltibuie, and was the postman's way until the advent of the mail bus. Many cairns marked the route, for by this hazardous mountain track coffins were carried from the numerous little townships which flanked the Coigach range to their last resting place at Ullapool.

In those days there were no houses down on the present shore as we see them now, and the oldest of them was not built eighty years ago. Those shore houses were an overflow from Ardmair village, in a fold of the hills where the track passed through it and the burn tumbled down its deep channel. Its waters are now piped to Ardmair's houses. Still within living memory sixteen of the ruined houses on the hill were occupied. Only two remain, modernized, one strangely numbered 47, and the crofter here farms three crofts along modern lines, and has utilized the walls of several ruined cottages for sheep fanks (enclosures).

Three-quarters of a century ago Ardmair on the hill had its blacksmith and its cobbler, two necessary tradesmen when the rough bridle track played havoc with the finest iron shoes and the stoutest leather boots. Then too a fiddler and a piper were among its inhabitants and in great demand at weddings and ceilidhs.[1] I cannot find that a shop ever existed here but with their own milk, butter, cheese, and eggs there was little need. They grew potatoes, corn and hay, milling the oats between quern stones, two of which can still be seen. They had fish from the sea and salmon from the river; and white fish, herring and mackerel were salted for winter use. A sheep, or pig was killed as required, sheep's wool was spun, dyed with vegetable dyes and knitted, or woven on hand-looms. Linen they made from flax, which grows well here, and clothes were fashioned at home, with buttons, ribbons and laces from the pedlar's pack for finishing: and Ardmair, like most other townships, was self-supporting.

One day we climbed up through the hills from the old village to find the postman's track; a stiff climb but the reward was a

[1] Ceilidh—pronounced 'caely'—meaning an impromptu sing-song party.

Old Kinloss Village
A quiet corner of Kinloss Abbey
Elgin Cathedral

superb panorama of mountains, lochs and peninsulas. To the north Cul Beag's twin peaks rose behind the mighty Coigach range and southward reared Ben Goleach beyond Loch Broom, and the Challich Hills with glorious An Teallach, 3,483 feet, towering to the sky. Out in the Minch 'floated' the Summer Isles with Isle Martin lying greenly in our bay.

St. Martin's Isle is this island's real name, for here that saintly man, sent out from Iona by St. Columba, landed and made this his base while he taught the people of these parts. He built a chapel on the island's southern side, the ruins of which remain. Close by are the graves of many of his followers, and his own is marked by a headstone on which the cross is carved with double arms.

St. Martin's cave is also on the island, because on the sides facing the Minch and Ben More Coigach there are tremendous red cliffs, frightening to look up at from a small boat, with black caves and strange rock formations. Yet in places they are gloriously draped with honeysuckle with exceptionally large and very beautiful flowers; and alive with birds, for out from rock-holes and caves fly scores of cormorants, shags, fulmars and rock-doves.

But this is no barren island, and much of its 398 acres are good grazing. Topping the island's hill is a lochan which no drought ever shrinks, because it is fed by springs and bubbles up fresh, pure and cold. The island's most enterprising laird piped this water to the four good houses facing Ardmair, giving each a fine bathroom. His tenants were his flour-millers, and his farmer who looked after his herds of cattle, cows and sheep grazing on the green cliff tops.

The flour mill was converted from a red-herring factory originally built in the eighteenth century. Until well into this century fourteen families lived on the island, and the ruins of their sturdy stone cottages are still to be seen, while the tiny one-roomed school is still in good repair. They have outlived the island mill which was demolished in 1949 when building material was scarce, and the laird had another use in Ullapool for its slates and timber. I remember seeing, on my very first visit to Ardmair, the laird's full-rigged schooner, bringing grain from Liverpool, coming in silhouetted against the glory of the sunset, to tie up at his fine new pier. Already that pier is disintegrating but the older stone jetty, which the fishermen of long ago used, is still there.

Now the main harvest around the island is lobsters; but trolling below its cliffs we have caught countless numbers of big lythe, inshore codlings and mackerel. Only when stormy days make boating impracticable are we without fresh fish. The great rollers come in from the Atlantic, curling and glinting like silver before crashing on the beach, churning the shingle, and sucking it back in the undertow with a thunderous roar and rattle. After such a storm many more semi-precious stones are to be found on the beach which is famous for agates, cornelians, rose quartz, topaz, jaspers and amethysts.

The bay's northern sheltering wall is the great rampart of Ben More Coigach; massive, riven by a million storms, red sandstone yet changing colour with every passing cloud and glint of sunshine, and always amazingly beautiful. Coigach's ridge is knife-edged, so one can sit astride it. "One has to," the gamekeeper told us whimsically, "because the wind up there makes it impossible to stand." Between Coigach and the bay is the outlet of Loch Kanaird and here, on a shore rock only approachable by boat, we saw an oyster-catcher's chicks crack their eggshells and emerge. We re-embarked speedily to allow the parent birds' return, but the thrill remained.

At the head of this short sea loch where the river enters the sea, the salmon fishers are busy during the season, and sometimes heavy catches are taken in their ring-nets. There is no lack of life, interest and work in this little corner of Ross-shire, and from our windows we watch the fishing boats make in past the islands towards Loch Broom and Ullapool. Lovely morning pictures, sometimes with heavy cloud and the sun glinting through and under in patches, with a beam lighting a pair of drifters which, with their bright orange-coloured sails, look like golden galleons against the dark Summer Isles.

In spite of stormy days, peace is the key-note of this delightful place, especially of St. Martin's Isle, on which is the sweet serenity peculiar to the island homes of saintly men.

With 'Golden Eagle' at Ardmair, our shopping centre is Ullapool. I love Ullapool. Admittedly its people take a bit of getting to know, but once known they are friends for life. Ullapool is a gem, gay and exotic, where even palm trees and fuchsia hedges grow. There is no need for a promenade nor places of amusement here, no need for any artificial embellishment, for this west Highland village stands supreme in its superb setting, with dignity in its very simplicity and naturalness, full of life and laughter and salty breezes, of boats and mountains and blue sea. Its rows of houses, thick-walled to the winter's blast, are snow-white. For backcloth are vivid green hills, till flowering heather turns them glowing purple-red, for forecloth, the blue sea; and over all is that clear shine peculiar to west Highland air, which lifts the scene from ordinary beauty and burnishes it to brilliance, lovely beyond words.

Ullapool is built on a long, narrow spear-point of land which runs out half-way across Loch Broom, a loch so deep that the largest naval vessels can anchor safely off the peninsula. It was in 1788 that the British Fisheries Association saw the advantages of this long spit of land, providing sheltered anchorage and commanding Minch ports. They built streets of sturdy stone houses and cottages, terrace-fashion, so that from the higher levels one looks over roofs of the Shore Street houses and catches one's breath anew at the grandeur of Loch Broom, stretching away to the glorious blue mountains at its head, seen in even greater splendour from this height. They built fish stores and factories, all in stone with thick walls and slated roofs. There white fish was smoked, cod salted, and herring salt-cured and kippered. Most important of all they built the sturdy pier; and that same pier has just been enlarged to accommodate the ever-increasing herring fleet, with bigger boats, fishing the Minch and landing their catch here.

In the eighteenth, nineteenth and early twentieth centuries most of the cured fish was shipped to Baltic ports. It was fortunate that on the inward voyage the boats carried timber as ballast, because here was the wood necessary for the pier and for beams in the houses and stores, without the cost and labour of felling trees and hauling from some distant inland forest. Those beams can still be seen.

For those who like exploring by sea there is a cruise by motor-launch to the Summer Isles, landing on the largest, Tanerra More, for a picnic lunch, and returning by the foot of Ben More Coigach and round Isle Martin. No one seems to know why those fabled Summer Isles are so named. My own theory is that winter's storms and mists hide them completely from the mainlander, while in summer they are clearly visible, sometimes close in, at others appearing more distant and as if afloat on the Minch.

But back we come to Ullapool—busy, gay Ullapool with all the bustle and excitement of the auction ring at the pier, when the drifters and ring-net boats follow each other in quick succession up Loch Broom and round the point to unload their catch with all speed. Far from detracting from the holiday spirit it adds living interest; and lucky is anyone who samples those Minch herring, fresh landed, or kippers fresh from Ullapool's kippering factory—there are no equals.

With deep waters on three sides, the long peninsula held a fishing village long before the Fisheries Association's building in 1788. First there was a small township of black houses with turf and heather thatch, and legend tells how in those early days large shoals of fish came each year to the waters off Lewis, but because of a witch's curse none entered Loch Broom. This intolerable state of affairs took a deal of cunning and careful planning to rectify. The wives of the fishermen of the 'Big Loch' eventually broke the spell and brought herring to their home waters by having a beautiful silver herring made and a boat prepared against all witchcraft. It sailed to the Lews, then, turning for home, the silver charm on a silken line was trailed behind and the greatest of all herring shoals lured into Loch Broom. To ensure that herring would stay there for ever the charm was finally dropped into the loch.

Being so old, Ullapool has a wonderful store of legend—but the romance of Murdo Mackenzie was more than legend, because his descendants are in the village to this day. The story goes that tall, handsome Murdo, a splendid fisherman, traded his catch by sailing his fishing smack round coastal townships farther south. Reaching the Island of Luing one evening he found a ball in full swing. On entering the ballroom he saw the fairest of ladies, the beautiful daughter of Lord Breadalbane, and she, with fluttering heart, beheld this stalwart, most handsome of men. Dance followed dance. Deeper and deeper this splendidly matched pair fell in love, till, when the stars were dimming with the dawn, she boarded his smack and sailed off with him to Ullapool, where they were married.

Lord Breadalbane, beside himself with anger and grief, offered a big reward for his daughter's recovery. He learned that she had been carried off in a nameless fishing smack, so he persuaded the King to pass a law that all boats should henceforth bear names or numbers—which they do to this day. Our hero must have had a sense of humour for he chose a novel way of introducing himself to his father-in-law. He sailed to Oban, procured a horse and rode across country to Taymouth Castle, and was soon closeted with Lord Breadalbane.

"You'll get the reward," said his Lordship, "when you tell me where she is."

"I'll tell you when I get the money," said Murdo. The money changed hands.

"Now," said Murdo, "for another £300 I'll tell you where the man is who stole her!" He got the money, and holding out his hand said, "There is the hand that stole her from Luing."

So pleased was the girl's father at Murdo's courage and manliness that he gladly accepted him as his son-in-law and gave his beloved daughter a handsome dowry.

It was in 1912 that the silver charm failed and the herring deserted Loch Broom and the Minch. This black disaster forced the fishermen of Ullapool to other trades, and many turned their nimble fingers from making and mending nets to tailoring, until there were sixty tailors in the village cutting and stitching tweed woven on cottage hand-looms from the wool of local-bred sheep, and selling their durable suits and coats throughout the north and islands. Then, too, the foundation of today's rich tourist trade was laid when hard-pressed housewives turned their attention to summer visitors—only the discerning few in those days, who did not mind more than thirty rough miles of road from Garve; lovers of magnificent scenery, sport, and peace beyond dreams.

Then about 1950, in the inexplicable way of their kind, great shoals of herring returned to the Minch, and Ullapool, overnight, became once more the centre of a great fishing industry. All Minch ports are controlled from Ullapool by the Herring Industry Board's representative. Salting stations were set up on Morefield Hill, and on the peninsula's western shore, by fishermen from the great east coast fishing ports and from Ireland. Once more barrels of salted herring are shipped direct to Germany and other countries—America being a good customer for the early season, or Matja herring. And fleets of lorries race over the narrow, twisted roads day and night carrying this valuable fresh food to the big kippering factories at Wick, Fraserburgh, Peterhead and Aberdeen, or, with the fish carefully iced, to the English markets via Hull and London; they also travel in huge refrigerated vans.

Ullapool is busy in all seasons. An exciting competition, the deep-sea angling one, takes place towards the end of September each year. Deep-sea anglers come from all over Britain and Ireland to demonstrate their prowess with rod and line; but in September, 1965, they came from all over the world, because this week of intensive angling saw the battle of the European Sea Angling Championships. Sportsmen from twelve nations took part, and at the start their flags were ceremoniously raised. The heaviest fish brought in was a 135-pound skate and, in contrast, the smallest, caught on a large skate hook, was a spotted dragonet, weighing $1\frac{1}{2}$ ounces and only six inches long.

There are also deep-sea angling competitions, which are local, throughout the summer, and visitors delight to participate. Every Saturday there are also yacht races, which are enjoyed by the landlubbers as well as the yachtsmen.

When we go exploring farther afield, one way we love is by Destitution Road, which starts at Braemore junction beyond the head of Loch Broom. In 1846 the disastrous failure of the potato harvest caused famine among the crofters of the north-west. To alleviate their distress a Destitute Committee was set up in Edinburgh, and grants made to give them work, mainly on road improvements and building new roads from Gairloch to Loch Maree, and by Dundonnell to Braemore—this latter section became known as Destitution Road. In the making these were roads of great toil, as they went across peat-bogs, bridged deep chasms, climbed through mountain passes to over 1,100 feet, wormed around cliffs by cutting out rock, or, with hair-raising gradients and bad overhangs, carried shelf-like roads down cliff faces; laborious, too, must have been ways across the shifting sands of wide bays.

In winter, with rain and mist blotting out mountains and loch, Destitution Road must appear desolate enough to justify its name. But go over it when our Highlands are ashine on a clear, sunny day; coming from the wild Dirrie More, past Loch Droma and the towering peaks of Beinn Dearg and Squrr Mor, or from the pass where rushes the River Broom, and where, in its incredible chasm, thunder the Measach, or Corrie Halloch, Falls, dropping in foam and fury over 300 feet. Magnificent larches grace this wooded way to Braemore and by the bridge over the River Droma to Destitution Road. But this old road has had a face-lift, and is a lot less hazardous now. However, in spite of the construction work just completed, it is still beautiful and more in keeping with modern traffic. Far below the wooded valley of Strath More stretches to Loch Broom, and in the distance, Ben More Coigach with silver-edged clouds cleft by its knife-like ridge. Then for a spell the road runs high and a cooling wind tempers the hot sunshine; a wind fragrant with heather, peat and bog-myrtle, but not strong enough to keep the clegs, or horse-flies, at bay.

Sgurr Mor, 3,637 feet, backed by white clouds came into full view, massive, comely, like a great St. Bernard, and with snow-wreaths lingering in its eastern fissures. We were now in Gleann Mor, where the Cuileig River foams over its falls and rushes down into amber pools between fern-grown rock walls with tiny birch trees. Crossing the bridge, with 3,276-foot A'Chailleach towering over the glen, the scene changed to bogland, where black, peaty tarns were fringed with scarlet and orange mosses and spangled with silken cotton grass. Ahead the great peak, An Teallach, pierced the skyline, followed by many pinnacles sharply defined against banked clouds. The whole of this amazing range of wild mountains is called the Challich Hills, and is said to be the oldest rock in Europe. This home of the golden eagle, ptarmigan, buzzard, red deer and fox crowded our skyline until reaching Strath Beg, where Strathbeg River leaped down its glen in a series of glorious falls over and between jagged rocks of vivid red sandstone. Seated on a fragrant, thyme-cushioned dyke, I gloried in its wildness and its laughter as it gleefully sprayed rowan trees, clinging tenaciously in spite of scanty root-hold, and making more lovely its way.

At the hill-foot, by the head of Little Loch Broom, is Dundonnell, a township frequented by geologists looking for topaz, moss agate, rose quartz, amethyst, and other treasures which rocks of the district yield. Its Youth Hostel is a vital link in the north-west chain, because from here goes that lovable old road

Sueno's Stone near Forres

which served before Destitution Road was made. It crosses the river, climbs along the side of Beinn nam Ban and drops to Aultnaharrie on Loch Broom with a mile's ferry across to Ullapool.

Leaving the loch our wayward road climbed inland, to reach the sea again at Gruinard Bay, then on through a narrowing glen with the rollicking Gruinard River, and Scotch pines, spruce, birch and rowan on one side, and the massive conical Goat's Hill on the other. The Gruinard boat-repairer told us that there are still about twenty wild goats on this hill, but they are difficult to pick out among the welter of tumbled, white rocks. Across an old Scotch pine plantation, remnant of the once great Gruinard Forest, a buzzard flew to alight high on the rock face. We crossed Gruinard River and by the gamekeeper's house looked far up this lovely glen to glorious An Teallach, now dressed in softest lavender.

Dropping steeply down Cabeg Hill, now tamed from the once harum-scarum hill with its wicked little bridges, we again reached sea-level at Fisherfield's white sands, and had the good fortune to see a golden eagle fly up the glen which backs the green machair. His was the freedom, and his the way to An Teallach's sublime heights.

Up along the cliff-face we climbed on a steep gradient with grand seascape views over Gruinard Bay before rounding the cliff-point. Then through the clachan of Second Coast and First Coast, and, finding a grass-grown road, down to the sea we stopped for a snack. This little road led to a sandy bay at the foot of the spectacular Needle Rocks, and here were preaching caves with pulpit and rock seats used up to a century ago for open-air services, with the vast congregation gathered from miles around and often numbering over 2,000.

We turned inland through a land of neat crofts, reaching the sea once more at Aultbea, where we usually lunch in its good hotel before continuing round Loch Ewe with its beautiful sea-scapes, until we come to Inverewe and the famous gardens.

The designing and laying out of the gardens was started on this wild little peninsula, which was then just a barren hillside, in 1865 by Osgood Mackenzie, who realized that here, where the warm airs of the Gulf Stream prevailed and prevented frost, anything could grow. Wind, of course, was a big hazard, but

9

Culbin Forest, planted to anchor the shifting sands of Culbin
The graves of Rob Roy and his wife beside the old Kirk of Balquhidder

trees, shrubs and hedges controlled that difficulty in time. Here are many tropical trees and plants, and my most enjoyable visit was when we took an Australian friend to see the gardens. She came from Brisbane and knew the names of all foreign trees and shrubs; she made them live for me in that tropical outpost of Australia.

The gardens were given to the National Trust for Scotland by Osgood Mackenzie's daughter, and the Trust has improved them greatly, with more little walks, and steps climbing to viewpoints. They have also added a splendid restaurant, and a large car park. The best time to see the gardens is in June, when the rhododendrons and azaleas are in bloom, but later the little rock pools are gay with water lilies, and at all seasons the seascapes are magnificent. It is a place I never grow tired of visiting.

A short distance round, at the very head of this great sea loch, lies Poolewe, a delightful anglers' rendezvous, because here the glorious River Ewe, having run only a few miles from Loch Maree, enters the sea. We climbed inland for a few miles until we looked down on the wonderful sandy beaches of Gairloch. This is a good holiday place and caters well for the visitors. There is a great deal to explore close by on the big peninsula which forms the western side of Loch Ewe. There is a fine caravan site here, but again it is one that can become crowded. South from Gairloch is an enticing little road which goes to Badchro, where there is a tiny hotel on the sea's brink, a delightful corner with wild rocks, islands and small boats. The road continues to Red Point and here, on the machair, many caravanners find a happy landfall.

From Gairloch we are soon running east through beautifully wooded Kerrysdale, a pass which brings us to Loch Maree. Much has been written about this famous angling loch, but it is its beauty which holds one spellbound. Its little islands, its wooded, rocky shores and the magnificent, massive Slioch mountain, 3,217 feet, on its farther shore, dominating the loch yet adding such beauty. This mountain, so different in shape from any other, creates the unique Loch Maree picture.

Just past the head of the loch is Kinlochewe, and here the road goes off for Torridon, not the old rocky road of bygone days but a new through-way of unsurpassed beauty. But our way for the moment is on through glen Docharty to Achnasheen, with its busy railway station on the Kyle of Lochalsh line, and on through Strath Bran, past pretty Loch Luichart, with its great electric power-house, to Garve and our return journey to Ullapool.

Ardmair is only the starting point for all the magnificent scenery to the north. It is no dead-end, and one can go from here right round the top; to Cape Wrath, to Thurso and Wick, or perhaps to Lairg, and down Loch Shin to Dingwall and Inverness. It takes time to do it all, in fact, it has taken us many summers, but we know it all well now and many of the small roads off.

There is one particular road, and it is my favourite, the route to Achiltibuie. Except for a lick of tar and some better passing-places, this is still the old road, narrow and winding high above Loch Lurgain for miles, with the glory of the mountains making a background to every picture. Across the big loch, with its crocodile-shaped island, we look on the great Coigach Range, and how different it is from this angle with smaller, out-jutting, peaked mountains of wonderful beauty. Cul More and Cul Beag are comely and huge, then An Stac, commonly called by mountaineers Stack Polly because from its northerly side flows the River Polly.

Stack Polly is an unusual mountain, its whole long ridge is serrated with tall pinnacles like fine teeth, and all summer there are people climbing it. We see their cars parked in little roadside quarries, their tents pitched among the heather, but rarely do we see the climbers, because through the day they are on the hill.

Achiltibuie is a long straggling village with a small hotel; but before reaching it there is a small road which runs down to its pier. This road climbs high into the hills with glorious seascapes. It continues to Reiff, a seacoast clachan of half a dozen houses, and an emergency landing strip of machair for the 'mercy planes' bringing patients from the north and west islands. From here the Ullapool ambulance can take the patient to hospital at Inverness.

But today our road does not go to Reiff; we branch off and climb high to run down the Brae of Achnahaird, and here we have a magnificent panorama of mountains: An Stac, Cul Beag, Cul Mor, Suilven, Canisp, and all backed by the glorious Quinag Range.

One of the most spectacular roads in those parts is the sea-road to Lochinver. It starts a little way back before reaching Achilti-buie. It drops to the Inverpolly estate, which nestles in a green cup of the hills with the River Polly flowing through; and this glorious section is a nature reserve. This shore-edging road is very narrow. It climbs, dips and twists right round Enard Bay, which with its rocks and islands is beautiful. If we have not lunched by the River Polly, we lunch at Enard Bay.

After passing the little township of Inverkirkaig, we run steeply down past Loch Culag, a small loch backed by beautiful hills, behind which rises the round top of Suilven, the Sugar Loaf. And here is the Lochinver school and schoolhouse, delightfully sited on the loch's edge, and a mile out from the village.

From Lochinver we can return to Ardmair by the splendidly remade road which skirts Loch Assynt for many lovely miles and goes through pretty Elphin village, Elphin of the rowan trees, for here they grow prolifically, making dull autumn days glow with their scarlet berries and crimson leaves. Overshadowing, towers Ben More Assynt, where wild cat, fox, ptarmigan and golden eagle all have their habitat.

But going north from Lochinver we find a little road, which wanders along the hillside and drops us down into Achmelvich's sandy bay, with an open caravan park on the green machair. This is Lochinver's caravan park, and a delightful one beloved by many caravanners, especially with children who love sand and bathing. On the surrounding hills we have often found white heather, so it is a lucky site.

Still farther north, through wild and beautiful hills, we climb steeply up Clach Toll; why so named I cannot find, perhaps in stage-coach days there was a toll on this steep hill. I always laugh when we climb this hill, because I remember friends from Perth who brought their little, tall, grey caravan to rest beside us at Ardmair. I asked why they called it 'The Elephant'.

"Because," she said, "we tried to take it up Clach Toll, but our little car just refused. So we unhitched, meaning to turn the caravan about and go down again. But on the steep hill the caravan took control and ran down the old narrow road and landed end-on in the ditch. It looked so funny with its towbar sticking up in the air, like a little elephant with a trunk, that we called it the 'Elephant'!" When they returned to Ardmair next year they had taken David's advice to reduce its gauntness, by making the top half a lighter colour than the bottom section. It was now cream and green.

"But you can't call it 'The Elephant' now," I said.

"No," replied Molly solemnly, "it is now 'The Caterpillar'."

At Clach Toll summit we halt and climb higher on foot among rock and heather to gaze far down and across to an amazing panorama of mountains, each so different in shape that they are easily recognizable: Cul Mor, Suilven, Canisp and Ben More Assynt. From this height they are spread before us like a map. Some kind soul in this Sutherland county has placed a seat on this elevated viewpoint.

Our next villages are Stoer and Drumbeg, where again caravanners use the machair among the sand dunes as a happy holiday resting place. There is nothing organized about this site; it is just naturally lovely and an ideal place for those who want a sandy beach. I could never imagine it becoming crowded because it stretches such a long way.

The road becomes wilder and steeper as we turn inland, and eventually it brings us to Kylesku ferry, which crosses Loch Cairnbaun to Kylestrom; the only free ferry and a very fine one now, with a splendid, remade road to it from Skiag Bridge junction just beyond Inchnadamph by Loch Assynt. This road, to us, was an engineering wonder. It was built over bogland, but the bog was 'thatched' with tree trunks, and those will not deteriorate because peat-bog preserves wood. On this firm base the new road took shape. It must have been an expensive operation.

Beyond Kylestrom lies a fairyland of all the wondrous beauty of Badcall Bay and Eddrachillis Bay, with their rugged rocks, beautiful little islands, and a pervading peace only disturbed by the sea-birds' cry.

11

Round the North of Scotland: Caithness and East Sutherland

Now to our farthest north-eastern county, which is one I love dearly. By road or rail it is a long day's journey from Edinburgh or Glasgow, but by air only a few hours separate the southern towns from this northern tip. Yet a hundred years ago the only sensible way to this aloof county was by sea, because two of its three borders are coastal, and its towns and villages were all at the river mouths.

The third leg of the triangle is its land border to Sutherland; a roadless hinterland of bleak hills and bog, but from there come the many rivers which make the remainder of that vast cliff-top plateau so fertile. Those same rivers, through the ages, have carved their way to the sea, sometimes at the last dropping in glorious waterfall formations down cliff faces where the hard rock has refused to yield to erosion, at others roaring through their rock-walled ravines far, far below where their original channels ran.

In those sheltered gullies trees grow in abundance in striking contrast to the almost treeless, windswept plateau. There the many lochs which these rivers feed seem bleak in consequence. They are grand fishing lochs, but being unsheltered are subject to violent storms, and many are the tales of unwary anglers scrambling ashore from upturned boats.

But Caithness is beautiful, with an unusual beauty which is found in the blue of the North Sea and the dazzling white fringe it throws around ragged, rock-toothed shores. It triumphs in the sheer magnificence of towering headlands, sometimes crowned with lighthouses; in the untrodden, lonely beaches, while the tree-less, flat terrain emphasizes the splendour of unbroken sky and throws into relief the dozen or more ancient castles which fringe its cliff-tops.

Journeying to Caithness, we find the roads splendid, although not without thrills after crossing the border at the Ord of Caithness. On a particularly dangerous point of the Ord is a stone slab with the grim inscription:

> William Welch perished here.
> Be ye also ready.

We are into the long parish of Latheron, one of the largest parishes in Scotland and over thirty miles long. What a lovely name it has. Latheron is derived from the Gaelic 'Laithair Roin', 'the Haunt of Seals'. Latheronwheel and Lathorn Village are lovely little coastal villages here. Between spells of cliff-top airiness the road dips to many a village of charm, but at Berriedale it topples clean from the cliff-top to the foot of the gorge and climbs as dizzily up the opposite cliff, with a hair-pin bend in the centre. But Berriedale itself is lovely with its pretty cottages deep in trees, while the gamekeeper's house makes an arresting picture, with its white walls gorgeously patterned with hundreds of antlers. It took two rivers to chisel this gorge, and these we cross by twin bridges, then a little farther and the rivers tumble into the sea at a pretty little rocky harbour, where small boats are drawn up on the shingle clear of the surge of that turbulent North Sea.

A short way on a fairy castle from Hans Andersen swims into view; snow-white, turreted, immense Castle of Dunbeath, perched on a mighty cliff above the rock-pierced sea. There has been very little history written about this ancient stronghold, but in my searching for information, I came on this gem in an old guide book.

> Dunbeath Castle had the distinction of being besieged in 1650 by the 'Great Marquis' of Montrose, and on that occasion was romantically defended by Lady Sinclair.

Dunbeath village, too, is like something from a fairy-tale; a glorious place, with spectacular cliffs and tumbled rocks, white-edged by breaking waves or ringed with gold of sand. An inn stands on the banks of Dunbeath Water, and anyone who has a taste for mountaineering will find this an ideal starting point for the ascent of Morven (over 2,000 feet). Here too are cliff-top tracks, narrow and scented by wayside flowers, and walks over hill-land, or up the green strath by the river where the brown trout splash in limpid pools.

The north-bound railway reaches a somewhat southerly terminus at Lybster, six miles farther on. Its route is strangely roundabout, for it shies clear of Berriedale's fearsome mountains and deep valleys and runs inland almost to Thurso, before turning east to Wick and doubling back down the coast to the fishing port. Lybster is a Norse name meaning 'Homestead on the Slope'. Besides being a fishing port, it once had a busy market which lasted three days and was held in the main street. It has a beautiful harbour, and at one time 200 fishing boats sailed from it, all local ones.

From Lybster gentle dips and rises and spacious seaward views carry us on to Wick, a fine old Norse town which figured in Sagas eight centuries ago, but which has many of the facilities of a modern holiday resort. Its busy aerodrome links it with Orkney and Shetland. Its splendid wireless station is a major and vital link with ships at sea. But to find the real pulsating life of the town is to follow its steep, narrow, winding streets, which all lead down to the harbours. Here are the kippering factories, salting yards, and fish-meal factory, and these get additional supplies by fast road transport from the Minch ports and from Scrabster on the north coast; but there is a great deal of white fish brought into Wick by the seine-net boats, too, and it is a busy, colourful scene when the fleet is in.

Wick's great day of festival is the crowning of the Herring Queen. Then fishing boats, harbour and town are decked with bunting and flags to welcome their new young Herring Queen as she sails in from the North Sea aboard a herring drifter. A great and memorable day of pageantry.

However, there are various industries in Wick now, apart from the fishing and the agriculture of the surrounding country district; and one which is both interesting and important is the glassware made by Caithness Glass Ltd. This company was started only a little over ten years ago by the Hon. R. M. Sinclair, who knew that when the main construction work at Dounreay was completed many local people would have to find other employment.

It had to be something that could be marketed all over Britain and then build up export trade, so it was decided that a glass factory could be the answer.

Scottish Industrial Estates agreed to build a factory at Wick, if the company to be formed could produce £50,000. The money was raised locally, the company floated, and a factory built. They procured the services of a glass technologist and designer, Domhnall O'Brian, who laid out the factory and prepared the first designs. They employed glass blowers from several European glass-blowing centres, and started to train some local apprentices in all the skills of hand-blown glass.

It was a tremendous enterprise by Mr. Sinclair and his friends, especially as it entailed massive inward transportation costs of raw materials and outward transport of the finished articles. Of course there were teething troubles, but these seem to have been cured, and during 1966 sales touched the £100,000 mark. This is now a growing export company.

Among others, they have a remarkably fine glass worker, Paul Ysart, a naturalized Briton, who has worked in glass for forty years. He is Spanish by birth and comes of a family famous in glass-making. His particular delight is making glass paper-weights, and he is one of the three best paper-weight makers in the world. His paper-weights and designs have been commissioned by the royal family and are generally much sought after. He is now a training officer in the factory, where 95 per cent of the labour force is local, and a very big proportion is making the full range of high quality, hand-made glassware, which one sees in good china shops and departments of big stores up and down the whole country. They also have a London show-room which is becoming very well known.

Our most northerly town is Thurso, on the top coast of Caithness, and another Norse port of great antiquity, which derived its name from the Scandinavian god, Thor. It went on growing as a trading port, and by the fourteenth century had become so important that David II made its weights legal throughout Scotland, declaring that "the weicht of Caithness shall be used by all men buying and selling within this realm". Now, with a modern cloak, it still maintains this tradition, if coupled with Scrabster, the busy fishing port farther round Thurso Bay, where steamers from the Islands also call.

Thurso Castle is an asset to the town, with its turrets and battlements and looking as a splendid, old Scottish castle should; yet it only dates from 1872 when it replaced one built by the Earl of Caithness two centuries earlier. It is the home of Viscount Thurso.

An ancestor of his, Sir John Sinclair, whose statue stands in the town square, was responsible for that invaluable record of his day, *The Statistical Account of Scotland*.

For the angler and botanist Thurso River is the lure; a glorious salmon river, earlier even than Tay or Tweed, and on its banks are many rare flowers including the golden flowered 'holy grass', found nowhere else in our land, and the dainty but hardy *primula scotica*, which thrives and blooms most in wild, stormy weather.

From Thurso we circle the golden sands of Dunnet Bay on our way to John o' Groats. It was a sunny morning the last time we passed that way, and a lone caravanner had those miles of glorious sands and sand dunes to himself, to his amazement, having come from London! We had camped the night before at Murkle Bay, near Thurso, and before leaving I asked at a nearby farm for milk; but such is the warmheartedness of Caithness folk I got a quart of cream—called milk—two dozen new-laid eggs, and a big bag of scones and pancakes fresh off the girdle.

We took the tortuous road to Dunnet Head, the most northerly point of our mainland, where, above the awesome cliffs, ringing with the cries of sea-birds, stands its magnificent lighthouse, which Thomas Stevenson built in 1823. A keeper took us up the spiral stairway until, 350 feet above the turbulent sea, we stood beside the great light and its gleaming magnifiers, which, rotating slowly in a huge bowl of mercury, cast a friendly, guiding beam twenty-five miles out over the stormy Pentland Firth.

With a telescope from the lighthouse parapet we got amazing views of Orkney, picking out houses and spires, besides the Old Man of Hoy, Orkney's 450-foot rock stack, and of the Pentland Skerries, Duncansby Head, and the nearer, storm-riven shore at Scarfskerry and Men of Mey. The bird-life around the headland was marvellous, and among those we saw were gannets, fulmars, kittiwakes, puffins, cormorants, guillemots, razor bills, and a peregrine falcon. On the face of this headland too is a cavern known as the Aukies' Hole, where an immense colony of auks have their abode.

From there, on our way to John o' Groats, we passed the wind-swept, old church of Canisbay. In the churchyard here lies John de Groat. Legend has it that he built an eight-sided house with eight doors, and used an eight-sided table so that none of his quarrelsome sons could take precedence one of another by entering first or sitting at the head of the table. With eight doors it must have been a draughty house on that windswept shore, especially during fierce winter storms! But on the day we were there John o' Groats was entrancing; a little harbour with white boats, a beach of finest silver sand, sea incredibly blue and tossed by a wind giving snow-white curly plumes to the waves, and the whole drenched in golden sunshine.

Caithness is full of spectacular vignettes, not the least being the great Atomic Research Station near Thurso, and, not so far from there again, the Castle of Mey, the so-loved Caithness home of our beloved Queen Mother. Yet the most unexpected scene we found was on the day we crossed the border from Sutherland on the northern road, and after miles of bleak moorland came suddenly on Forss Water. Here, on a crook of the road, was an old bridge by a weir, a wimpling river and two old meal mills, one on either side, splashing foaming water from their wheels. The whole was surrounded by an amazing mass of trees from which came the cooing of wood-pigeons to mingle with the homely clucking and gaggle of hens, geese and turkeys, and, to give beauty in good measure, the millhouse garden, in a riot of colour, spilled its blooms over the chuckling river.

By contrast was the picture we got a few days later when we stood on the battlements of Ackergill Tower, a fifteenth-century keep near Wick. We looked far over the plain, canopied by glorious, windswept clouds and unbroken by trees or even hedges. This flat, fertile land was for long the Norsemen's granary, and ever since the days of their occupation has continued to be tilled, sown and reaped. Where necessary the fields are sturdily fenced with Caithness paving stones by standing them on their edges. Those flat slabs of rock are mainly quarried at Castletown, a long, stretched-out village, which was always the main centre of the flagstone industry. From there, before cement or tarmacadam were thought of, came one of the county's biggest exports to pave sidewalks in our cities. They were also used as roofing slates.

But another of the county's biggest exports has always been her people. *Caithness Your Home* Herbert Sinclair called one of his books, and home this northern county is to many exiles in every part of the world. In our cities they band together to form associations; they write poems about the beauty and worth of their native county and dream of the day when retirement will let them go back.

Yet still they emigrate; it may be the restless Norse blood in their veins, or eyes that look out across stormy seas to far horizons beyond which youthful aspirations can find fulfilment. Recently I spoke with a Perthshire gamekeeper who said he left his home at John o' Groats forty years ago. I should have known he was descended from the Vikings with his high cheekbones in a lean face, his tall, spare figure, his fair hair, and blue eyes which looked beyond the mountains of that narrow Perthshire glen to a sea-lashed, rocky coast. I spoke to him about the amazing feeling I always have in Caithness of being physically fit, happy and serene, as if there was some special elixir in the air. He knew what I meant and explained it by saying that with its borders being mainly coastal, no matter from which airt (direction) the wind blows, fresh, health-giving sea breezes cover Caithness.

We took a notion one day to visit and explore the valley which the north-bound railway took preferable to the coast road which would take it over the Ord at Berriedale. On a rising road, bound northwards, flanked by the seemingly limitless, restless sea, and bordered to the west with the wild hinterland of mountains, we came to the inevitable dip from the cliff-top to cross the mouth of yet another river-chiselled valley. But our sudden descent into Strath Ullie revealed a superb picture; from between green mountainsides, patched with silver-grey rock and the rich reds and purples of heather, came the rushing River Helmsdale, then, matured and sedate, it wended through its wooded valley and on beneath the bridge into its estuary. And here lay the old Port of Helmsdale.

What a lovely place Sutherland's only eastern port is, with its pearly-white old village and sturdy, stone-built stores, clinging to the harbours and estuary. Climbing the hillside, and facing the headland where stands the ruins of Helmsdale Castle, was prosperous new Helmsdale, set in terraces and flowered gardens, with, over the brow of the hill and where wooded slopes spill their verdant way down behind the bridge to the river, more houses and its grand old kirk. From our vantage point we looked at this vivid village picture, enhanced by a blue sky and wind-tossed clouds, and the shining river mouth which, in its curving, gave shape to the streets.

Continuing downhill the road curved past a landmark of this century's building, the beautiful war memorial clock-tower, which stands four-square on the hillside with its face to the village and harbour, and to the fishermen in their home-coming as they cross the bar. Still down; then, bridging the wide mouth of Strath Ullie, the road north runs through the main street of the village. Here, in street and shops, it was pleasant to listen to the lilting voices of those north-country folk, who have so much Norse blood in their veins, and who, like their forbears of countless generations, have weathered the bracing winds of that breezy, north-eastern shore.

From the street to the water's edge is only a step. Here the fishing boats are in two harbours inside the great natural one, formed by the basin of the Helmsdale River and made more complete by stout sea-walls. In the palmy days when many boats operated from this, their home port, the old and new harbours, and even up the river a little way, must have been filled with fishing-craft when this was a busy, thriving port; but herring are fickle, and the disappearance of the shoals off the east coast for several years brought sore problems and lean years to this fair village. It caused many of the local fishermen to go over from herring to white fish, from drifters to seine-net boats, because white fish catches are more consistent and easily marketed, and there is no need to follow the shoals, as with herring which take the drifters and ring-net boats to Minch ports in summer and south to Yarmouth or Lowestoft in autumn.

Seine-net fishing allows the men home to Helmsdale each day, the catch being usually landed around five o'clock, and in the summer days of this far north-land there are long evenings in which to tend their crofts, small-holdings, or other business. In times when white fish are scarce, or days too stormy to venture out, those second strings to the fishermen's bows are splendid stand-bys. I think the purely English sense of the port's name is symbolical—the helms by which those men so successfully steer their craft, and the dale, or strath, where they toil on the land.

The castle atop the south cliff at its very point, sentinel and landmark through the centuries, is now a crumbling but picturesque ruin. Like most old castles, the only tales it has handed down are gruesome ones. Here, in the twelfth century, a Viking burned the lady of the castle; and in 1567 Isobel Sinclair, scheming to get rid of the heir to the Sutherland earldom, made an unintentional error and poisoned the earl and countess and her own son instead. So much for the good old days; but today the youth of Helmsdale, and its summer visitors, pass the old castle on their way to the foot of the cliff's southern side where there is such excellent bathing.

The main road, running through the village, goes on over the Ord into Caithness, but it is here that the railway, which has escorted the road for many a mile, deserts it and turns up Strath Ullie. And up the strath, too, goes a good road; a lovely road which winds for miles by the River Helmsdale and goes on gently climbing through the hills to nearly 600 feet, as it passes through Achentoul Forest before dropping down by a lang, lang, whang through Strath Halladale to the northernmost coast.

Lovely Strath Ullie with its river and burns is not so wild now as it climbs away from Helmsdale, but fearful, indeed, it must have been until less than three centuries ago, when the last wolf in Sutherland, some say in Scotland, was killed here. But wolves or not, through the centuries the lure of gold has made men disturb its peace. To the Kildonan goldfields they have come, generation after generation, but finding that fortunes were not easily made there, they have gone again, leaving the Kildonan Burn to chuckle and laugh as it hurries to join the River Helmsdale.

But even today there is some word of research work in connection with the Kildonan gold mines by the Canadian Highland Development and Exploration Company, so perhaps Helmsdale will once again find itself the centre of a thriving gold-digging industry.

This eastern side of Sutherland has more industry than around its northern and western borders. At Brora there is a thriving and prosperous coal mine, which is not nationalized. It is more or less owned and run by the miners. Its big lorry load of coal bags travels as far as Ardmair and Ullapool, which is a boon, as coal brought from the south, with its heavy transport charges, is exorbitant.

In this delightful village on the estuary of the River Brora is a hand-loom weaver of considerable skill. As with most of the people here, his surname is Sutherland, and he also runs the petrol station. Our Innes tartan is difficult to weave on a power loom because of its many colours, but Donald Sutherland, using my beautiful Langholm-woven scarf as a pattern, wove me a length of Innes dress-tartan.

Dornoch, at the mouth of the Dornoch Firth, is the county town. It was made a royal burgh by Charles I in 1628, but is one of the smallest county towns in Scotland. There are good hotels, but its chief claim to distinction is its miles of golf links; there are two 18-hole golf courses. Golf here dates from 1619, and the Dornoch golf links are the third earliest mentioned in history.

There is a wonderfully open, breezy, municipal caravan park at Dornoch, which takes at least 150 touring caravans. It is on the links and only twenty yards from the beach, which is splendid for bathing. But at a little coastal village north of Dornoch called Embo, which has its own railway station and pier, there is an interesting caravan site delightfully named 'Grannies's Hielan' Hame' (Highland Home).

North of Dornoch, road and rail cross the head of Loch Fleet, not by bridge but on an embankment called The Mound. This was built by Telford, the famous bridge builder, who made here a unique design of sluice gates, which allow the River Fleet through into the sea but automatically close against the rising tide and prevent the sea from entering. We find these ingenious sluice gates fascinating.

This brings us to Golspie, a ducal town with a huge statue of the Duke of Sutherland, which was erected by the Sutherland tenantry. A mile and a half from Golspie is Dunrobin Castle, which is the Sutherland main seat. At certain times permission can be obtained to visit the beautiful gardens and even the castle. To visit this princely castle is on our list of future 'musts'.

I cannot leave Sutherland without mentioning one more village, because it is the one I like best, Bonar Bridge. This charming, wind-swept, sunny village is at the narrows of the Kyle of Sutherland, which are joined by a beautiful red-sandstone bridge of Telford's building.

When we come from our base at Ardmair, we lunch in a hotel, looking from its enormous picture windows over the great, expansive stretch of the Kyle, backed by high mountains. The food is first class, but that means less to me than that superb view. I could live there and never tire of that outlook, because I love an expansive view. I think I would pine away if I had to live in the close confines of a town or city! There is a particularly fine climate at Bonar Bridge and along the Dornoch coast.

The head of Loch Lubnaig

12

On Tour to Banffshire:
Maggieknockater, Honey and Whisky

It was the capricious month of April, when any kind of weather can be anticipated, that David and I once more set out with 'Golden Eagle', a Sunday and a glorious day harmonizing with the joy we felt to be on the road again. The countryside was ashine with the soft, lustrous green of spring, and gean trees (wild cherries) were already in full blossom. The gardens, as we passed through towns and villages, were full of colour, with golden daffodils and multi-coloured tulips, borders of dainty blue forget-me-nots surrounding beds of fragrant, velvety wallflowers, and the pink of almond trees blending with the greens of hawthorns already in full leaf.

As the afternoon wore on and the miles slipped by, people came out, till sidewalks and road-edges were gay with new spring fashions, all light and bright colours, as if everyone realized that the old, drab winter was past at last. Our road carried us through Stirling, where the stern old castle was softened by the heat-haze so that it forgot to frown, and the Wallace Monument on its green hill was more picturesque than ever. We skirted Dunblane, whose old town and beautiful cathedral are only for those who tarry and seek them out. Our thoughts were of places beyond the Tay, so pretty Strath Allan and wilder Glen Eagles too slipped by, but sweeping down from Auchterarder's stone-built mile we stopped; never had the River Earn appeared more beautiful— there it coiled lazily, caressed by the low sun, a sparkling silver, gold, and red ribbon, serene and lovely in its setting of emerald. Tearing ourselves away from this bewitching picture, we crossed the river, and our desire now was to find a place to rest for the night. Very soon we came on just what we wanted; it was a wide grassy part in the shade of a belt of Scotch pines and spruce, and evidently used freely for picnics because we backed 'Golden

The Brig o' Rome over the Alyth Burn

Eagle' on top of the still smouldering ashes of a wood fire, while farther down in a hollow, beside a small brown burn, about a dozen sun-bronzed cyclists had another fire alight and were brewing their tea.

Six miles' journey brought us the next day to the fair city of Perth where we left the Great North Road, crossed the wide River Tay, and went on through New Scone. We were on the A.94, a delightful motoring road, gently dipping and rising with long straight stretches and wide bends, running right through wide and fertile Strath More. To the south-east ranged the Sidlaw Hills, and to the north-west all the glory of foothills and mountains which go on piling up until they merge into the Grampians.

Going through Coupar-Angus, I remembered the tale of how King Edward VII—Edward, the Peace-maker—presented the station master with a beautiful gold watch in recognition of the splendid, clear way he called out "Coupar-Angus" as the royal train passed on its way to Ballater. Coupar-Angus is on the borders between Perthshire and Angus and on the beautiful River Isla. Not far from here is Meikleour where the famous beech hedge is. It is over 200 years old and over 100 feet tall, and on a windy day it is an amazing thing to see it swaying and to hear the wind sighing through it.

Beyond Coupar-Angus there were trim fields of raspberry canes and wide fields flushed with the soft, new green of spring-sown corn, or deep in rippling lush winter wheat. Occasionally we passed a farmhouse, but the farms in Strath More are big, with many miles between, and the farmhouses themselves large and square, with so many outbuildings and cottages that in some cases they look like complete villages.

We twisted through Meigle then crossed out of Perthshire into Angus, and shortly, going slowly over a level-crossing, I saw bread in a van drawn up beside the railway cottage—and the lilt in that van-girl's voice was like enchanted music in the ears of one whose forefathers too belonged to Barrie's country. She said the baps were "just ordinary", but she was wrong, for when we stopped a few miles on for lunch we found that they were as light as thistledown and simply melted in the mouth—as they should do, coming out of such a fairy-tale village as Glamis, where a little girl grew up to marry a prince and become our queen.

Where we stopped for lunch, our windows framed a very different view from the deep, closed-in pine forest of breakfast time; now it was a vast panorama of the wide green strath, and its distant rampart of deep indigo-coloured hills with, in its spaciousness, the very breath of freedom. Then, as we looked, a rift in a far-away cloud spilt a slanting sunbeam to illumine a streak of white in a mountain cleft, and we were reminded that this was still just April in spite of the summer-like days.

At what seemed the end of the road we came to a stately and very old gateway. Of course the road curved past it, but it is a charming introduction to the pretty, old-world village of Glamis. The castle gateway has many quaint figures carved in stone, but the gates of wrought-iron and brass are modern, having been erected in 1931 to commemorate the golden wedding of the Earl and Countess of Strathmore, father and mother of the Queen Mother. They bear the dates 1881–1931. An old lady in the lodge told us that for many years the brass-work was kept polished, making them like golden gates, but shortage of labour had let the glitter go.

The Earl of Strathmore's fine old baronial castle and gardens are open to the public on Fridays. There is a deal of history connected with Glamis but at least one king was murdered within its hoary walls, Malcolm II. There is supposed to be a secret chamber and only three people must know its secret at a time, the Earl, his heir, and a third person in whom they have implicit trust.

Another six or seven miles, delightfully tree-edged, brought us to Forfar, the county town, which has, besides tales of kings and queens and shoemakers, one about a bell which hung for a century without a tongue. This bell was sent from Holland by the Provost's two sons and arrived at Dundee, the nearest port, but Dundee said it was far too grand a bell for wee Forfar and decided to keep it. But the souters (shoemakers) of Forfar were inclined to disagree, so a battle took place on the shore, and in the mêlée the tongue was torn from the bell and thrown into the sea. Dundee then agreed to relinquish the gift if Forfar bought all the land over which it must travel from the port; this Forfar did and paid a very stiff price for its tongueless property.

The next town on our journey was Brechin and it was extremely busy, as befitted a town which for hundreds of years has specialized in good markets, and where in olden days the burghers could buy timber to make furniture and to line rooms in their sturdy stone houses, as well as heather for brooms, peats for fuel, wool for weaving into warm homespuns, and wildfowl for the pot.

From Brechin we were in the Howe o' the Mearns, another green and richly fertile strath stretching to blue hills across which skimmed cloud shadows but whose very clarity denoted rain. We ran through Laurencekirk, a canny and kindly-looking country town, and climbing steadily found, a few miles on, a good stopping-place on a strip of old, disused road. After tea I followed a track down to a farm in the valley, where I got my milk pitcher filled and a basket of fresh eggs. But now the wind had risen to gale force, and the barometer and temperature were falling rapidly. We laughed at the way things turn out, because the night before had been warm and stuffy when we were sheltered by the pine forest, but for this night of storm we could not have chosen a pitch more open and completely exposed to the elements.

In spite of having our powerful Tilley radiator alight all night, there was ice inside the windows in the morning; outside the air was piercingly cold, the wind shrieked as if all the demons of winter had been loosed, and sleet and icy rain lashed the bonny spring world mercilessly. It is on such a day that we really appreciate the comfort and spaciousness of our mobile home, and we both got a rare lot of work done while the storm blew itself out.

By late afternoon there were blinks of sunshine between the flying, storm-riven clouds, and those bursts of sunlight momentarily lit distant scenes in an amazing fashion; from our lofty pitch we could see far down the Howe o' the Mearns, and suddenly a whole village appeared as if by magic: church, school, large houses, cottages, lit by the sun, and framed by the dark mass of shadowed country surrounding it. We decided from our map that it must be Drunlithie, a village not on the main road and until then quite unnoticed by us. The distant hills were now white with snow and dazzling where sun shafts caught them up.

Our only visitors were two drivers, near bedtime, seeking some spare petrol; they were delivering two new lorries to Aberdeen and had run short. The night was now bitterly cold and they were glad of a warm-up in the caravan, but terribly afraid of falling asleep for it had been a difficult and tiring journey through a night and day of storm since they had left Birmingham at 10 p.m. the night before.

Next day we were thankful that we had adhered to our resolve to stay put on bad days when travelling with the caravan, for we would have been loth to miss any of the eighty-four miles we covered on that magnificent day of brilliant sunshine, of startling, rain-washed clarity, of blue hills and snowy mountains, blue sea and sky and great white clouds; a day of such exquisite loveliness in all its spring freshness that it was sheer joy to be alive and on the road with 'Golden Eagle'.

Stonehaven was approached by a long, curving road, following the bends made in a deep little dell by a sparkling brown burn dancing joyously seawards, and canopied by beech trees all agleam. This county town of Kincardine was very quiet, for we were early abroad, and in the clear, cold light it looked very clean and trim with a salt-tanged air which altogether was very invigorating. The restless blue waters of the North Sea splashed on the shore fringing the town and beyond rose steep, rugged cliffs with outcropping rocks.

Our road followed those cliff tops for some time then went helter-skelter for Aberdeen. Never did the Granite City look finer with the sun sparkling on its beautiful houses and municipal buildings, but the flower of them all was the Marischal College. I held my breath at its sheer, wondrous beauty; it was like something built by fairies, yet, in spite of its slender, ethereal-looking pinnacles and towers of exquisite Gothic design, the whole building is built of granite—clean, silver granite, which shone as if each mighty block had been newly hewn.

Our next stop was at Inverurie, a charming little town where I found a baker's shop in West High Street which sold bridies and veal pies, cream tarts and feather-light jam rolls. With my luncheon problem so speedily solved it seemed natural to find a perfect place to stop a few miles on; this was a wayside quarry, from which we looked down across the valley of the River Urie. A little way farther down the valley a meal mill, quaint and very old but still working, made an arrestingly beautiful picture embowered in lovely gean trees. On the other side of the road from us was a little farm, where we filled our drinking-water pitchers from a pump while the snow petals of yet another great gean floated down about us. So long had the dry spell lasted through March and April that the water in that deep well was too low to start the pump working, so it had first to be primed by a bucket of water kept handy for the purpose. The pure, delicious water coming from such a depth seemed warmer on that cold day than it would have done at midsummer.

Lunch finished, we followed the gently flowing Urie into wilder country. The road became hillier, more austere, with fewer trees as we climbed towards the Hill of Tillymorgan. Nearing 1,000 feet, the road careered up and down like a scenic railway and then turned into lonely Glen Foudland. Here there were snow-clad hills all about us, and when we stopped to gaze enraptured at the wild scene spread out below cotton-wool clouds in the bluest of skies, the air struck through us cold and chill.

But in the comfort of the car we left the high tops behind and were soon crossing Strath Bogie where, in its fertile cup, lay Huntly, a lovely, solid, old stone-built town surrounding its spacious square. Past Keith, which is another north-country town hiding a deal of history behind a modern look, we turned south towards the parish of Boharm. Our road which now climbed the glen between Ben Aigan and Knockan, was beautifully wooded; yet high above on their slopes were arable and pasture lands, an unusual but very pleasing combination, which kept with us all the way to our destination, the village with the delightful name of Maggieknockater.

How places got their names has always intrigued me, and Maggieknockater was no exception; but we soon learned that this name was appropriate; 'Maggie', meaning arable land, and 'knockater', meaning forests on the lower slopes. This way of using the hills was practical, because high on the hills the slopes were gentle, making good farmland, and the farms were up there, too, with a good road serving them, high in the hills and running parallel with the main road in the valley. The lower hill slopes were steep down to the River Fiddich, and so were suitable only as forest-land.

Our host, Mr. George McLean, an Aberdonian by birth, we had met first in Galloway and had been then enticed to promise to bring 'Golden Eagle' to his village in Banffshire. To make our welcome doubly sure he had put a new gate to the field in which

'Golden Eagle' was to park, the widest field gate I have ever seen, and had pushed it well back, leaving a wide space between gate and farm-road for easy turning.

From this gently sloping field, our front window looked farther down across the narrow valley, with its wild, dancing burn, to trees with their first flush of green on the foothills of Ben Aigen, and above the trees to the pasture lands with brown and white cattle grazing. My kitchen window framed a wheat-field rising steeply to the skyline, with a tantalizing farm chimney stuck on top. To the west we looked far out along the winding road to Dufftown and up the steep road to Craigellachie. Between those wide forking roads lay the deep, twisting way of the River Fiddich, bowered in trees and with an occasional trail of white smoke etching its course as an unseen train followed the river's bends. And far beyond this valley rose the Convals and Ben Rinnes, snow-capped, lovely, and ever changing, as sunshine and cloud shadows raced across them.

To the east our view brought us sharply back to Maggie-knockater, to look across dozens of beehives to our host's house and the many outbuildings which formed the centre of Maggie-knockater's activities. I have called this place a village, yet it was scarcely that, a clachan might describe it better, for there were not more than half a dozen cottages, a school and schoolhouse, a little church hall and Mr. McLean's establishment.

Besides being one of the biggest bee farmers in Scotland and Secretary of the North of Scotland Bee Association, Mr. McLean manufactured all kinds of bee accessories, including beehives and honey extractors. Being the blacksmith, for this was great farming country, he included with this ancient craft the manufacture of beautiful wrought-iron gates.

He was general merchant, and in the north such an emporium lives up to its name—grocery, bakery, fruit, boots and shoes of every description, hardware, including everything for house or farm use, and oil heating and lighting appliances, soft goods, underwear, towels, knitting wools, haberdashery, patent medicines, and confectionery.

I wondered at first where the custom came from to keep such a thriving shop going, but I soon learned that miles meant nothing and his customers were scattered over a wide district. Friday was the day when sturdy young farmers staggered in from their cars with great baskets and hampers of eggs, for here, too, was the packing station's egg collector for the district.

There was passing trade, too; attractive windows and three petrol pumps saw to that. Among the outbuildings there was a huge garage with every conceivable up-to-date appliance, including a spraying plant. There was also a thriving hiring business, with two cars and a brake in almost constant demand. At one end of the garage was a section for bicycles, with a large window displaying new motor-cycles and ordinary cycles, tyres, etc. Mr. McLean was also a farmer, with fields of potatoes and corn, a couple of cows, sheep and a few hens; and a fruit grower with amazing wall-trees of apples, black currants and gooseberries. Except for one girl, who helped Mrs. McLean in the house and in the shop, this varied business was a family affair, with three sons playing their part.

Our visit this time was a short one, but on our return later in the year we found Maggieknockater a splendid centre for much of interest, including the real Highland mixture of honey and whisky. Already the bees were on the heather and we followed them to their hives, which had been brought up to the heather-clad Conval Hills and Ben Rinnes. It was wonderful to watch those velvety little creatures as they flew away with their leg baskets full of brightly coloured pollen or laden with nectar, trundling in their loads of pollen food for the young and nectar for their winter honey store; heather honey which, to the bee-keeper, is the best and the last of his harvest for the season.

But the work of the bees and the beekeeper started away back in the spring, when, Mr. McLean told us, difficult autumn conditions had been overcome by careful feeding with sugar and water, and a mild winter and glorious spring have left him with stocks in fine condition. At that time the air vibrated as, in their millions, the bees swept in and out of his apiary to the clover fields.

Assuring us that the bees were far too busy to pay any attention to us unless we got in their way, he lifted the top off a well-stocked hive and with his smoker blew puffs of smoke over the frames, which sent the bees hurriedly below.

Lifting out a frame, we saw how the cells were being drawn out from the artificially-made wax bases, and that those towards the centre were completed and being filled with honey, a few even being sealed.

Levering off this honey chamber, he disclosed a seething mass of bees, but another whiff of smoke sent them down. This was a brood chamber with larger frames, and, fascinated, we watched the top being loosened and a frame gently lifted out for our inspection.

Our demonstrator's unconcern as he puffed his cigarette reassured us. With our faces in distinct danger, we examined the beautifully-formed cells, some holding newly-deposited eggs, just like tiny bits of thread, some bee grubs, growing fat in a jelly-like food of pollen, nectar and water served by the workers, and some with grubs turning to larva and being sealed over; and the wonder of one breaking its seals and emerging as a young, woolly worker bee.

In another frame we watched the queen laying eggs while her attendants fussed about. There, too, were knobby-looking big drone cells housing the young male bees, and towards the bottom some queen cells, even larger, which looked like crooked monkey nut shells.

Busy bees! The ingathering of their honey store is only a small part of their activities. They make wax for the cells to hold the honey and the cells to take the eggs. Like any careful housewife they keep their home clean. They feed, tend, and nurse the tiny grubs. In cold weather they huddle together to keep the eggs and grubs warm. In warm weather they flutter their wings like fans to cool the air in the hive. They carry in food and water, and it takes three workers to keep a drone supplied. But woe betide the drones when famine sets in! A beekeeper knows it is time to feed his stock when he sees the dead drones being flung out.

A good many of the cells made for eggs are for workers, a few are for drones, and some very special ones are constructed if a new queen is wanted. Then the young queen is sent out on her maiden flight, mates with a drone, and returns to lay her eggs. There is nothing special about the eggs she lays in the large queen cells. The making of the new queen is the workers' job, and their method is to feed the grubs in these cells with an abundance of rich food called 'royal jelly'.

The beekeeper carefully watches for a new queen appearing, no easy matter among so many. He can remove her and prevent half of the hive swarming. Mr. McLean collected her quite simply in a match-box, and a lovely little creature she was. He said he would put her into a hive where perhaps the queen had not returned from her maiden flight, or had not mated.

But when bees do swarm it is no mad stampede. They know exactly where their new home will be, because they have sent out their scouts in advance to locate it. It may be in a tree, a chimney, under a roof, but the beekeeper usually has a few empty hives handy so that their choice may be simpler and more satisfactory to him.

Up on Ben Aigen one day, having a look at his hives, Mr. McLean lifted his head, listened, then looked towards a black ball coming out of the sky.

"A swarm," he said. "I wonder where they will land." To his and our amazement the zooming mass of bees made a bee-line for an empty hive and covered it. Then, slowly but surely, all disappeared inside. I'm sure Mr. McLean's laughter could be heard far down below in the valley where from his apiary the swarm had probably come.

With the clover harvest extracted and the combs back in the hives to be filled from the heather he was happy, but it is not always like that. Cold winters, famine and disease play havoc at times and it is then the the big bee-farmers at home and abroad help with fresh stocks. It was in this way that we met the Dutch bee-farmer, Mr. J. de Meza, who was superintending the distribution of 400 new stocks to Scottish beekeepers; 2,000 other stocks went to England. Into Leith sailed the Dutch bee-ship, and from all parts came bee-farmers to watch the unloading of the precious cargo, and to enjoy the spectacle of dancing seamen as they swatted and swore at the escaping and angry livestock.

Fifty stocks went from Leith to Craigellachie by rail, and the last two miles to Maggieknockater in Mr. McLean's and David's cars. David found twenty leaky skeps unpleasant company and stopped half-way to open windows and let out the many lively bees which were buzzing merrily around. A few stings? More than a few for he took many wonderful photographs and declared that he ought to remain immune to rheumatism for the rest of his life!

Our interest in the making of real Highland malt whisky was first roused when Mr. McLean introduced us to the brewer of Mortlach Distillery, which is one of several in Dufftown and the largest.

We arrived in time to see the sacks of barley being unloaded from railway trucks straight into a hopper feeding a form of elevator, which drew the grain upwards to conveyor belts and carried it across to the granary. When we reached the granary the barley was pouring down on to the floor in golden streams, and there was a haze of dust mingling with the sunshine streaming into that spacious barn, which measures 200 feet by 60 feet and has a smooth wooden floor. We were told that occasionally barn dances were held there, and that the barley-polished wood made a perfect dance-floor.

Malting, the first process, is continuous day and night and starts by steeping. At one end of the granary there were two 'steeps', a steep being a large tank with its top level with the floor, and each taking 11 tons of barley. In the steep the grain is covered with water and allowed to soak for three days, the water being changed each day to keep it fresh.

From the steeps the grain drops down through manholes to the malting floors below, where it is spread damp over the floor and left to germinate. In summer it starts right away, the growth taking eight or nine days to complete, but in winter it takes three or four days to start germinating and fourteen days to grow. During this period the grain is frequently raked with a 'malt plough' to aerate it, and turned with large wooden shovels, each turn taking it farther away from where it started and making room for the next consignment from the steep.

When the growth, or acrospire, has reached three-quarters the length of the grain sufficient germination has taken place. The maltsters of old used to know if it was ready when, by splitting a grain, they could write on a slate with it as if they were using chalk. The grain, being now malted, is shovelled into travelling buckets which carry it to an elevator. To see the next stage we had to climb steep, narrow, ladder-like stairs, up and up till we reached the kiln, where the grain was spread over a wire floor, through which rose hot air from the peat and coke fire below; and the more peat used for the kiln the better the flavour of the whisky. Three times a day the drying grain is turned and the five men we saw doing this work were finding it very warm, although in winter, we were told, it is a good job to have. In the turning over on the wire floor most of the root growth is rubbed off and this falls down a chute and goes for pig feeding. The dried malt now goes to huge storage bins, and is drawn off as required each week.

From there the grain is crushed, emerging as dry malt, in appearance like flour and chaff, to travel on conveyor belts to a hopper above the mash tun. This tun, in which the mashing takes place, is a large circular vessel 21 feet in diameter, which is filled with a mixture of malt and water. Each mash consists of 500 bushels of malt, and water to the proportion of 23 gallons to each bushel.

When all the mash has been fed into the tun the remaining hot water required to bring it to the measured quantity is forced up through the perforated floor of the tun and bubbles up through the mash. A mechanical mixer with fork-like arms is then set in motion and travels round and round in the tun, while three men energetically assist in mixing with large flat shovels. This complete process takes about forty minutes, and the mash is then allowed to sit for an hour. The tun looks like a steaming cauldron full of porridge, and it has the pleasant smell of porridge in the making.

After the mash has soaked, the liquor is allowed to filter through the perforated false bottom of the tun, then a second quantity of water is run in. This in turn is run off, and a third amount of water is run in, so making sure that all the substance is removed from the malt. This third water is too weak to use, so it is run back into the coppers, the water storage and heating vessels, reheated and used as part of the first water for the next mash. When this third water is run off, the residue in the tun is now draff, which drops down direct into wagons and is dispatched to the farmers for cattle feed; so after all the farmers get back something of the barley they grow. Each complete mash takes seven hours, and there are six mashes a week, starting at 1 a.m. every Monday morning and continuing day and night until completed; the men working in three shifts.

The liquor which comes off the mash is now called wort; it is non-alcoholic and we were told we could drink gallons with no ill effect. This wort passes into an under back, which is a huge storage tank, and then on for fermentation in the wash backs. A wash back is like a gigantic wooden barrel with the top above floor level, but the remainder of its 21 feet of depth reaching far down to the floor below. Just under its lid there is a power-operated mixer. In the tunroom there are seven of these huge wash backs.

The wash back is filled three-quarters full by 12,000 gallons of wort, to which yeast is added. Fermentation takes about forty-eight hours, and after it has ceased the wash, as the mixture is now called, is ready for distilling. This wash looks just like thick lentil soup, and 4,000 gallons of it are pumped to the wash still for boiling. The still is an enormous copper vessel shaped like a flat-bottomed pear, with a long, tapering neck stretching upwards and its foot resting on top of a carefully regulated furnace. The neck curves gracefully through the roof, forming a pipe of over a foot in diameter, which goes to a worm tub which is the cooling system; the cooling water required in the worm tubs for the six stills is 30,000 gallons an hour. In this great tub the pipe coils downwards, like a huge tapering worm, emerging far below as a three-inch pipe which returns to the still room.

When the first, or wash still, has been charged, as the wash is rich in yeasty solids it is stirred, and the bottom scraped continuously by revolving copper-webbed chains to prevent it sticking and being burnt. As it starts to boil, the light, easily evaporated alcohol separates from the wash and, rising as rich vapour, enters the worm-like pipe, and is cooled by the cold water circulating round it in the worm tub. Condensing, it becomes liquid and flows back along the three-inch pipe, emerging at a check-point in the still room called the safe, as a steady stream of unpurified, weak alcohol called low wine. This first distillation takes eight hours and stops when all alcohol has gone; by then the spent wash, also called burnt ale, has reached the boiling point of water. The furnace, which has been carefully tended so as to give slow but ever-increasing heat to the still, is now drawn, and the useless burnt ale discharged.

From the low wine receiver the weak spirit is pumped into a low wine still, and, as before, heat is applied carefully, until the resulting vapours condense and emerge as a steady stream of rich spirit at the safe. In whisky-making the safe plays a most important part; it is a brass-bound, plate-glass showcase, six feet long, which, for excise reasons, cannot be entered. At one end is test apparatus, which is made to be operated from outside, at the other end are three large glass funnels; the first leads the low wine from the wash-still worm to its receiver; the second collects purified spirit from the low-wine still, and the nozzle of its feed pipe is movable so that impure and weak spirits, called foreshot and feints, collected at the beginning and end of distilling the low wine, can be directed into the third funnel and so back to the low-wine receiver to be redistilled. The individual skill of the brewer at this point can be detected by experts, five, ten or twenty years afterwards, even to the extent of identifying the distiller.

The pure whisky gravitates to vats in the vat house below. Here, under the eagle eye of the customs officer, it is carefully reduced to 11 overproof, then casked, the customs officer selecting samples from a cask in each batch, which he checks with the brewer by means of a hydrometer and thermometer.

The empty casks, which had their number and weight checked on entry, are, after filling, weighed, and the proof and weight of contents noted by customs and distillery officials. From this they know the number of gallons in each cask. With 8,000 gallons of whisky coming off towards the end of each week, it is an amazing sight to see the casks being rolled into the bonded warehouses: 100- and 110-gallon fat puncheons and tall butts weighing 10 and 11 hundredweight each, and then, inside, the rows and rows of them, catalogued and put in week by week and year by year.

These casks were filled with water-clear whisky, termed white, and which is unfit for consumption until it has matured in the wood for at least three years, and normally eight to ten years. Fifteen and even twenty years are allowed for a very superior liqueur whisky. During these periods a subtle and yet undiscovered chemical change takes place, the whisky mellows, loses proof strength, and goes down in volume, and if in old sherry casks turns to the rich tawny gold colour so appreciated by the connoisseurs. The Mortlach whisky, when it is drawn from the cask will have dropped its overproof strength of 110, but it will require further reduction before sale at the usual strength of 30% underproof or 70% proof, and colouring also if not in a sherry cask.

Mortlach Distillery, like many another, started as a smuggling bothy and, in fact, was carried on as such until the business was officially established under Government licence in 1823, which was thirty years after distilling was made legal under licence. The firm's name then, as now, was Cowie, although exactly one hundred years after being established the business was sold to

'Johnnie Walker', By paying the licence of £10 in 1823, Cowie was able to enlarge his plant and expand his business, and through the years it steadily grew, buildings spreading out on all sides, and in 1897, when there was a boom in whisky, extensive alterations and rebuilding took place, till now it is one of the largest malt distilleries in Scotland.

In the glass, whisky from Mortlach has the fragrance of the winds over bog-myrtle and peat, and the sparkle of the waters of a granite spring in the Conval Hills.

13

Old Towns:
the Laich o' Moray

We have various well-loved autumn pitches, but a favourite has often been a sheltered place on the River Findhorn's estuary about five miles from Forres in Morayshire.

It is a beautiful autumn pitch, and the welcome from our farmer friends was always a heart-warming experience. To the west we were completely sheltered by the Culbin Forest; to the east a great wide, expansive view swept across the estuary, over which flooded the morning sun. Here we got all the sunshine there was from morning until early evening. As dusk enfolded us a fairyland of twinkling lights gleamed and sparkled as Forres lit up and also Findhorn village and the great aerodrome at Kinloss.

With the season so well advanced, we have never used the boat here, which allowed us more time for exploring the interesting surrounding country and to visit and entertain the many friends we have in the district. Forres was our shopping centre and a truly delightful one, where, although there are modern self-service stores, one can still find the pleasant old family grocer, butcher and baker. There is a first-class laundry, and the fruit shop I like has local-grown apples, pears and tomatoes with superb flavours.

Forres lies in the Laich o' Moray, and for over 3,000 years the Laich o' Moray, or Moravia as its old name was, has been inhabited by man; but for the first 2,000 years and more only its fringe bordering the Moray Firth, because its hinterland was part of Scotland's vast primeval forest. Of those early centuries and its settlers there is little record save in flint and bronze and stone, and of these a great deal has been brought to light. Picts, Romans and invading Norsemen all left their mark and disappeared before any written history lifted the veil of obscurity. For that we are

Alyth's Auld Brig
Tithe Barns at Meigle

indebted to the early Church and two of its learned, fifteenth-century historians, John of Fordun, a secular priest of Aberdeen, and Andrew of Wyntoun, an abbot of St. Andrews. Fordun wandered throughout the country seeking its history and recording it in Latin, while Wintoun wrote his *Kronikles of Scotland* in old English. Then in the sixteenth century a great effort was made by the historian, Boetheus, then Principal of Aberdeen University, to search out and record the earlier history of Moray.

With such enormous forests in Scotland, our early kings were great hunters, and those bordering the Moray Firth were in good favour as royal hunting forests; indeed all this part of Scotland was dearly beloved by kings. Yet it was a place of ill omen during the tenth century, for three successive monarchs were done to death at Forres between 900 and 970. First Donald, son of Constantine, king of Scotland for eleven years, was murdered in the Castle of Forres; then his son, Malcolm, who had a long reign but was eventually slain while trying to bring his unruly and too powerful people of Moray to subjection; only to be followed a short time later by King Duff (or Duffus) who, while taking shelter in Forres from a rival to his throne, was cruelly murdered by the governor of the castle.

But still Forres Castle continued to be a royal residence, while around it squatted the town, its houses built of wood from the great forest and thatched with marram grass from the Culbin shore. Forres Castle has disappeared, but there were, and still are, many more castles near Forres, some, in those days, royal, and some the seats of the powerful Moravian earls, who were such a thorn in the flesh of the early Scottish kings. So we come to the early spring of 1150, when the history of Kinloss started, when we find King David I in residence in Duffus Castle. As was his wont he set off for the forest with his hunting party one fine morning. But David, bringing enthusiasm to all he did, soon outstripped his followers, and, when the undergrowth and thickets became too much for his horse, he dismounted and continued the chase on foot.

At length he turned to retrace his steps and regain his party, only to find very soon that he was completely lost in the almost impenetrable depths and gloom of the dense forest. As his repeated shouts remained unanswered, King David realized how

The Hermitage showing Ossian's Hall above the River Bran

serious his plight was so he knelt on the ground in prayer.

No sooner had he finished, than, looking up, he beheld a snow-white dove hovering in front of him, and, as he followed, breaking through undergrowth and shrubs, the dove hovered always a short distance ahead. At last, to his intense relief, he came on a clearing of green pasture-land where a shepherd was tending his flock. The dove, its work done, flew away and was seen no more. With night fast approaching, tired and hungry, King David gladly accepted the shepherd's offer to share his humble dwelling and frugal fare.

That night in his dreams the Virgin came to David, telling him that for his deliverance from the forest that day he must build a church in the clearing where he had met the shepherd. In the morning he hurried back to the clearing and there, in the bright sunlight of a new day, he cut on the greensward with his sword the outline of the sacred building he would erect.

Back at Duffus Castle he sent dispatches off at once to his architects, quarriers and masons, all busy on other royal works in various parts of his kingdom—for David, son of Malcolm Canmore and saintly Queen Margaret, was a great builder and founded abbeys at Kelso, Dryburgh, Melrose, Newbattle, Dundrennan, Cambuskenneth, Jedburgh and Holyrood—and on 20th June 1150 the foundation stone was laid of the beautiful Abbey of Kinloss. All that summer David supervised and spurred on the work, but when autumn came affairs of state called him away from Moray so he gave over the task of supervision to Asceline, a monk from Melrose, and when the abbey was completed Asceline was made its first abbot, with twenty monks, also drawn from Melrose.

One of the biggest assets in making this the perfect site for such a magnificent abbey, as Kinloss undoubtedly was, was the same one that has made Moray's seaboard so favourable through thousands of years for man's habitation: its exceptionally fine climate, low rainfall and high percentage of sunshine. Its situation too was superb, at the head of Findhorn Bay and close to the River Findhorn; and it was King Robert the Bruce who gave the monks sole fishing rights on that splendid river.

But David and each successive king gave royally, until Kinloss was rich in land without and treasure within. Abbot succeeded abbot, and some were of great noblemen's families, princes in their own right, and some were very scholarly, so that the abbey library became famous. Several of its old vellum manuscripts have been preserved in the National Library in Edinburgh, and also the list of volumes which the abbey once contained. The abbey reached its peak of power and magnificence when Robert Reid was abbot, between 1526 and 1540, and so short a time before the devastation of the Reformation.

Abbot Reid, who later became Bishop of Orkney, was both scholarly and practical. From Dieppe he brought a French gardener, by name Guillaume Lubias, who was highly skilled, particularly in planting and grafting fruit trees. When the last of those ancient trees, a pear tree, was blown down in a storm, not so long ago, it was found that it had been underpaved with flat flagstones; and much of the delicious fruit grown in the gardens of Forres today owes its origin to Abbot Reid's French gardener. But Robert Reid's greatest love was learning, and when he died he left 8,000 Scots merks to found a college for the education of youth in the Capital; in this way he founded what later became Edinburgh's famous university.

The years rolled on. Kinloss Abbey, a ruin, became a quarry for the building of much of Forres in stone; for surrounding farmhouses and steadings and dykes; and Cromwell, it is said, used its beautiful red stones, hewn hundreds of years earlier, to build his castle at Inverness. Little wonder there are but scanty remains to tell of the grandeur that once was Kinloss. There is a small chapel, built in a part of the abbey left standing, by an Episcopalian clergyman, the Rev. Mr. Dunbar-Dunbar, who inherited the estate on which the abbey stands. However, he and his family worshipped in the parish church, and the chapel has never, at any time, been used for public services.

Some of the graves in and around the abbey precincts are very old, several, it is believed, of monks and possibly abbots, especially those under one of the remaining arches of the abbey, which, perhaps for that reason, the despoilers shrank from desecrating. Legend ascribes one grave to be that of a king, perhaps it was that of King Duff, whose body was hidden for long under a bridge over the burn at Kinloss and would probably be, at first when found, buried close by. But in this quiet God's acre there are over eighty graves which are not old. They are marked by simple little crosses and are of airmen, mostly Dominion men, killed near here on service during the last war, whose bodies could not be sent home.

Close by is the great aerodrome—which swallowed up five farms on that highly productive terrain by the Moray Firth—and it is not now the white wings of doves but the silver wings of aircraft that fly over the old abbey. From here, on their urgent missions of mercy, they fly out to bring sick people with all speed from lonely islands for hospital treatment; and from here, all too often, goes out that splendid mountain-rescue team, to find lost or hurt climbers in the Cairngorms or Glen Coe's wild mountains.

The village of Kinloss has practically dwindled away, although the beautiful parish church remains. But east of the church is a thriving, virile colony of young people in about two hundred married quarters, then another section of dwellings for officers, and then Findhorn village, also in the parish of Kinloss; windy, bracing, sea-fringing Findhorn, with its pretty houses, its salmon fishers and its boats. Originally the village lay a mile north-west of its present position, but when the mouth of the River Findhorn became choked with sand, it changed its course to the sea, choosing the lower level of the village. So sea and river, encroaching from either side, during a terrible storm swept the old village, already deserted, away.

Eight hundred years have passed since David I dreamed a dream and saw a vision there in the deep royal forest. In that time the sea's erosion has caused considerable shrinkage of the land here, but on the other side of the river land has been reclaimed and, like the swing of the pendulum, immense new forests cover 7,500 acres and thereby anchor the great shifting waste of the Culbin Sands.

Great is the heritage of the people of this corner of Moray, but its history will continue to be written because forestry and air forces are young men's work and the name of Kinloss lives on, although its original name, I think, would be 'Kinglost'.

Now I feel I should tell you more about the amazing Culbin, partly because the Culbin Forest is a bulwark between our caravan pitch and the prevailing westerly autumn gales.

For centuries Culbin has been one of Scotland's eccentric freaks of Nature, stirring imaginary visions of something sinister and altogether out of place in the serene picture of the fertile and well-husbanded counties of Moray and Nairn. A desert some seven miles long and over two miles wide of fine white sand, in places forming great sand dunes and hillocks, which moved ever eastward before the prevailing west wind.

But today this shifting, miniature Sahara, bordering the southern shore of the Moray Firth has been anchored by the Forestry Commission. They have changed it from the Culbin Sands of yesterday to the Culbin Forest of today. When first we explored this great forest the last of the trees, fringing its eastern boundary, had been planted, covering in all 7,546 acres and completing the Commission's herculean task started over forty years ago.

We chose a calm day to explore the labyrinth of little roads which criss-cross the forest, and our wheels and our feet drew puffs of sand from their hard-rolled sand-and-gravel surface as we drove and walked. Some led us by narrow, ravine-like passages between high, tree-topped dunes to the shore with its shell-strewn beach and widespread views. Others took us through glades of early plantings, with the mellow sunlight dappling our way. Those were to the west, where already thinnings for pit-props and telephone poles were beginning to make the forest pay its way. But to the east the roads were less hard-packed, and the trees diminished in size, until those newly planted could scarcely be seen among the deep thatch.

With no secure roothold, and every gale of wind a potential uprooting and sand-smothering agent, the foresters resorted to 'thatching' with fairly heavy birch branches, pressing the butt ends into the sand in a windward direction. Much broom brush-wood, lighter in weight, was also used; and broom is plentiful in the district, in places growing to over ten feet in height. After this laborious sand-stabilizing operation, the little trees were planted, five feet apart, in through the thatch. As they grow, weather and time decays the thatch, which becomes humus for the otherwise barren ground, and dead needles from the trees also gradually lay a stabilizing carpet on the turbulent sands.

The trees planted are mostly Scotch and Corsican pines, with some lodgepole pines, which are doing well here, and a few Maritime and Monterey pines planted experimentally. The Corsican pine is proving a splendid choice, somewhat to the forester's surprise, since it is so far from its natural home in the Mediterranean. But I think perhaps the Sahara-like 'soil', coupled with the district's unusually small rainfall and abundance of sunshine, makes Culbin more home to it than to the Scotch pine, whose natural habitat, I have found, is peat-soil, wet hillsides and rock cracks, crannies and islets washed by loch and river waters. Besides being admirably suited for Culbin's sterile soil, the Corsican pine stands up well to the salt air on the dunes adjoining the Moray Firth; but in frost-hollows and on shingle beds only Scotch and lodgepole pines have proved suitable.

The most newly planted trees, on Culbin's eastern side, were sheltered by the Binsness Woods which fringe the estuary of the Findhorn. Here the pines are from forty to eighty years old and constitute some of the pioneer work of landowners to stop the encroaching sands from engulfing their estates. But even some of those tall trees, which have through the years impeded the sand's progress eastward, are so buried that we had the strange experience of moving about among the treetops like birds on the wing.

In the quiet glades of Binsness there was beauty in the expansive view, glimpsed through the trees, across the estuary to Findhorn village. On the rugged shore too there is beauty, where swans with their well-grown cygnets make a sheltered corner their favourite haunt, and the piercingly-sweet cry of oyster-catchers shrills above the chorus of sea-birds, which find such rich feeding on the sandbanks and mudflats. In the forest itself are pigeons and capercailzies, and the latter, which love the tips of pines with their turpentine flavour, are numerous. Roe deer also have adopted Culbin Forest for their happy hunting-ground.

That is Culbin today, a vast forest, securing the shifting sands and in time burying them beneath good soil. Centuries ago too there was also good soil. Great numbers of bronze and pottery vessels and ornaments, flint arrowheads and old coins, uncovered by the moving sands, are evidence that Culbin was well inhabited from early times. Indeed in the seventeenth century the Culbin estate comprised, besides the mansion house and polices of the Kinnard family, some sixteen farms, a good sprinkling of crofts and many fishermen's cottages. It was one of the most fertile and richest estates in the county, and was often called 'the granary' —or girnal—of Moray.

On a fine August evening in 1676, the farmer of Culbin's west-most farm looked with pride on the field of barley ready for the harvesters in the morning. Never had there been such a mag-nificent crop, and only some of the old folks at that night's ceilidh shook their heads and called it a 'fey' crop. But the har-vesters' scythes needed no sharpening for the next day's toil, because a fierce wind rose in the night, and by daybreak only an ear or two of barley showed above the devastation of burying sand.

It is thought that many subsequent storms of great violence lay between that first devastating night and the final act of the com-plete obliteration of the estate in 1694. The Findhorn, which until then reached the sea at The Bar and formed the boundary march between the counties of Moray and Nairn, became so choked with sand that it changed its course, sweeping all before it, in-cluding the village of Findhorn.

The year following the Culbin disaster the Scottish Parliament passed an Act making it illegal to pull marram grass for roof thatching. Previously it had been used in great quantities through-out a large area, so weakening its stabilizing effect on the shifting sands. That Act has never been repealed. But except for attempts by local landowners fringing Culbin to stay the encroaching sands by planting trees, little was attempted to reclaim this lost land until the Forestry Commission started operations. For many generations the wind had full play. Sandhills rose, sometimes as high as 120 feet and 440 yards long at their base.

Shaw, in his *History of Moray*, graphically describes an alarming visit to Culbin during a westerly wind. Between the sandhills, he says,

the wind poured through the hollow as through a funnel. The quantity of drifting sand was immense. I caught it in handfuls as it passed. Nearing the gorge the wind had acquired a rotary motion, and the sand drifted about lashing me with severity. Under the lee of the hill the wind was somewhat broken and the sand came pour-ing down in torrents, and sometimes in masses. These, again broken, whirled about with a most bewildering effect. Moving onwards, my eyes shut, for to open them would have sacrificed them, I ex-pected the worst would soon pass and I could grope my way out of this horrible place, but beyond the shelter of the sandhill I was met by such a powerful blast of wind, that came sweeping round the hill, as seemed to be a work altogether beyond the common operations of nature. I felt as if a dozen thongs were lashing me round the body, and actually felt as if the points of them had reached upwards, twitching my face. Once beyond the sand-drift I felt something about me which was quite unaccountable, making me exceedingly uncomfortable, even qualmish. I felt a pressure and weight on my body which had the effect of dragging me down and retarding my progress, as if the power of gravitation had been increased tenfold. . . . I stood like one petrified. . . . I put my hand in my pocket . . . it was crammed with sand. Every pocket was filled with sand, my clothes were completely saturated with it, my shoes were like to burst and eyes, ears, nostrils and mouth were all partakers of it. Moving, the minute particles of sand poured from my clothes as thick as drizzling rain.

Adding to the treasures secreted by the moving sands was that of some smugglers. Dark was the night that a foreign ship stole up the Firth and chose lonely Culbin on which to land their valuable cargo of contraband. Being unable that night to convey it farther they stowed it under the slope of a great sandhill. Overnight a strong westerly wind blew up and raged incessantly until the following evening. When it abated the smugglers returned with carts to collect the treasure. But the shifting sands had obliterated every visible sign of its whereabouts, and to this day no trace of that valuable cargo has ever been discovered.

Now, what of this river which has its estuary on our doorstep; literally, as it turned out one night when a strong wind and an unusually high spring tide swept the waters back to flood over the wide machair in front of us and engulf both car and caravan. Fortunately it did not quite reach floor level before the tide turned, but it was an alarming experience at 2 a.m.

The Findhorn is one of our most beautiful and most impetuous rivers, yet it is not generally well known. It has its source in the heart of the dark Monadliath Mountains and is fed from their highest peak, Carn Ban. From its flowing out of Strath Dearn, its valley is for miles a deep, rock-walled gorge, precluding the possibility of verging roads, so that the wayfarer and tourist can only view this secret river from the five bridges which carry roads across it.

For that reason its beauty remains wild, only fully divulged to the angler or any who can negotiate its precarious fishing tracks. In its seclusion bird life is varied and interesting and many rare and lovely flowers, ferns, sedges and grasses are to be found. Yet from its bridges one gets enchanting glimpses, the finest being from Dulsie Bridge, which spans the magnificent torrent cascading over huge rocks into boiling pools, pushing a turbulent, crooked way through the lovely gorge.

A few miles below Dulsie, the river, its tempo slower as if not to disturb the worshippers, passes Ardclach parish kirk which was built at the river-edge, far below the road, to suit parishioners from both banks. High above on its lofty perch stands the ancient white Ardclach Tower, a bell-cum-watchtower built high so that its bell would be heard throughout the widely-scattered parish. Had the bell been used only to call the worshippers, its sweet chiming might still be heard, but so enraged were the Highland caterans (hill robbers) when watchers tolled the bell to give the country folk time to put their cattle in hiding, that they captured the tower and destroyed the bell.

A grand stretch for the angler follows, then the river sweeps under Logie Bridge, to meander by picturesque farmlands till the cleft hillsides are clothed and guarded with great conifers overlooking Daltulich Bridge, a granite arch which spans the gash high above fine salmon pools.

Now deep forest closes in for miles, as the river tears its way through great cliffs and cascades from pool to pool; an amazing sight of whirlpool and rumbling fall with a last glorious plunge into the great, quiet pool at Sluie. From behind Sluie Farm, set high amid heather and birches, hazels, oaks, and gnarled old pines, one looks over the pool, downstream to a great vista of trees sliced in two by the river, and to high, red sandstone cliffs, which are topped with trees to their very edge. Wild cliffs these, holed and crumbling, the haunt of a great colony of jackdaws.

Between Daltulich and Sluie is Randolph's Leap, so called because after the Battle of the 'Lost Standard' Alastair Cumyn of Dunphail and four companions, finding themselves cut-off and closely surrounded by Randolph's forces, leaped across the eight-foot-wide chasm, and, although followed by several of Randolph's men, fought their way to safety. Below Randolph's Leap the River Divie, also wildly beautiful, joins the Findhorn which continues its turbulent way down to Red Craig past the

Meads of St. John. On this large, semi-circular, natural amphi-
theatre of meadowland, crowning and set into red cliffs, Mary
Queen of Scots and her lords and ladies attended a grand tourna-
ment in 1562. A picture of this brilliant occasion hangs in Forres
Council Chambers.

From Red Craig the Findhorn is a river of quiet charm, and
the delight of the local Angling Society. Beyond Forres road-
bridge it becomes tidal and in its bay is joined by the Muckle, or
Moy Burn, and the Mosset, or Altyre Burn. After widening out
into its tidal bay, or at low tide traversing a labyrinth of sand-
and-mud-banks, where wild-fowl abound, the river reaches the
sea by a narrow mouth, just beyond the Port of Findhorn. Prior
to the great storm of 1692 it turned west for another four miles
before flowing into the Moray Firth, where now lies a long, low
island offshore called The Bar. The river was then navigable to
the old Port of Findhorn a mile north-west of the present port,
but this was the one swept away when the shifting sands blocked
the river's passage and forced it to take the easier, nearer route to
the sea.

In our exploring we often go eastward from Forres, and the
road is a good caravanning one, almost level with very few
bends; a fast road yet pleasant as it runs like a silver ribbon
through the green velvet of the Laich's lush fields. Then come
stretches of forest, and deep-shaded in a belt by the roadside near
Elgin is a delightful motel with adjoining chalets all of wood,
almost like an old-time Canadian homestead.

Elgin is a cathedral city, and that is why it became the county
town, although compared with Forres, or even Burghead, it is
not so old nor has it so much history. Yet it is a pleasant place
on the River Lossie, with the remains of its once great cathedral
set in a beautiful park with wide herbaceous borders a riot of
colour as foreground to the red sandstone edifice.

The cathedral, called 'The Lanthorn of the North', was founded
in 1224 by Andrew, Bishop of Moray. But that was mainly
destroyed by fire in 1270, and what we see today was built later
only to be again destroyed by fire in 1390 at the hands of Alexander, Earl of Buchan, the hated and feared Wolf of Badenoch.

It was burned in revenge because the Church excommunicated
him for deserting his wife. However, he was compelled by his
half-brother, Robert III, to help repair the damage he had done

to the cathedral and the town. But when the Wolf became seriously ill he repented of his many sins, and recovering, in the few years which remained to him, he lavished the Church with riches.

In 1506 the great steeple fell, and with the Reformation came the final destruction, when in 1568 the lead was stripped from the roof to be sold to buy food for the Regent Moray's army. The lead went for about £100 to a mercantile company in Amsterdam, but the ship carrying it was sunk off Aberdeen at the Girdleness rocky headland.

After the ruins had lain for nearly a century the tumbled stone became a quarry for much of Elgin and the surrounding country villages.

Our main road continues south-east to Keith, but at the moment the little roads to the sea are luring us to explore, because many lovely fishing villages fringe the Moray Firth, and those of Spey Bay, where the great River Spey enters the sea, are particularly interesting.

A road goes from Elgin seawards to Lossiemouth, so there came the day when we decided to have a look at all the fishing villages on Spey Bay.

With the harvest of the sea good food for the taking, it was natural that villages, many growing into towns, should edge the firths and bays of our rugged, indented shores, especially where good fresh water was available. Spey Bay is well served by river and burn, and here, as elsewhere, the fishing ports are full of interest and a delight to explore.

From Lossiemouth on the Bay's western headland to Cullen, round the corner from Scar Nose, its eastern point, innumerable small roads link the ports like charms on a chain strung between the smooth green silk of fields and the sapphire satin of the bay.

Lossiemouth is Spey Bay's busiest fishing port—but one of its lads did not go to the fishing but to No. 10 Downing Street, because here was the birthplace of Ramsay MacDonald, the Labour Party's first prime minister.

It was a shining breezy morning when David and I left Lossiemouth to wend our way eastward to Garmouth, a village of steep little streets, quaint corners and old, picturesque houses set high above Spey-mouth, safe from the river's periodic flooding.

The traditional Maggie Fair is held here each summer, but

some of the older villagers told us that in their young days it was also market day with booths and stands lining the narrow, crooked streets and a great influx of people from neighbouring towns and countryside, with all the noise, laughter and friendly meetings which made Maggie Fair a red-letter day. The Fair originated when by Crown Charter, in 1587, King James VI made 'Garmoch' a burgh of barony. But it was about a century later that the Fair was given the name of the dearly loved Lady Margaret, wife of the laird, Sir James Innes, and took on the gaiety and colour of those joyous days following the Restoration. And, indeed, Garmouth had something to sing about, for the Merry Monarch landed on their Boat Green after his seventeen months' exile in Holland. Two commissioners from Scotland, one a Moray man, had obtained his pledge to uphold the Covenant. There followed three weeks of hazardous voyaging across the North Sea in a Dutch man-of-war, taking devious ways to avoid Cromwell's fleet and being belaboured by squalls and storms.

The story goes that they anchored off the mouth of the Spey just three hours after four Parliament ships had set sail from the same anchorage down the Moray Firth to intercept the Dutch ship, but, miraculously, an easterly haar (mist) descended, shrouding the ships from each other. The King was rowed ashore, but the small boat grounded, so on the back of a sturdy little ferryman King Charles II ended his exile. A commemoration stone in the wall of a Garmouth house shows where the laird's town house, 'The Laird's Toft', stood. In this mansion-house the King signed the Solemn League and Covenant, and dined with the laird before going on to sleep at Gordon Castle.

We ran down to the shore to see what used to be the Boat Green and what was left of the tiny village of Kingston. In the past few years erosion has caused the evacuation of several families, whose houses were gradually tumbling into the sea.

We had to go inland to cross the River Spey at Fochabers. Then over the Moray–Banff boundary and down into Portgordon. This clean, compact fishing village had a prosperous look, for, like other small Spey Bay ports, where few boats operate from their harbours today, their fishermen sail into the larger ports like Lossiemouth and Buckie where the fish markets are held. The small home ports remain pleasant places to return to at week-ends, as well as delightful holiday haunts for visitors, who love salty breezes, peace and the friendliness of those sturdy fisherfolk.

Only a few miles separate Portgordon from Buckie. Strange that this large, beautifully stone-built town should be named after such a tiny shell-fish, or did the buckie take its name from the town? There are no gardens or flowers about Buckie, but the grey austerity of its streets was redeemed by its scintillating harbour, where boats vied with each other in bright colours as if to match the brilliant sunshine, sparkling blue sea and gleaming white gulls on the wing. Probably most of the boats there were locally built because we saw one on the stocks, nearing completion, in a boatbuilder's yard.

Findochty and Portknockie—were there ever lovelier names?—were the next sizeable fishing villages we visited, and by both we were completely captivated. In Findochty the fishermen's houses are built close together with gable-ends to the sea, each gable with one or two windows. The old stone walls are not drab here but painted all over in lovely shades of grey, cream, green, black, brown and cinnamon; sometimes a dark colour picked out in a contrasting light shade, or light dove-grey with battleship-grey edgings. It is impossible to describe adequately the charm of those beautifully kept harbour-side cottages, or of the many quaint corners they form.

High on its hillock, like a protecting watchdog, stands the kirk, so that Findochty folk can raise their eyes to the hill from whence has come their aid in countless years of toil. When boats were less seaworthy and their calling more hazardous, it was quite usual on a still evening for the lovely tune of a fine old Scottish paraphrase to be carried over the water from one boat to another and to be taken up by each boat's crew until a male-voice choir of hundreds was raised in glorious unison. Wresting a living from the deep has never been an easy one, and always before shooting the nets the fishermen of these parts offered up a short prayer.

The fine harbour, which makes a safe haven from that stormy coast, grew bit by bit, its final extension being about fifty years ago at their peak fishing time; but by 1934 the local drifters were worn out and had to be scrapped, and most of the men went to man Aberdeen trawlers. Today a hundred men are on seine-net fishing here.

Coming near the eastern point of Spey Bay, where the land

rises to the headland well-named Scar Nose, we found Port-knockie high on the cliffs. This is a delightful village of beautiful cottages, with every window a shining picture-frame for lace-trimmed blinds, dainty, frilled curtains and flowering geraniums. As in all the Spey ports, shining cleanliness was Portknockie's keynote. At the very foot of the cliffs we found its story-book harbour sheltered by the crags and itself partly rocky, with about a dozen fishing boats close to the sea wall. The harbour was like a mirror, but beyond the harbour wall was the surge and splash of an almost full tide.

Round Scar Nose we ran down into where Cullen is on its own bay, and at the town foot a wide, high arch of the railway viaduct makes a spectacular entrance. Here is the harbour and the fishing section of Cullen, but the breezy, friendly holiday town is on top of the cliffs.

From Cullen we took the main road back to Lossiemouth and a busy, workaday finish to our day of exploring; 230 boats steaming into port and landing that day's enormous catch of white fish. One after another they crossed the bar, and we mar-velled afresh at the fishermen's expert handling of those big boats as they manœuvred them into seemingly quite inadequate spaces in the packed harbour. The bows were pointed to the quays, for let just the tip touch and the fish could be easily un-loaded. Wedged together, those beautiful seine-net boats were only separated by fenders, the modern type used by fishermen being old rubber tyres. Long after the harbour seemed to us crammed to capacity the boats still sailed in and the boxes of fish were landed and hauled into the roofed, but otherwise open, market, where continuous selling went on, the auctioneer going from catch to catch, steadily, swiftly clearing them to make way for fresh landings.

Fish! The harvest of the sea, that was what had put all the ports which we had explored that day on Spey Bay.

14

In Historic Perthshire:
Alyth, Meigle and the Braes o' Balquhidder

First let us visit the old town of Alyth, which is one I dearly love. There are several reasons: its serenity and sunny loveliness; much that is quaint and unusual about it; and the fact that here my paternal grandfather was cradled and in later years had his country house. We as children came many times; to fish in the burn and climb the hills and to know this little old Perthshire market-town intimately. Exploring it again, but for the first time in David's company, I knew the glad happiness of realizing that he, too, had succumbed to its charm and grown to love it as much as I did myself; only then I realized that I had been steeling my-self against disappointment in case he could not see it with my eyes. But it had not been all the memory of carefree child-hood days that had cast a glamour over Alyth, for now on this return visit, on April days when wind chased clouds in boisterous fun across incredibly blue skies, I saw Alyth with new eyes, with a deeper appreciation of its beauty and of the history which is its background.

You come into Alyth down Airlie Street. It tries so hard to be a real town street, but it just somehow isn't, for there is a farm at the top, and the houses are not quite straight-on. Farther down is the little railway station and a couple of garages. Then come the shops with houses above: one or two sweet shops, rather grander than the tiny one where we used to buy home-made 'burnt sugar'; a new stationer's shop, but still the old one on the opposite corner; a new baker's. But the old taxidermist and game-dealer's shop was just the same; I really don't think that the amazing array of stuffed birds in the window had been moved an inch since I was a child.

A draper's shop, a barber's, a shoe shop, two butchers, and the post office, and you are into the market square. Alyth Square is different from any other I have ever seen. It is big and wide, seeming even more spacious because one side is bordered by trees on the bank of the Alyth Burn. Facing this was a sturdy old red-stone building, long and low, which was the school in my great-grandfather's day, and a pocket-size garden where now rests the old market cross, also an obelisk commemorating three local men killed in the Boer War, one of them the Earl of Airlie.

The Royal Bank Building, in which are the town's offices, and the provost's large ironmongery shop gave a modern touch to the square, but the old buildings facing them took it back a century. Here too was a small, very old saddler's shop, with the white horse in its tiny window which I knew as a child, and still the name above the door which never failed to surprise me because it was the same as my father's and my grandfather's.

Across a stone bridge, built in 1884 at a cost of £900, is Commercial Street. It always seemed to me a far too business-like name for that road; with shops and the Commercial Hotel on one side it is true, but with such a pretty burn flowing down its centre for its whole length, and the music of it brightened by the clang from a smith's anvil. Over the burn are many little bridges, mostly wooden ones, and the Auld Brig, a real gem built of stone but narrow and steep. From all these bridges you can look into the deep amber pools and watch the trout darting like swift black shadows, or jumping when the flies are shimmering above the surface.

From Commercial Street you look up beyond the Auld Brig to the Auld Toon, rising steeply on the hillside, and your eyes are held by three beautiful arches. This old town and the arches are all very compact and near, so you hurry along Commercial Street, forgetting the lovely burn, to see if you can find the way up. You turn a bend, and there is Toutie Street.

After level and straight Commercial Street, Toutie is almost incredible. It is narrow, twisted, and so steep that you will need a stout heart for that stae[1] brae. An enchanting, exciting street up which have toiled, and down which have hurried, countless generations of douce[2] Alyth folk. There was nothing douce, however, about the two young scamps holding the centre of the street one day we climbed it; sturdy little imps of mischief, lustily

[1] Steep slope.
[2] Douce means decent, good-living people.

Dunkeld's old main street, the Brae
The new main street, carrying the Great North Road

kicking a perfectly good silk hat. Up the hill and down that hat flew and bumped and rolled, its silk ruffled and gleaming in the sunshine. And when I laughingly remarked to a woman who was entering her house, "Poor lum hat!", she made delighted reply, "It'll sune be a lum hat wantin' a croon." Where else but in Toutie could such a scene be so perfect?

At the top of Toutie you are into the old town proper. Here the wool market was held in olden times, and the little old market cross stood in its rightful place. But you are still seeking the arches; so you climb steps green with age, and there they are, standing in the quiet peace of the old burying-ground surrounded by old, old gravestones, some of them those of my own ancestors. The arches and a little bit of wall are all that remain of the old parish church which was in a "ruinous condition", unfit for further use and demolished after the new church was built in 1839. The arches were part of the inside of the old church but much newer than the main structure, having been built to support the roof of an addition about the time of the Reformation.

Another delightful road from the square goes past the jute factory, where Alyth folk have worked for hundreds of years and always for the same family, generation after generation. Grand old trees embowering a bridge make a pretty picture as you cross the burn and pass the old sawmill, which has grown considerably since I last saw it, and so on up the hill to the parish church. A lovely church built of local rich red sandstone with its spire rising high, a landmark to the countryside. To me an unusual feature is its great arched gateway into the churchyard, with a heavy, nail-studded door.

A little farther along this road a track runs down into the Den o' Alyth, a sylvan retreat, where the path winds for fully a mile beside the burn. Here the water is even more amber, more limpid, yet sometimes swift and sparkling as it splashes into deep pools, where fleeting black shadows betray the many trout darting from rock to rock. Here and there great walls of rock edge the burn's further side, and elsewhere rustic bridges cross to tempt the rambler to explore. Except for those little bridges, the Den has been left in its natural state, and on this spring day the anemones lay like splashes of snow on the banks while celandines, flat open to the sun, were shaped from shining gold, and tiny violets, so fresh and sweet, peeped from rock crevices.

12

The West Front and Tower of Dunkeld Cathedral

Another ramble we enjoyed was to the Brig o' Rome. It was difficult to find, I remembered; so we decided to follow the burn from the Square. We found later that it would have been quicker to go by car to Pitcrocknie farm, yet although it meant a good few miles of walking, and some of it over fields and climbing barbed-wire fences, I would not have missed that walk by the burn. The aniseed, of which great quantities grow here, was just coming into bloom and scenting the air, the kingcups, too, were opening the first of their golden flowers, while above us the blue and cloud-flecked dome of heaven was filled with the rapturous song of larks.

The Brig o' Rome is an old packhorse bridge, high-arched, narrow, without parapets, and has natural sandstone piers on both banks. There is some doubt as to its actual origin; but its beautiful arch is typically Roman, and a Roman camp was only a few miles south. It was still being used as a footbridge by the farm folk.

Was there ever another town blessed with such priceless environments as Alyth; so we thought as we delved deeper into its countryside. Three miles northwards is the Loch o' Lintrathen, now Dundee's principal reservoir. But what a beautiful seven-mile stretch of water—its irregular, tree-shaded shores, its verdant islands, and the invariably drifting boats with anglers tirelessly whipping its waters. Of such, amidst rising hills and racing clouds, was the picture each vista framed as we circled the loch on its splendid road.

But the day we chose for the Den o' Airlie was the pick of them all, sun, wind, blue sky and clouds. We left the car at Kilry and took our way across a field where shepherds were tending their sheep and lambs, many of the latter only a few hours old. Then through trees our rugged little track, interlaced with tree roots, led us looking down on the River Isla, till its gurgle and splash were lost in the thundering roar of the Reekie Linn.

Farther down this wild and glorious Den are the Slugs of Auchrannie, where the river bunches together to pass through a chasm less than three yards wide, a sight to leave one breathless, especially when the Isla is in spate. And yet a little farther is the Bonnie Hoose o' Airlie. In the absence of the Earl of Airlie in 1640 the Earl of Argyle, hereditary enemy of the Ogilvys, burned down Airlie Castle. But a tower and wall of the old castle remain and a new castle rose on the old foundations.

The castle stands on a high promontory of rock, with a sheer drop on three sides to the rivers Melgam and Isla where they join, and is quite inaccessible. On the fourth, or front side, a moat with drawbridge 30 feet wide and a wall 35 feet high and 10 feet thick protected the stronghold to the land side, but the moat has been filled in.

The castle is built so close to the precipice on one side that there is no foothold below the walls and any repairs have to be done by men lowered by ropes. The day we visited Airlie Castle was one of such wild gales that the ploughed fields around Alyth were lifting in the air and flying across the strath like clouds of smoke, and on the high castle promontory it was difficult keeping our feet while we looked far, far down into the Den.

Alyth has its hills, too. A little to the east is Barry Hill, 668 feet, an old watch-tower site from which could be seen the southward beacon points of Dunsinane and Kinpurnie on the other side of the strath, eight miles distant. Legend has it that on Barry Hill the Picts imprisoned Queen Guinevere, the faithless wife of Prince Arthur, and, not content with that, legend has this luckless lady torn to pieces by wild beasts on her way to Meigle, where she was buried.

Behind Alyth is Alyth Hill which, in olden days, was part of a royal forest. In 1214 Alexander II gave the monks of Cupar Abbey a right-of-way through this 'Forest of Alycht' to their lands in Glenisla. Later, this 'way' became a drove road, and sheep and cattle from the busy markets of Linton Roderick—now West Linton—were grazed on those hills. Today the old track makes an easy and delightful climb, and from the hill-top we looked down on the lovable town—on its red church and tall factory chimney, its winding burn and splendid town hall—and thought happily of the days we had spent there.

Each evening from Alyth we returned to 'Golden Eagle'. After quite a bit of searching we had found a delightful pitch in a little lane running down to the River Isla and got permission from the farmer to stay there. We were close to the village of Meigle.

"Of course you know that this is the oldest village in Scotland," said one of the villagers after she had directed me to Meigle's butcher's shop. The butcher's shop was not easily recognizable, as it was undergoing a face-lift, and, as I waited for my order to be cut and weighed, I thought how symbolic that shop was of Meigle itself. There is nothing to tell the stranger passing through on that main road to Aberdeen that here is a priceless thing. To the majority it is just another Perthshire village with a busy road running through and a twist that necessitates care and a change of gears. We had done it often enough ourselves. "Meigle? Nice little place, yes, we know it." But we didn't, not until we brought 'Golden Eagle' to rest in that little leafy lane running down to an old ford across the Isla.

Meigle cannot substantiate its claim with actual dates, other villages claim the distinction, but so rich is Meigle in old buildings and ancient stones and history that no one who has really explored it will grudge it its age-old title. There is something different about it from most Scottish villages. Usually there is one road with houses on either side, but Meigle has the parish church in the centre with the village grouped round it. This gives roads, houses and shops at all angles, just as if everything had been built in a nice, free-and-easy style wherever a space offered. And if the space was not wide enough then the house would be built sideways, a style which has kept the village very compact, and its irregularity is rather pleasing.

In the square, which is not at all square, is the hotel, an exceedingly old building but with a top storey which was added some time in the last century making it look rather quaint and top-heavy. Opposite the hotel is the old Temple Hall, now a first-class grocery store with houses above. But looking back down the centuries we find the Meigle Knights Templars with their Temple on this site, and several sculptured stones, believed to have been erected to the memory of those who fell in the Holy Wars, were discovered as part of the foundations of a corn kiln when it was pulled down here.

Those stones, with others garnered from the churchyard and other parts of the village, are now housed in a splendid museum of their own which was once the old school but was altered to preserve these precious relics from damp and decay. The stones are now in the safe keeping of the Ancient Monuments' Trust and are renowned far beyond our shores. There are twenty-two of them, beautifully sculptured; the largest, measuring 8 feet by 3½ feet, is said to be to the memory of Queen Guinevere who was buried in Meigle kirkyard. Many bear the symbol of Christianity in the form of Celtic crosses, while others may have been carved even before the Christian era, and some of them date from the years of the Roman occupation.

Back in the little lane beside the Isla we were on the Cardean estate, and between where we were and Cardean House Agricola had a great camp in A.D. 84. Many have been the Roman relics turned up by the plough on this land. Cardean was then 'Caer Dean', the camp on the Dean. A little way along the road the River Dean is crossed by what was reputed to be a Roman bridge. Although it seemed to us rather sturdy for that period, we learned that it had been partly demolished to keep people from using it instead of the new road bridge, and that it had been rebuilt by James Cox who bought the Cardean estate in 1878. During the lovely spring days we stayed at Meigle all about the bridge was gay with multi-coloured primroses and primulas.

Beside the old bridge was the estate saw-mill, which in olden times was a lint mill, for lint was grown extensively in this fertile strath and every cottage had its loom for weaving fine linens. Over at Ruthven, called Riven, a few miles from Meigle, we found another mill which was, in weaving days, a pirn[1] mill. Its wheel was turned by the Isla, and here the river is wild and rocky, particularly where it flows under the road bridge. On looking over the bridge, we found, far below, the remains of an older bridge, on part of which a pretty flower garden was now growing. This belongs to adjoining cottages which also once comprised a lint mill. It was the Meigle postman who told us where to find the pirn mill when we met him at Ruthven on his daily round.

Close to Meigle is historic Belmont Castle, which took its present magnificent form when, in 1885, it became the property of Sir Henry Campbell Bannerman. In 1906 Sir Henry became prime minister and then, more than ever before or since, Meigle became a place of importance with a busy post office, and matters of great moment were discussed and planned in the Premier's beautiful home. Now Belmont Castle belongs to Dundee and is leased to the Church of Scotland for use as an Eventide Home so that in this beautiful and historic place fifty-nine old people have their permanent home, "relieved of all cares and worries of everyday life".

[1] Pirn means thread-reel, or bobbin, used in weaving.

Here were smooth green lawns and fine old trees; one, a magnificent copper beech, was particularly beautiful, while three other beeches in soft green leaf were, we were told, known as 'The three sisters', and Sir Henry used to salute them every morning, and when driving past them always raised his hat.

Inside the castle the superintendent took us through the main rooms. The walls and ceilings had been cleaned, revealing magnificent papers embossed in heavy gold and velvet. The little room with high-domed ceiling in one round tower was a powder closet, and walls and ceilings had been hand-painted on canvas and were very beautiful. Some of the rooms had very ornate ceilings and cornices and some had magnificent marble fireplaces, one reputed to have belonged to Napoleon.

At the entrance to the village was Meigle House. It dates from 1796 and retains much of its old-world charm, although it is now a comfortable guest house. At the entrance to the drive and close to the main road are some ancient and beautiful buildings. Their history is unknown; some call them the old monastery and some tithe barns, but, whatever those fine old buildings were originally used for, they have stood the test of time; built of stone throughout, even to their arched roofs, which are just a continuation of the walls, they are in very good repair.

We were taken to visit other members of the Cox family, Mrs. Cox, widow of John Cox, and her daughters in the ancient and beautiful house of Drumkilbo, about a mile to the east of Meigle. This is now the property of the Queen's cousin, Lord Elphinstone, and a place where she frequently spends a week-end when in Scotland. But this house dates back before any records were kept, and is thought to have been owned by some Pictish family when Nechten ruled the Picts and Pictish courts were held in 'Midgill' the oldest village.

There was a Drumkilbo vault in old Meigle Church where a Celtic stone was found. It is called the Drumkilbo Stone and is with the others in the museum. On the top of it is a zoomorphic design of three intertwined snakes with their tails in their mouths which is quite unlike any other known carving on Celtic stones.

Drumkilbo belonged to Robert the Bruce who gave it to Morice de Tiry, who fought with The Bruce in the War of Independence. A descendant owned the famous horse, Kildaro, which he raced at Perth on Palm Sunday in 1631 and won the very first cup there, which was made from the silver bells which, until then, had been the prize. In 1644 Charles I asked for a loan of the grey gelding, promising to return it, but there is no record of it having come back to Drumkilbo.

Down through the centuries this old house took a prominent part in Scottish history. In conjunction with the Ogilvys of Airlie this became the headquarters from where they sallied forth to attack patrolling parties of Monk's army, when the latter was trying to bring the people of these parts to subjection, and so harassed them that they asked to be withdrawn to England.

It was in 1920 that John Cox commissioned Sir Robert Lorimer, the famous Edinburgh architect, who designed the Scottish Shrine at Edinburgh Castle, to enlarge the house to meet the needs of a growing family. Sir Robert fell under the spell of the old house with its thick walls and steep-pitched roof. He removed additions which had been made by a previous owner to the east and north and added a beautiful new wing to the north and west in keeping with the old building. The dining-room to the north was rebuilt, and a storey added to correspond with the roof's pitch. Mrs. Cox told us that Sir Robert was very pleased with the new room which was so in harmony with the old house that he said it might have been there for over a hundred years. During the alterations an old sword was found in the walls, it was a claymore made at Soligren.

There are several other old houses around Meigle with interesting history, and also many stories of churches, but I like best the account sent to the minister by J. Jones, a joiner, for services rendered:

Rev. J. Maquire.		Novr. 1st 1605
To J. Jones, Joiner.		
For solidly repairing St. Joseph.		£0 0 4
Cleaning and Repairing Holy Ghost.		0 0 6
Repairing M. behind and before and making her a new child.		0 5 6
To making a nose to the devil and fitting a horn on his head and giving a piece to his tail		0 6 6
		0 12 10

Before leaving Meigle I must just mention their Meigle Book.

This fine chronicle of Meigle's history was compiled by members of its Scottish Women's Rural Institute about thirty years ago and tied with another village for first place in a competition called 'Village Books'. In its community effort there is a varied freshness of style, and as the reader follows Meigle people down through the centuries, he realizes what a vital place this oldest village has had in Scotland's history.

Still in Perthshire and still springtime, we cross the County to Loch Lubnaig.

Nowhere can spring be lovelier than by this Perthshire loch. A week of sunshine has starred its banks with primroses and violets and spangled a tree at our caravan windows with the pink and white of apple blossom. The black branches of lochside alders are lit with green fingers, and even the fat buds on the stubborn old ash trees are bursting into yellow-green fronds of leaf; but most glorious are the whins (gorse or furze), a blaze of gold, lighting hillside, roadside and lochside with the torch of spring.

Each morning we are awakened early by such a glorious chorus of birdsong. By day our hearts lift to the ineffable sweetness of the curlew's mating call. All along the lochside lambs are at the fat, cuddly stage, and their baa-ing is a constant accompaniment to the passing hours of each spring day.

Loch Lubnaig—the Crooked, or Bow-shaped Loch—is so called because Ardnandave's crag, Creig-na-co-Heilg—Rock of the Joint Hunting—forces it to bend in the middle. Its sparkling waters are surrounded by glorious, tree-clad hills, and at this season the rich, changeful spring greens gives names to the forest belts, especially those on the slopes of the Ardchullarie range; the almost black of Douglas firs, the pale green of larch, brown-tinged Norwegian spruce, a few magnificent old, red-barked Scotch pines, and a belt of beech in shimmering new leaf which, when sun-lit, turns the forest to a thing of rare loveliness.

On the opposite shore the main Oban railway line clings to the mountain-foot just above the waterline, and its stone embankment is like a rock-garden, with little flowers and beautiful ferns uncurling their tender green fronds. From across the loch the railway is only seen when a train snakes its way north or south, or at night when trains have a fairy-like appearance, being only visible as a double line of travelling lights; the train-lights and their reflection on dark waters.

Few are the lights of houses by Loch Lubnaig, yet lights gleam round its shores on Saturday nights as camp fires flare, like the watch-fires of primeval men warding off wild beasts of the forest. They are lit by men from towns and mining villages farther south, who roar up on motor-cycles to stake their claim to their favourite section of the loch and fish throughout the night. Tough those men are, for not even the icy winds of early spring can daunt them, and the tea they brew is with fresh-drawn water from brawling mountain burns, which tumble as foaming water-falls down from the heights.

Springtime brings other lights which gleam and fade and re-appear in endless succession as the streaking-for-home motorists of Sunday nights follow the winding road which fringes Lub-naig's shores. On weekdays the road is quieter, with only its workaday traffic and an occasional band of tinkers with ponies and carts, or all their worldly goods in old prams. The women, with tousled hair blowing in the wind, carry babies in tartan plaids, the men, bairns and dogs slouch along; gangrel (homeless, wayfaring) buddies, but with the love of freedom and the lilt of spring in their hearts, and a smile for us as they pass 'Golden Eagle'.

Round the crook and beyond the railway, the farm work of spring is going on apace at the old farm of Laggan. This farm had to be moved back from the loch's edge when the railway crept up this length. It was from Laggan farm that Rob Roy carried off his bride and crossed the loch one dark spring night. Being an outlaw, by stealth and in the dark would be the only method he could employ, no matter how willing the farmer's daughter was to wed him. It may be that her family was less willing and would have betrayed him rather than have Helen married to a Mac-Gregor.

Already at the loch's head and at its foot, water lilies are appear-ing, which later will unfold waxen petals to the sun, and those at the loch's foot form a perfect fairy-ring. Here the River Leny leaves the loch and flows softly past the remains of St. Bride's Chapel and burying-ground, lying in the shadow of Ben Ledi. The foundations of the chapel were identified and restored in memory of Sir Walter Scott in 1932, his centenary year. Three lonely, rugged, but beautiful old Scotch pines keep vigil and underfoot crunch their brown cones. Amongst the grass around the old foundations wild hyacinths bloom profusely, and in this sweet, hallowed place is the joyous song of many birds.

Shortly beyond the chapel the Leny thunders in two magnificent falls on either side of a great rugged rock which, defying the river's erosive tactics, splits it into two masses of tumbling, cream-foamed water. As it hurtles down, the water bunches together again in a boiling, roaring turmoil of dissipating power. All around is the shining beauty of beech, oaks with the rusty tinge of unfolding leaves, and Scotch pines in their rugged splendour, many with scanty root-hold on the ragged, grey and moss-grown rock-walls, through which the turbulent Leny has carved its way.

So, by the Crooked Loch, the days weave their pattern to the accompaniment of all the wonder and beauty of new life which is spring's awakening.

For one small section of Perthshire Strathyre, walled by its green braes, holds an abundance of legend and is clothed with beauty; yet its key-notes today are careful husbandry of the land, and an angler's and a hill-walker's paradise. Near its foot lies the lovely little village of Balquhidder, tucked snugly in the bield of the Braes. Farther up the glen, like two great mirrors lying on its floor, are Lochs Voil and Doine, windswept and glorious.

The road to this interesting, rugged bit of country is a little one, which leaves the main A.85 at the old King's House, north of Loch Lubnaig, runs under the railway bridge and climbs into the hills. A rough road to the village, which was peculiarly Rob Roy's own and where he and Helen and some of their sons were laid to rest in the old kirkyard.

This glen must for ever be associated with the history of the MacGregors. The story of this clan in the late sixteenth and early seventeenth centuries was one of intrigue by Argyll in pitting one clan against another; Macdonalds against Mackenzies and Mac-Gregors against Colquhouns and others, and, through more cunning manœuvring in Edinburgh and at the instigation of Argyll, the MacGregors were made the scapegoats and not only outlawed but condemned to death in 1603 by the Lords of Council. Taking to the hills, making caves their homes, this unhappy race became known as the Children of the Mist. Many who found that way of life too hard, being unable to mix freely with ordinary folk while bearing their own proscribed name, took the strange remedy of changing their name and tartan to that of an enemy clan. Those with more strength of character and physique, and less cunning, fought their way through life, harried on every side. Of such was Rob Roy, renowned for the amazing strength of his sword-arm and its tremendous length, champion and protector of the weak, taking from those who had plenty and giving to those who wanted. It was Wordsworth, after visiting Rob Roy's grave, who wrote these words of Rob and his followers:

> For why?—because the good old rule
> Sufficeth them, the simple plan,
> That they should take, who have the power
> And they should keep who can.

Recumbent stones cover the graves and, because of their Celtic carving, are said to be of a much earlier period, probably removed from nearby ancient, forgotten graves. Sweet rest in that quiet place after a life of turmoil, yet the Braes which stretch up the glen, although green and velvety to look at and good hill-pasture, are steep with great rocks reminding us of the wild years when they were the Braes of the Broken Men.

Although in the safe fastnesses of the hills which guard that narrow glen, the MacGregors were not isolated, because many are the passes through the hills, north, south and west. To the keen hill-walker those old tracks and ways through small glens and high passes are today a sheer delight; and when dusk falls and evening mists fill the valleys, it is perhaps no wonder that the feeling persists that they are still haunted by the wraiths of the Children of the Mist. Rob Roy's house, which was burned by Government troops, was near the head of the glen, about a mile beyond Loch Doine, at Inverlochlarig. From there west, up the River Lochlarig, a track, now indistinct, climbed through the Bealach nan Corp—Dead Man's Pass—at nearly 2,000 feet and dropped steeply down to Ardleish on Loch Lomond; about ten miles from Rob Roy's house, with another two miles or so round the head of the loch, or a short ferry across to Ardlui. Bealach nan Corp got its rather 'wild-west'-like name from the funeral processions which used the pass in olden times, and, reaching the summit, made that a resting place before continuing to Balquhidder kirkyard or to the quiet God's Acre beside the ancient Chapel of St. Bride at the foot of Ben Ledi.

A matter of seven miles, rough and steep-going, round Stob a Choin would take Rob Roy from his house to his birthplace, Glengyle, at the head of Loch Katrine. This may have been the route he and the redoubtable Helen took before the approach of the Government troops who burned their house. But not even Glengyle was safe then, so they made their temporary home in a cave north of Inversnaid on Loch Lomond.

Five miles north from Inverlochlarig would bring him up Inverlochlarig Glen below the precipitous slopes of Ben Am Beinnein, and down by the Glen More Burn, with great, lumpy Ben More rising sheer to the east; and so to the shores of Loch Dochart near Crianlarich. Another lovely way north starts from Balquhidder up the bonnie Kirton Glen and through the pass by little Lochan an Eireannaich at 1,000 feet, to drop down by the Ledchary Burn to Glen Dochart.

South, a longer way, but one which Rob Roy must have traversed many times and driven his 'lifted' beasts over, goes up Glen Buckie from Balquhidder. At Bailemore it veers west, then south through the pass, Beallach a Chonnaidh, and descends by the sparkling, rollicking Allt Gleann-nam-Meann in the shadow of Benvane to the once Royal Deer Forest of Glen Finglas. Then this wild but glorious track continues down by the River Turk to the Brig o' Turk. But at the head of Glen Buckie one has a choice of ways because another delightful path goes east by Immercon, round the end of Beinn-an-t-Shithen and down into Stratyre, or connects the little road to Laggan at the foot of Benvane, from whence Rob Roy carried off his bride, Helen.

It was blossom time when last we followed the tortuous windings of the glen road, and the lower slopes of the Braes were a gorgeous blaze of golden whins. Here and there a large house and occasionally a farm added a tamer note, yet even the sheep here look wild, with great curled horns. On and up, to Loch Voil and Loch Doine, with the road climbing high above them till they lay below like a section of coloured map. But how beautiful; satin-smooth with the green Braes slipping into them and only separated from each other by a long green field, tree-fringed down both sides, through which flowed the connecting short, wide river. On both lochs boats were out, for here fishing is good.

Of bird-life there seemed little, although beside us, flitting about the wayside bushes, were yellow hammers, perching close as if seeking our admiration and uttering their sweet call of, "Little-bit-of-bread-and-no-cheese"; and we watched a hawk wing its way out over Loch Doine to become lost against the opposite Braes.

It was as we came down the glen again to the old kirk at Balquhidder that we recalled Sir Walter Scott's story of the minister of Rob Roy's day who wished to have his stipend increased. But Rob Roy, knowing that the poor people of the Parish could not meet that, persuaded him to abandon the idea, and during that year, and each succeeding one, as compensation, presented him with a cow and a fat sheep, which the minister glady accepted, carefully refraining from asking how Rob Roy acquired them.

There was another, who was for some time minister of Balquhidder, and succeeded his father as minister of Aberfoyle, who became a legend in a rather unusual fashion. Robert Kirke was his name, a seventh son, which may have had something to do with it, for in 1691 he wrote a very knowledgeable book *The Secret Commonwealth of Elves, Faunes and Fairies*. He seemed to know their ways, so perhaps it was natural that when his mortal life ended he was spirited away to fairyland—or so he told those to whom he appeared after his mortal remains were laid to rest.

Yes, the Braes of Balquhidder shelter one of the richest in story of Perthshire's many lovely glens; here lived and walked a proscribed clan and a brave man with a strong arm, Government troops with their red coats and their quarters at the King's House at the road-end, strange ministers of a strange flock, and our greatest historian, the Wizard of the North, who wove the legends into tales that will live for ever.

15

History and Autumn Days:
in and around Dunkeld

We are still in Perthshire, this amazing county which would take several lifetimes to thoroughly explore. There is Dunkeld, for instance. You may have passed through Birnam—and you probably glanced in passing at the tweed shop with its lovely tartans hanging outside and resolved to have one of those beautiful rugs when you return south—then across the wide and beautiful River Tay by the old bridge and on through Dunkeld on the Great North Road; a lovely stretch through leafy Perthshire.

David and I like this corner, particularly in autumn when the wealth of trees put on their golden and crimson cloaks; and our favourite pitch, for perhaps a week's stay, is a wide wayside one between Dowally and Dunkeld. It makes a splendid centre for a large section of this enormous county, and from it we look far down to the swift-flowing Tay.

The little town of Dunkeld is our shopping place, but it is hardly a town. In fact, it is an ancient cathedral city of great renown. Its foundation is lost in antiquity, before records were kept, except in cup-marked stones, standing-stones and stone circles. This hill-sheltered corner where Tay and Bran meet, and glens and straths strike off in every direction, was a natural place of security, yet a central spot of easy access for communal worship, a strategic place for gatherings of invaders and the gateway, through a barrier of hills, to the Highlands.

Near here Agricola made a great Roman camp in A.D. 84, and here for centuries Picts had their fortified stronghold; but Dunkeld's real history started with the coming of Christianity. St. Ninian and St. Colm brought light to the peoples of the Tay valley as early as the fifth century, but St. Columba became the Patron Saint of Dunkeld when Kenneth MacAlpine brought part of the saint's relics from Iona and the depredations of the

Danes, to Dunkeld, when he made it the centre of the early Culdee monasteries.

So from strength to strength until, in the twelfth century, the bishops of Dunkeld Cathedral had charge of a see reaching to Iona, right down Kintyre, to parts of Angus and Fife and also the Lothians, including Newbattle Abbey and the island of Inchcolm. Bishop followed bishop and some were great builders, so Dunkeld Cathedral grew in magnitude and beauty through troublous centuries until the Reformation put an end to the old order and despoiled that beautiful edifice.

Many skirmishes raged in and around this key position between Highlands and Lowlands, but the worst recorded battle was in 1689 when the Highland force again defended Dunkeld against the Covenanters. The Highlanders had won the Battle of Killiecrankie, so short a distance northwards, but had lost their leader, 'Bonnie Dundee', and were in low spirits when they came to grips with the Government troops at Dunkeld. However, fierce was the battle, and when the Jacobites at last occupied most of the houses, the Government troops, running short of ammunition, tore lead from the cathedral roof to use as shot. Their leader, Colonel Cleland, was killed, as was his second-in-command, Major Henderson, after which Captain Munro set fire to the town and burned out the Jacobites.

After the conflagration only three houses remained, so a new town had to be built. Then the choir of the cathedral was partly restored, and in 1762 a Government grant of £300 allowed further work on it, and the tower was roofed. In 1815 the Duke of Atholl continued the good work by raising £5,000 and obtaining £1,000 from the Government to make the choir suitable for Dunkeld's parish church. Nearly a hundred years later, in 1908, Sir Donald Currie of Garth re-roofed the choir with Caithness slates; inside much that was old and hidden behind plaster was uncovered, oak was used for the interior woodwork, and the beautiful stained-glass East Window, which is such a fine feature of the cathedral kirk today, was added. In 1922, the Duke of Atholl gave the cathedral to the nation, when preservation work was begun on the nave and tower by the Ancient Monuments Department of H.M. Ministry of Works.

Before the Battle of Dunkeld the town stretched west beyond the cathedral to the ferry near Inver, and east up the Brae to where, below the townhead, another ferry operated. Even in those days this was the Great North Road, and those ferries and fords carried and were crossed by many illustrious people, many armed forces and their brave leaders, and many ordinary folk. In 1842 Queen Victoria got her first glimpse of the Highlands here and wrote in a letter: 'The situation of Dunkeld down in a valley surrounded by wooded hills is very, very pretty.' The bridge, designed by Telford, superseded the ferries only thirty-four years earlier, for although General Wade used the Great North Road as an arterial road to open up the Highlands, a difference of opinion with the Duke of Atholl decided him to bridge the Tay at Aberfeldy. There he built his finest bridge, no doubt to the chagrin of the duke and the citizens of Dunkeld.

Following the building of Dunkeld Bridge, a new street of houses, shops and hotels took shape, running north and crossing the old street. Progress was the keynote until, in 1856, the Perth to Dunkeld railway was inaugurated, with the terminus and station at Birnam to save bridging the Tay. But Dunkeld's citizens were resentful, for they had to pay toll crossing the road bridge to the station, while the people of Birnam, a village growing lustily with the advent of the railway, paid no toll. So were instigated the Toll Riots; the toll-gates were repeatedly thrown into the river, and disturbances became so bad that a detachment of Royal Highlanders was drafted into the city to keep the peace. In 1879 the bridge was taken over by the county, and the toll-gate removed. The old toll-house, a pretty little house at the bridge-end, remains and is still occupied, its windows ever watchful, while across the old, 685-foot-long bridge, with its five principal and two land arches, the traffic roars day and night.

But Birnam has history, too. From the great woods on its shapely, 1,324-foot hill, which towers above the village, Malcolm Canmore's men-of-arms cut branches and marched to Dunsinane on the Sidlaws to avenge his father's death; and Macbeth, seeing them coming, remembered the witches' prophecy that he would be safe until Birnam Wood should come to Dunsinane. So Shakespeare put Birnam Hill on the world's map, basing his play on actual happenings of the eleventh century.

Birnam Hill was where King Duncan, Malcolm's father, had

his camp, but much earlier there was a vitrified[1] fort here, and many cup-marked rocks were discovered. The hill's position at the southern end of the Grampians was a strategic one, commanding the entrance of several glens and overlooking Strath More with the Sidlaws on the farther side.

Between Birnam and the bridge there is the remnant of a village called Little Dunkeld and its parish church, because Little Dunkeld is a parish of considerable size and separated from that of Dunkeld and Dowally by the river. Dowally, the small, ancient village five miles north, also has its church, where services are now taken by the minister of the cathedral kirk. At Dowally, close to the Great North Road, there are some fine specimens of standing stones.

In Dunkeld we trace the old main street, east to west, and find it quaint and interesting: the narrow, steep Brae, the square, and the way by the cathedral to Inver Ferry. In the square the ornamental, pillared fountain superseded the old Mercat Cross in 1865 and was erected by the townsfolk in memory of the sixth Duke of Atholl; a natural form of memorial, as the Atholl family had recently defrayed the expense of piping water from the hills to the town. The square has a pleasantly old look, yet there is a freshness about it. Several of the derelict houses were rebuilt in harmony with and carefully resembling the old architecture of the square, in commemoration of the coronation of Queen Elizabeth II.

Off the square westward runs Cathedral Street, where the old houses are National Trust of Scotland property, and they have done a superlative job in restoration and modernization work, keeping the properties in the old style, because they embodied some of the finest traditional, domestic architecture in Scotland. So, much that is old and much that is lovely is being preserved in this little old city.

Another simply designed but old-styled building was the headquarters of the Territorials, the Scottish Horse. A more ornate eighteenth-century building is now a pleasant restaurant. It was built by Jane, Duchess of Atholl, as a school for girls. But Dunkeld Royal School for boys dated back to 1567, when

---

[1] Made by Picts. The stones were welded together by using magnesium-limestone and building fires of brushwood and heather inside and out. The intense heat thus generated caused the limestone magnesium to liquefy.

James VI made a grant for its erection and endowed it under royal warrant. Now the school for boys and girls is across the bridge at the cross roads.

From time immemorial markets and fairs were held in the square, "the city lying in such a commodious pairt near to the Hielands", making it the perfect rendezvous of merchants, millers, cattle-men, horse dealers, weavers—of which there were many in and around Dunkeld—and farmers. Those markets are all things of the past, but still a wall-fixture on the old building known as St. George's Hospital is a bronze ell-measure gauge for measuring cloth, and also on it are 'hand' marks for measuring the height of horses. A little gift shop in this old building bears the name 'The Ell', and it is a gift shop worth visiting. All the merchandise is of Scottish make, most of it local, and much of it useful as well as beautiful.

The pretty house nearest the cathedral gates was at one time a rectory and is one of the three houses which escaped destruction by the fire of 1689. One of the most charming views of old Dunkeld is seen from inside the gates looking along Cathedral Street to the Square. The Brae, the old continuation eastward of Cathedral Street, wafts one back centuries. It climbs, and a stout heart is required to breast its twisted, steep way between old houses. Here we found the bairns, laddies and lassies, standing on their heads, and skipping, while they chanted old rhymes, all in the middle of the narrow little road; so vastly different from the street passing the foot of the Braes with its ceaseless rush of traffic.

High on the Brae is a pretty cream-walled cottage, but dropping downhill on a tiny road which curved round its side we found it to be a four-storey house to its river front. This precipitous little road was the old Boat Brae connecting the East Ferry, and still brings one swiftly from city-head to river-edge.

Where the West Ferry used to be it crossed to Inver; a picturesque village of a scattering of cottages and an old mill, lying snugly between the rivers, Bran and Tay, and reached by lovely old Invar Bridge. This village was the home of Niel Gow, the famous fiddler, who even played before Prince Charlie when the prince was the guest of the Marquis of Tullibardine at Dunkeld House. Raeburn painted the fiddler's portrait, which hangs in the

County Buildings, Perth. Gow died in 1807 but his cottage at Inver is still occupied and in good repair.

A little beyond Inver a rough road leads to the Hermitage, which the Duchess of Atholl presented to the National Trust for Scotland in memory of her husband, the eighth duke, who was the Trust's first president from 1931 to 1942. The circular-walled, domed building, called Ossian's Hall, is cleverly built on a rock-spur, hiding the scene until the railed front is reached, where one looks down 40 feet to the tremendous rush of the Bran hurtling over the falls. Fine spray rises high like mist, and the roar in the hall is terrific. In former days, when twenty wall and roof mirrors reflected the whole tumultuous scene, one must have felt oneself drowning in the rushing waters. Below the falls the river boils through a narrow slug, and spanning it high is a small stone bridge; an enchanting corner with rugged, moss-grown rock, beach and pine trees and a beautiful *cedrus Libani*, cedar of Lebanon.

A mile higher up the river is spanned by the Rumbling Bridge where, in a terrific rush of foaming water, it hurtles over great, jagged rocks, throwing spray high, losing itself under arching rock 80 feet below the bridge, and emerging to force its passage through a narrow, straight-walled slug, the rock chiselled by the water's force like gigantic blocks of dressed stone. With the river in spate, the noise is tremendous, and the constant rumble under the rocks and bridge is like thunder grumbling in a ravine, deep, hollow, vibrating.

The Five Lochs are also on Dunkeld's doorstep, three within easy walking distance, uphill, following an old pilgrims' route; and where pilgrims first glimpsed Dunkeld's cathedral, a dean placed a cross. Beset by robbers and highwaymen, who often relieved them of their gifts for the cathedral, the cross, reached safely, was a sign for thanksgiving. This was an old drove road too, and many a skirmish was waged between Highland drovers, returning home from Dunkeld markets with their sporrans lined with gold, and the caterans skulking in the hills.

The lochs are pretty, tree-fringed, scented with bog-myrtle, wild thyme and meadowsweet, occasionally enriched with water-lilies, edged with the heavenly blue of wild hyacinths, with snow-white hawthorn and pink and white roses, their sweet peace only broken by birdsong. First comes Loch of the Lowes, its name thought to be derived from Lucius, meaning pike, because the monks stocked those lochs with pike too, knowing their good food value.

Loch of Craiglush, colourful with yachts and dinghies afloat, is now joined to the Lowes by a burn, but they were once one. Loch of Butterstone is close by the road as it curves through pretty Butterstone village. It must have known a great coming and going in olden days for here, a glen road climbs to the Den of Reichip where was found a Druid's circle and other Druidical remains beside a spring called Grew's Well, probably from Sancta Crux, Well of the Holy Cross. Its waters had healing properties and were taken on the first Sunday of May. Many centuries ago there was a chapel here for those living at the summer shielings in the hills, and for thousands of pilgrims who came yearly to the well.

Loch Clunie has more history. On its island a palace was built by George Brown, Bishop of Dunkeld, 1484 to 1514, and became the 'Key of the See of Dunkeld'. After the Reformation it ceased to belong to the Church and in 1562 became the castle-home of Robert Crichton, kinsman of a former bishop, and his wife, Elizabeth Stewart, of royal descent, with their two-year-old son, James.

James, later called the Admirable Crichton, was the prototype of J. M. Barrie's play. This youthful prodigy of learning could dispute with anyone on "literature, science and art, in prose or verse, in Hebrew, Syriac, Arabic, Greek, Latin, Spanish, French, Dutch, Flemish or Slavonic". He spent his childhood in the Castle of Clunie, had some schooling in Perth before going to St. Andrews, the greatest seat of learning in his day, and met his death at the early age of 22.

But as we began our exploring there, so let us finish at the cathedral where green lawns slope to the wide, swift-flowing Tay, where trees are old and beautiful and where peace enfolds the venerable ruins and the beautiful cathedral kirk.

The week before our caravan windows looked out on the rushing waters of a Border river. Two days later we drew on to this pitch beside Loch Earn, one of Perthshire's loveliest lochs; for myself I think I would say the loveliest. The pictures that 'Golden Eagle's' windows now frame are so surpassingly beautiful that you will think I exaggerate in even my simplest attempt to describe them.

What a delight our little bay is; it changes its colour a dozen times a day. When the hour is kind it reflects the blue of the sky but adds its own clarity, it froths with coffee-coloured spume when storms suddenly take control, it sparkles like glittering gold when sunshine drenches it, and when no breeze stirs it lies smooth like soft, green velvet, deeply reflecting the green of trees which sparsely edge it. After heavy rains the loch is high, and many of those trees are standing deep in water, their trunks green with moss above the waterline, while one gorgeous oak tree has its lower, gold-laden branches fanned out like a huge, down-curving canopy, their leafy points pricking the loch's surface.

We are only a few yards from the loch's edge and close to the narrow, winding road, where twelve magnificent, gigantic larch trees stand sentinel to all who approach. Straight, of great girth and tremendous height, those are some of the survivors of the second lot of larch trees to be planted in Scotland. The laird tells me that his great-great-great-grandfather got the saplings in 1780 from the Duke of Atholl, who had already planted at Blair Castle the first great batch of this Scandinavian tree and found that it thrived in our cold, northern clime.

From the opposite edge of the tiny road the hill rises steeply, green, roughly wooded, and broken by the rush and splash of a cascading burn on its joyous descent over rugged, grey rock and between golden bracken and green ferns. From this delightful mountain burn of crystal-clear waters we fill our water-cans.

By the side of the burn a foot-wide track wriggles steeply up the hill to reach an old drove road which winds, high up, along the hillside. David and I set out to find that old road last night, but as we picked our way up over rivulets and the rain-sponged hillside, we found ourselves in a hazel-wood. By the time our pockets were bulging with nuts, the darkening was on us, and we must needs leave the old road for another day. As we descended, we stopped to watch a small hedgehog rooting among the ferns; although not a yard from us, and although we talked while watching it, it seemed quite unafraid. Back in the cara-van the making of hazel-nut tablet was a delightful evening ploy.

With such an abundance of hazel-nuts and acorns, it is natural that this is a haunt of the red squirrel, and never a day passes but we see some of those lovely, furry creatures sitting on the bank, with their great bushy tails arched over their heads, while they crack and eat the nuts, or cleverly, with cupped paws, test their weight, disgustedly throwing faulty ones aside, then going off with the good nuts.

This is a quiet time of the year for birds, but pretty wagtails haunt the rain pools between the caravan and the loch, and for a few moments today I watched a woodpecker run swiftly up one of the giant larches. Several times we have seen a sparrow-hawk hovering above the trees, while from high up in the hills comes the gentle, mewing cry of buzzards. Flitting among the trees and swimming at the loch's edge, we have glimpsed dainty little birds, but their passage is too swift for us to name them. On the water's edge too there is occasionally a flock of small gulls, with the silver-grey and white of them gleaming when stray sunbeams slant through the larches. At night, eerily breaking the stillness, comes the hooting of an owl, and by day the best songster now is our friendly, fat little robin, who sings his thanks for the crumbs scattered round the caravan door.

This afternoon we chose another and easier way up to the old road. Half-a-mile from our pitch a muddy and partly grass-grown track, wide enough for a tractor but very steep, climbs and curves uphill. High up on a tree-sheltered shelf, we looked out across the trees and up the loch to Lochearnhead and the glorious mountains about Glen Ogle. And now we were on the old road, which took us past a small farm and across rivulets and burns, by stepping stones and sapling-sparred bridges, to bring us down again on to the Queen's highway. Our road ended near another lovely bay, which had as background pretty St. Fillans and where in summer the flourishing Yacht Club has anchorage for its many boats.

Our walk back along the rugged road was a leisurely one, with a stop to talk with the roadman and another to look at a wayside tombstone. It marks the spot where Major James Stewart of Ardvorlich was temporarily buried in 1660. After a stormy life his enemies were many, particularly the MacGregors. No one of that name had ever received mercy at his hands, because of their terrible crime in killing his mother's brother and bringing her the head, thus causing her to lose her reason just before he was born.

As the MacGregors threatened to attack the funeral cortège, and lay in wait near Dundurn, the mourners hurriedly buried their laird by the roadside; but some time later he was lifted and re-interred in the family burying ground at Dundurn, near St. Fillans.

Another small tombstone, close to the gates of Ardvorlich, the laird's fine old house about a mile up the loch from our pitch, interested us. A feud existed between the Stewarts of Ardvorlich and the MacDonalds of Glen Coe. In 1620, in a fit of reprisals, seven MacDonalds set out to burn down the Stewart's house, and coming through Glen Dochart picked up a guide.

At this time the stormy Major James Stewart was in hiding in a cave at St. Fillans, called Ardvorlich's Cave, when word was brought to him. In all haste he came to defend his house, arriving in time to see a MacDonald struggling with a dairymaid in an endeavour to set fire to the thatch of the dairy. The Major took aim with his gun, as best he could, at the struggling couple and, with the prayer, "May God guide the shot," fired. Some said the gun, known as Gunna Breac, or spotted gun, was a fairy one, but at any rate the MacDonald fell dead. Meantime Major Stewart's men had dispatched the other six MacDonalds, and even the guide, Clark, who escaped, was chased and killed in a wood, ever since called Coille Clerich, or Clark's Wood.

The MacDonalds were buried close to the loch's edge, and about 150 years ago, when altering the road, their bones and metal buttons were unearthed. Those were moved to the road-side, reburied and the stone erected. Interest was aroused some years ago by a Canadian visiting the 'old country'. His name was, I think, Hutchison, and being in Aberfeldy he asked a newsagent to which clan Hutchison belonged. He was told MacDonalds of Glen Coe. After much spiering[1] he decided that the seven Mac-Donalds buried by the shores of Loch Earn were his ancestors, so, having been bitten by his lang pedigree, he did honour to those warriors by ceremoniously placing a heather wreath at the stone, while a piper from Aberfeldy marched up and down playing the MacDonald lament.

In the hall of Ardvorlich Mrs. Stewart showed me the famous old Gunna Breac, which has its place there among many more guns, targes, a two-handed sword, and pikes, all of which are

[1]Spiering means asking or inquiring.

steeped in the ancient history of this very old house, which has stood beneath mighty Ben Vorlich for countless generations.

Nearer the head of the loch and far below the road, there stands an imposing castle, uninhabited but in perfect condition. This is Castle Edinample and was built about 1630 by Sir Duncan Campbell of Glen Orchy, who was known as Black Duncan of the Seven Castles. This Campbell seems to have had a flair for castle-building, and to build seven in one short lifetime seems quite an achievement; but Edinample has had a singularly tranquil existence with no history recorded. Perhaps the original owner was so busy scurrying about the country setting up his castles he hadn't time to fight, and subsequent owners would have had so many castles that they couldn't be easily found.

Clustering about the head of the loch lies the village of Lochearnhead; a scattering of houses, a post office, village shop, garage and the hotel—and the main thing is the hotel. From a central building the hotel has grown and grown until now it is a big and beautiful hotel, where comfort, service and good food are the keynotes. In summer, at the head of the loch, water ski-ing is the sport which brings throngs of people to Lochearnhead, but in autumn, like birds of passage, they have all gone.

Opposite the hotel a tempting, red-surfaced road lures the explorer from the main one north; nor will it let him turn back, for it winds the whole seven miles close by the edge of the loch. Slow miles with many stops, as fresh and beautiful pictures unfold, of close, warmly coloured hills or distant blue peaks; of gleaming water, and, across it, the darker, tree-clad hills of our shore, until they open out in wide and sunny Glen Vorlich. And right at the top of the glen rises the mighty, snow-capped Ben, dazzling in the sunlight, yet with cloud-shadows constantly changing its appearance.

At the foot of the loch lies St. Fillans, like a jewel at the end of a gold and silver filigree chain; and with our eyes drawn to the small, tree-clad island off-shore, from the 'Drummond Arms' I tried to piece together a strange tale I heard a long time ago. This little island, as well as the one near Lochearnhead, is artificial, both thought to date back to the era of the lake dwellers. At one time a causeway connected the island to the shore at St. Fillans. Later a castle, or possibly a keep, was built as a royal fort, and a small harbour and landing stage took the place of the causeway.

But little would be known of its history had it not, at one time, been the stronghold of Clan Neish.

The story goes that the Neishes of Loch Earn had a feud with the MacNabs of Loch Tay, so, when some of the former clan found a servant of the latter returning from Crieff with large quantities of provisions and liquor for the MacNabs' Christmas celebrations, they relieved him of his burdens and, after some ill-treatment, sent him on his way. With so much good cheer at hand the Neishes proceeded to hold high revel in their island home, until the potent liquor took effect and they all slept deeply.

Meantime the old MacNab chief, with a weather eye to the black night, hinted to his stalwart sons—some say twelve in number—that, "The night is the night if the lads were the lads." It was a long trek from Tayside up over the hills and down Glen Tarkin to Loch Earn, but those young warriors carried their boat the whole way and there embarked for the island. The poor, drunken Neishes were easy prey, and none escaped alive except one small boy who hid under a bed. Their gruesome work done, the MacNabs returned over the hills, but, weary, they abandoned their boat in Glen Tarkin, and two hundred years later, in the nineteenth century, its remains were said to have been there.

There is much more of history in and around St. Fillans, but as it is today is perhaps more interesting. High on the hill slopes above the lochside road are beautiful houses with sheltering trees, and here and there a terraced garden ablaze with flowers. Lower on the roadside are pretty village houses and cottages, and the Drummond Arms Hotel in its glorious setting of vivid golden trees, backed by rugged hills and fronted by the silvery loch. There are no unsightly buildings, such as tumbledown cottages, and those residents who have come from other parts to make their homes here are happy and contented, for the local people welcome the incomers warmly into their friendly circle of village life, and old cottages, instead of being left to fall into ruin, have been enlarged, modernized and transformed into lovely homes of character.

One of the most interesting of the rejuvenated cottages is the old toll-house at the junction of the two lochside roads and the road to Comrie. We were on our way to Comrie—that lovely old, and interesting, nearby town where we do our shopping— when we stopped to look at this old toll-house. Here was a two-roomed cottage, which had had another storey added, with dormer windows, giving three lovely bedrooms and bathroom upstairs. The but-and-ben (two-roomed cottage) of the toll-house are now a comfortable dining-room and lounge, and opening off the former is a neat, beautifully equipped and all-electric kitchenette, with a door from it into a large storeroom. Being on the roadside, there is no real garden, yet there is no lack of flowers, for the present owners have them growing in large tubs on the cement in front of the house. From the porch too hang baskets of geraniums, and on the roadside verge, in front of a tiny paved court and summerhouse which adjoin the house, there are gladioli and other autumn flowers in a riot of colour, making altogether a beautiful corner and approach to this lovely village.

Well, already the deer are belling on those hills as the days shorten and the snows whiten the mountain-tops, and it is time for us to move homewards; but it will be with great reluctance that we shall leave lovely Loch Earn.

There is always a tinge of sorrow in our last run home for the year. The summer has sped, the golden days of roving are over until the spring. But my notebooks are full, and David has many photographs to process, so the winter months will be busy ones. Yet we cannot spend our last night of the season in 'Golden Eagle' without having the maps out and planning our next year's routes. They may be drastically changed in the interval, but it is a heart-lifting occupation before we garage 'Golden Eagle' for the winter.

Index

Index